"I enjoy reading Phil Moo[...]
the Christian life wi[...]
– [...]

"In taking us straight to the heart of the text, Phil Moore has served us magnificently. We so need to get into the Scriptures and let the Scriptures get into us. The fact that Phil writes so relevantly and with such submission to biblical revelation means that we are genuinely helped to be shaped by the Bible's teaching."

– Terry Virgo

"Fresh. Solid. Simple. Really good stuff."

– R. T. Kendall

"Phil makes the deep truths of Scripture alive and accessible. If you want to grow in your understanding of each book of the Bible, then buy these books and let them change your life!"

– P J Smyth, GodFirst Church, Johannesburg, South Africa

"Most commentaries are dull. These are alive.
Most commentaries are for scholars. These are for **you**!"

– Canon Michael Green

"These notes are amazingly good. Phil's insights are striking, original, and fresh, going straight to the heart of the text and the reader! Substantial yet succinct, they bristle with amazing insights and life applications, compelling us to read more. Bible reading will become enriched and informed with such a scintillating guide. Teachers and preachers will find nuggets of pure gold here!"

– Greg Haslam, Westminster Chapel, London, UK

"The Bible is living and dangerous. The ones who teach it best are those who bear that in mind – and let the author do the talking. Phil has written these studies with a sharp mind and a combination of creative application and reverence."

– Joel Virgo, Leader of Newday Youth Festival

For more information about the Straight to the Heart series,
please go to **www.philmoorebooks.com**.
You can also receive daily messages from Phil Moore on Twitter
by following **@PhilMooreLondon**.

STRAIGHT TO
THE HEART OF

Mark

60 BITE-SIZED INSIGHTS

Phil Moore

MONARCH
BOOKS

Oxford, UK & Grand Rapids, Michigan, USA

Published by Monarch Books
an imprint of
Lion Hudson plc
Wilkinson House, Jordan Hill Road,
Oxford OX2 8DR, England
Email: monarch@lionhudson.com
www.lionhudson.com/monarch

ISBN 978 0 85721 642 7
e-ISBN 978 0 85721 643 4

First edition 2015

Acknowledgments
Scripture quotations taken from the *Holy Bible, New International Version* Anglicised. Copyright © 1979, 1984, 2011 Biblica, formerly International Bible Society. Used by permission of Hodder & Stoughton Ltd, an Hachette UK company. All rights reserved. "NIV" is a registered trademark of Biblica. UK trademark number 1448790. Both 1984 and 2011 versions are quoted in this commentary.
pp. 33–34, 55: Extract from *Mere Christianity* by C. S. Lewis copyright © C. S. Lewis Pte. Ltd. 1942, 1943, 1944, 1952. Reprinted by permission.
p. 69: Lyrics from "Still" by Reuben Morgan copyright © 2003, Reuben Morgan. Reprinted by permission of Hillsong.
p. 165: Lyrics from "Poverty" by Jason Upton copyright © 2001 Key of David Music (BMI) (admin by Watershed Music Co.). All rights reserved. Used by permission.
p. 195: Extract from *Dead Poets Society* copyright © 1989, Touchstone Pictures. Reprinted by permission.

A catalogue record for this book is available from the British Library.

Printed and bound in the UK, March 2015, LH26

This book is for my four children:
Isaac, Noah, Esther and Ethan.
May it help you to step deeper into the story.

CONTENTS

PART FIVE: THE UNFINISHED STORY

About the *Straight to the Heart* Series

On his eightieth birthday, Sir Winston Churchill dismissed the compliment that he was the "lion" who had defeated Nazi Germany in World War Two. He told the Houses of Parliament that *"It was a nation and race dwelling all around the globe that had the lion's heart. I had the luck to be called upon to give the roar."*

I hope that God speaks to you very powerfully through the "roar" of the books in the *Straight to the Heart* series. I hope they help you to understand the books of the Bible and the message which the Holy Spirit inspired their authors to write. I hope that they help you to hear God's voice challenging you, and that they provide you with a springboard for further journeys into each book of Scripture for yourself.

But when you hear my "roar", I want you to know that it comes from the heart of a much bigger "lion" than me. I have been shaped by a whole host of great Christian thinkers and preachers from around the world, and I want to give due credit to at least some of them here:

Terry Virgo, David Stroud, Dave Holden, John Hosier, Adrian Holloway, Greg Haslam, Lex Loizides and all those who lead the Newfrontiers family of churches; friends and encouragers, such as Stef Liston, Joel Virgo, Stuart Gibbs, Scott Taylor, Nick Sharp, Nick Derbridge, Phil Whittall, and Kevin and Sarah Aires; Tony Collins, Jenny Ward, Simon Cox and Margaret Milton at Monarch Books; Malcolm Kayes and all the elders of The Coign Church,

Woking; my fellow elders and church members here at Everyday Church in London; my great friend Andrew Wilson – without your friendship, encouragement and example, this series would never have happened.

I would like to thank my parents, my brother Jonathan, and my in-laws, Clive and Sue Jackson. Dad – your example birthed in my heart the passion which brought this series into being. I didn't listen to all you said when I was a child, but I couldn't ignore the way you got up at five o' clock every morning to pray, read the Bible and worship, because of your radical love for God and for his Word. I'd like to thank my children – Isaac, Noah, Esther and Ethan – for keeping me sane when publishing deadlines were looming. But most of all, I'm grateful to my incredible wife, Ruth – my friend, encourager, corrector and helper.

You all have the lion's heart, and you have all developed the lion's heart in me. I count it an enormous privilege to be the one who was chosen to sound the lion's roar.

So welcome to the *Straight to the Heart* series. My prayer is that you will let this roar grip your own heart too – for the glory of the great Lion of the Tribe of Judah, the Lord Jesus Christ!

Introduction:
Step into the Story

He jumped to his feet and came to Jesus... and followed Jesus along the road.

(Mark 10:50, 52)

Mark may be the shortest of the four New Testament gospels, but it is also by far the most intense. Mark is like the driver of a Formula 1 racing car. He puts his foot to the floor in the very first verse and he doesn't let up the pace until he brings it to its sudden surprise ending. Mark's gospel is a breathless succession of exhilarating highs and lows because that is precisely how it felt to be one of the twelve disciples of Jesus. Mark wants us to experience what it was like for Peter and his friends when Jesus called them to leave their old lives behind and step into his story.

Mark wrote his gospel in Greek, the educated language in the first-century Roman Empire. His favourite Greek word is *eutheōs*, which means *immediately, at once* or *straightaway*.[1] He uses it forty-two times in just sixteen chapters. That is how it felt for Peter and his friends when they came into contact with Jesus, a man of action who burned with an incredible sense of purpose. His call to them was not a question: *"How can I help you?"* It was a command to *"Come and follow me."* He told them to wave goodbye to their quiet lives so that he could catapult them into a whirlwind adventure with God.

Mark loved this about Jesus. His parents had named him

---

[1] Sometimes Mark even finds the word *eutheōs* a bit too long. He often abbreviates it to *euthus*.

Marcus, a Latin name made famous by two of Rome's greatest action men. Marcus Tullius Cicero had opposed the rise of Julius Caesar, and Mark Antony had helped Caesar to overcome him. We can tell from the way Mark peppers his gospel with words imported from Latin that he was brought up on Roman history books about such men and on myths about Hercules, Aeneas and Romulus.[2] Mark therefore writes his gospel at a lightning pace in order to present Jesus to his Roman readers as the ultimate man of action. Jesus is far greater than any Roman action hero and he invites us to play our own part in his great story.

Mark also had a second name. The New Testament calls him *John Mark* because, although his parents courted favour with the Romans, they never forgot that they were first and foremost Jews.[3] *John* was Hebrew for *The Lord Has Shown Grace*, and it had been the name of high priests, warriors and generals throughout Israel's history.[4] Mark's Roman education must therefore have been supplemented with Old Testament hero stories about men such as Gideon, Samson, David and Jonathan. Mark's parents told him about God's promise that he would one day send an even greater hero to save the Jewish nation from its oppressors, making all of these Old Testament action men look like nothing more than warm-up acts for the Messiah. No wonder, therefore, Mark is excited as he writes his gospel. He is the first to chronicle the arrival of this Messiah.

Mark's gospel is technically anonymous. He does not name himself as author or list any of his sources. He is too busy narrating the non-stop action. However, several ancient writers

---

[2] None of the other gospel writers use as many imported Latin words as Mark – words such as *spekoulatōr* meaning *bodyguard* (6:27), *quadrans* referring to a Roman coin known as a *quarter* (12:42), or *phragelloō*, which describes being flogged using a special Roman whip known as a *flagellum* (15:15).

[3] See Acts 12:12, 12:25 and 15:37.

[4] The Hebrew name *Johanan* became *Iōannēs* in Greek and so it entered the English language as *John*. See 2 Kings 25:23; 1 Chronicles 6:10, 12:4, 12:12 and Nehemiah 8:22–23.

tell us that Mark wrote this gospel as scribe when the disciple Peter spoke his memoirs. Eusebius tells us that

> *Peter's hearers... were not satisfied with a single hearing... but with all sorts of entreaties pleaded with Mark whose Gospel we have, seeing that he was Peter's follower, to leave them a written statement of the teaching which had been given them verbally. They did not give up until they had persuaded him, and so they became the cause of the written Gospel which bears the name of Mark.*[5]

The second-century bishop Irenaeus of Lyons confirms this, telling us that *"Mark, the disciple and interpreter of Peter, handed down to us in writing what Peter preached."*[6] Mark listened to Peter as he preached the story of Jesus throughout the Roman Empire, then he wrote it down so that we might know how to become part of the story too.

Peter was a man of action whose shoot-first-ask-questions-later attitude kept on getting him into trouble. But his weakness was also his greatest strength. He became the leader of the Early Church because nobody was more willing to step into Jesus' story than he was. While the other disciples were content to watch Jesus walk on water, Peter asked him, *"Lord, if it's you, tell me to come to you on the water"* (Matthew 14:28). While the other disciples turned their boat and rowed 100 metres to the shore to have breakfast with the risen Jesus, Peter leapt into the water and swam on ahead of them (John 21:7). Mark's gospel still bears the voice of the rough-and-ready fisherman who first spoke it. Peter could not slow himself down as he preached excitedly about Jesus. Nor could Mark as he preserved Peter's words for the likes of you and me.

Mark 1:1–7:23 is set in Galilee and it recounts the early

---

[5] Eusebius of Caesarea wrote this just after 300 AD in his *Church History* (2.15.1).

[6] Irenaeus of Lyons wrote this in c.180 AD in *Against Heresies* (3.1.1).

days after Peter was invited to play a part in **the Messiah's story. Mark 7:24–9:29** is set among the pagans and it chronicles Peter's growing realisation that what is happening in Israel is **the world's story. Mark 9:30–10:52** takes place on the road to Jerusalem and charts Peter's growing awareness that it is going to be **a costly story. Mark 11–15** records the week leading up to Jesus' death and marvels at the fact that this is such **a surprising story. Mark 16** is the grand finale of the gospel, describing Peter's mixture of fear and delight as he finds Jesus' tomb empty and realises that he has been called to continue **an unfinished story**.

So get ready to experience Jesus as Peter knew him. Get ready to experience the emotional rollercoaster ride of following Jesus around with his twelve disciples. Mark describes how Peter felt at every bump along the road because the same call to follow Jesus is ours today. Mark expects God to surprise us and to teach us and to humble us and to transform us, just as he did Peter, while we read the pages of his gospel.

Let's get ready to discover what it was like for Peter and his friends to travel around with Jesus. Let's get ready to hear Jesus still speaking to us today. Let's get ready to step into the story.

Part One:

The
Messiah's Story

(Mark 1:1–7:23)

Journey's End (1:1–8)

The beginning of the good news about Jesus the Messiah, the Son of God.

(Mark 1:1)

There is no Christmas in Mark's gospel. There is no stable. There are no angel choirs. There are no shepherds or wise men. Mark covers in his first 13 verses what it takes Matthew 76 verses and Luke 182 verses to say. Mark has no time to beat around the bush. He takes us straight to the point where Peter came face to face with the adult Jesus.

There is a reason for this. Matthew wrote for Jewish readers and needed to explain how Jesus fitted into the Jewish story. He begins with historical background because he needs to prove that Jesus is the much-prophesied Jewish Messiah. Similarly Luke wrote for Gentile readers and he needed to explain how a man who was crucified as a criminal could be the Saviour of the world. He locates the life of Jesus in the history of the pagan world. But Mark is different. He isn't writing about the Jewish story or the Gentile story. He is writing about one man's encounter with the story of Jesus and about what made him step into the story.[1] He does not mention the early life of Jesus because Peter was not there. He takes us straight to the moment where their two stories collided.

Jesus does not appear in these opening eight verses. Mark builds anticipation for the moment when he appears in verse 9. In comparison to the other gospel writers, Mark tells us

---

[1] Mark reminds us in 1:1 that the Gospel isn't primarily our story. It is the story about Jesus the Messiah.

very little about what John the Baptist said. Instead he fills our senses with vivid detail so that we can sense how Peter felt at the beginning of his journey. Eyewitness detail is a major feature of Mark's gospel. Jesus doesn't just go to sleep in a boat; he goes to sleep in a boat *on a cushion* (4:38). Jesus doesn't just make people sit down to eat; he makes them sit down *on the green grass* (6:39). A blind man doesn't just leap up to talk to Jesus; he *throws his cloak aside* in his eagerness to talk to him (10:50). Mark sets the scene with vivid detail in these opening verses. He describes the clothing and the diet of a strange preacher who appeared in the wilderness.[2] He describes the crowds that gathered to him at the River Jordan. He tells us little about what John actually said.[3] What matters more is that we feel we are there at the start of Peter's journey.

Mark invites us to participate in Peter's confusion. He quotes far less from the Old Testament than Matthew does because his Roman readers are largely unfamiliar with the Jewish Scriptures, but he begins his gospel with two Old Testament quotations in order to convey to us just how confused first-century Jews were about what to expect from their Messiah. In verse 2, Mark quotes from Malachi 3:1, where God says *"I will send my messenger before **me** to prepare the way for **me**,"* but note the way Mark changes the words so that it hints at the divinity of the Messiah: *"I will send my messenger before **you** to prepare the way for **you"**.* In verse 3, he quotes from Isaiah 40:3, which says this messenger will prepare *"a highway for our God,"* but he changes the words again: the messenger will *"make straight paths for **him"**.* Mark therefore invites us to share in the

---

[2] Elijah had made this the traditional dress of a Jewish prophet (2 Kings 1:8; Zechariah 13:4). It linked John's ministry to a prophecy in Malachi 4:5, which described him as "Elijah".

[3] Matthew 3:1–12 and Luke 3:1–20 fill out Mark's brief account by recording much more of John the Baptist's teaching, and Luke records John's parentage. Mark tells us nothing more than Peter and the rest of the crowd knew at the time. He wants us to feel as though we are there.

crowd's confusion. How could the Scriptures prophesy that the Messiah would be a man and yet be God?

Mark invites us to participate in Peter's offence. Southerners from Judea looked down on Galilean northerners such as Peter. When he heard that swarms of Judeans had adopted John the Baptist as their own, it did not endear him to the Galilean fisherman.[4] Worse still was John's message. Non-Jews who wanted to embrace the God of Israel needed to be baptised in water as a confession that they were dirty Gentiles who needed a bath before they could become part of God's holy people. John's message was therefore outrageous. He told the Jews that their ethnicity could never save them; it could only lull them into a dangerous sense of spiritual pride.[5] They needed to humble themselves by accepting that they were just as spiritually unclean as any pagan. The Greek word for repentance means a change of mind, which is why in verse 4 it is repentance, rather than simply confession of sin, which brings forgiveness. John told them to confess their sins, to repent of their spiritual pride and to prepare their hearts for the arrival of the Messiah by being baptised in the River Jordan. He called them to admit that they were just as sinful as people from any other nation.

Mark invites us to participate in Peter's excitement. He summarises John the Baptist's message in two short verses: The Messiah is so much greater than the Old Testament prophets that John is not even worthy to take off his shoes like a common slave, and the Messiah will fulfil the great promise of the Old Testament by baptising with the Holy Spirit those who follow

---

[4] Mark is not claiming in 1:5 that every single individual in Judea came to listen to John the Baptist. This is a Hebrew way of saying that anyone who failed to do so was the exception rather than the norm.

[5] Matthew 3:7–10 and Luke 3:7–9 state this in more explicit detail. When Paul talks about *making a straight path* in 1 Thessalonians 3:11, he means dealing with every obstacle which might keep him away from Thessalonica. Pride is one of the biggest obstacles that prevent people coming to faith in Jesus.

him.[6] Whoever this Messiah might be and however offensive his message, Peter could see he was worth giving up everything to follow.

Mark therefore begins his gospel with a vivid description of how it felt to live in Galilee in the weeks leading up to the start of Jesus' public ministry. He ignores the Christmas story because he wants to take us on the same journey of discovery as the crowd. Jesus told Peter to follow him and now Mark tells us to walk with Peter.

But Mark is too excited about the journey to leave us in the dark completely. He is like a TV newsreader who blurts out the final score of the big match, even though he knows his viewers have not yet had a chance to watch the game. He reveals the end of Peter's journey in the very first verse of his gospel. Peter discovered that Jesus is the long-awaited *Christ* or *Messiah*,[7] and that he is therefore *the Son of God*. Mark uses the Greek word *euangelion* (the word used by Roman emperors when they claimed that their rule was *gospel* or *good news* for the world) in order to tell us that what Peter and his friends discovered was the ultimate Gospel.[8] Mark cannot resist encouraging us as we set out on the same journey of discovery as Peter by telling us what amazing treasure we will find at journey's end.

Can you sense Mark's excitement as he prepares us for the moment when the Messiah finally walks onto the stage of history? Can you feel the anticipation in these first eight verses as he builds up to the climactic moment in verse 9? Then come alongside Peter and walk with him in the early days. Mark is inviting you to step into the story.

---

[6] This was prophesied in Old Testament passages such as Joel 2:28–29, Isaiah 32:15, 44:3, Jeremiah 31:33–34, Ezekiel 36:26–27, 39:29 and Zechariah 12:10–13:1.

[7] Mark uses the Greek word *Christos*, which translates the Hebrew word *Messiah* and means *Anointed One*.

[8] Our word *Gospel* comes from an Anglo-Saxon word for *Good News*. Mark uses the Greek word *kērussō* in verses 4 and 7 to emphasise that John *heralded* a better message than the one proclaimed by Caesar's heralds.

A Single Step (1:9–20)

He saw Simon and his brother Andrew casting a net into the lake, for they were fishermen. "Come, follow me," Jesus said.

(Mark 1:16–17)

An ancient Chinese proverb tells us that *"A journey of a thousand miles begins with a single step."*[1] But what the Chinese proverb fails to tell us is that the first step is usually the hardest. That was certainly the case for Peter when Jesus appeared on the beach and shouted to him in his fishing boat that it was time to set out with him on a journey. Peter had plenty of reasons to refuse when Jesus commanded him to *"Come, follow me."*

Mark goes out of his way to emphasise Peter's ignorance of Jesus in these verses. Mark wants us to grasp that we already know as much about Jesus as Peter did at the start of his journey. He does not even mention Peter until the moment when Jesus calls him to take a first step of faith in him. Nothing should stop us from taking a similar first step of faith in Jesus too.

In verses 9–11, Mark tells us about the rumours Peter heard from the River Jordan. When Jesus obeyed John's call to be baptised, something happened that set him apart from the crowds of people who were baptised with him. The divine voice rang out from heaven and proclaimed that the carpenter from Nazareth was in fact God's own Son.[2] When the Holy Spirit descended upon him in bodily form and anointed him to begin

---

[1] Lao-Tzu wrote this in the sixth century BC in chapter 64 of his *Tao Te Ching*.

[2] Mark's Roman readers are too unfamiliar with the Old Testament for him to quote its prophecies that the Messiah would come from Nazareth. We are reminded of this in Matthew 2:23 and 4:13–16 instead.

his public ministry, God the Father, Son and Spirit testified together with one clear voice to the Jewish nation that the Messiah had finally come. Peter's first step on the journey with Jesus was difficult, but he was helped by the rumours he heard from the River Jordan. Faith means acting upon what we hear.

Mark's original Roman readers were used to hearing their emperors claim to be sons of the gods. We will discover later, in 15:39, that one of the most natural ways for a Roman to express conversion from paganism to Christianity was to exclaim that *"Surely this man was the Son of God!"* But to the Jewish ear this announcement meant something more. It meant that Jesus was the long-awaited Messiah. The Lord had promised King David that one of his descendants would be known as *"the son of God"* and would rule on the throne of Israel forever.[3] This event struck Peter so profoundly that he quotes these words in 2 Peter 1:16, reminding his readers that *"We did not follow cleverly devised stories when we told you about the coming of our Lord Jesus Christ in power, but we were eye-witnesses of his majesty."* Peter took a first step of faith because he believed the eyewitness accounts of Jesus' baptism. So can we.[4]

In verses 12–13, Mark tells us what happened next. No sooner had Jesus been revealed as the Messiah than the Holy Spirit drove him away from the crowds to endure forty days of testing in the desert.[5] For a Jew like Peter, the words *forty* and *desert* meant only one thing. Jesus had re-enacted the forty years which the Israelites spent in the desert after their exodus

---

[3] 1 Chronicles 17:11–14; Psalm 2:6–8; 89:20–29. God's words also refer back to Isaiah 42:1.

[4] Peter was not there to hear God's voice at Jesus' baptism (2 Peter 1:17) but, because he believed the word of others, he heard the same voice at Jesus' transfiguration (1:18). Unless we take an initial step of faltering faith based on the testimony of others, we will never experience Jesus powerfully for ourselves.

[5] The Greek word *ekballō* in 1:12 is the same word that Mark uses throughout his gospel for Jesus *driving out* demons. The Holy Spirit looked like a dove but he was very firm with Jesus. He is firm with us too.

from Egypt but, where they had succumbed to temptation and sinned, he had passed the test with flying colours.[6] Mark does not give us any detail about how Satan tempted Jesus, because Peter was not there to hear it.[7] Peter responded to faith in an incomplete story. So must we.

In verses 14–15, Mark tells us that Peter began to understand what it meant for Jesus to be Israel's Messiah. After John was imprisoned for daring to question King Herod's actions, Jesus started preaching all around Galilee that *"The time has come. The kingdom of God has come near. Repent and believe the good news!"*[8] Mark uses the Greek word *euangelion*, or *gospel*, in both verses and he uses the word *kērussō*, or *to herald*, in verse 14 because these were the words used by the Roman imperial machine. He tells us that Jesus proclaimed he was a greater King than Caesar's sinful governor Herod, and that he told the Jewish nation it was time for them to step into God's great story. Jesus demonstrated his Kingdom rule as well as preaching it – turning water into wine, healing many people and giving Peter a miraculous catch of fish before he called him to follow him (Luke 5:1–11; John 2:1–12; 4:46–54).[9] Mark omits this detail in order to take us swiftly to the moment when Jesus commanded Peter to step into his story and when Peter acted *at once* on the evidence he had seen.[10] Immediately he left his fishing nets behind and followed Jesus.

---

[6] Jesus was the true Son of God and therefore the true Israel (Exodus 4:22–23; Jeremiah 31:20). Matthew 2:15 quotes from Hosea 11:1 to make this point explicitly.

[7] *Satan* is the Hebrew word for *Adversary*. The Devil is called this at least 18 times in the Old Testament.

[8] Jesus proclaimed that he was the promised King of Israel who would demolish anything that dared resist heaven's rule. The Gospel isn't primarily about our need. It's the announcement of Jesus' identity.

[9] Luke has a different chronology for some of the events in Mark 1. Mark uses the Greek word for *straightaway* 11 times in this chapter to express that all of these events happened on top of one another.

[10] In fact, almost a year passed between Jesus' baptism in 27 AD and his calling Peter to follow him in 28 AD.

When Neil Armstrong became the first man to walk on the moon, he exclaimed in triumph that *"That's one small step for a man, one giant leap for all mankind."* Mark tells us that for Peter it was the same. In verses 16–20, he emphasises that Peter was a nobody. He calls him by his original name Simon, even though John 1:42 tells us that by this time Jesus had already renamed him Peter, which means *Rock*.[11] Mark wants us to understand that, at this stage, he was not yet a rock with which Jesus could build. He was more like his namesake Simeon, the son of Jacob who was cursed for his rash enthusiasm. Mark wants us to understand that Peter set out on his journey of faith in Jesus even though he had more questions than he had answers.

Mark wants to prevent us from treating our questions as excuses not to step into Jesus' story. Peter and his brother Andrew had better reasons to delay making their first step of faith than we have, yet they believed Jesus when he promised them in verse 17 that, if they followed him, he would teach them how to fish for the souls of men and women.[12] They believed that he would turn nobodies like them into great apostles.[13] You may have more questions than answers at this early stage in Mark's gospel, but don't let that stop you from praying and telling Jesus that you want to take a first step of faith into his great story. Your single step will be a giant leap into the adventure of a lifetime.

---

[11] Mark only switches from *Simon* to *Peter* when Jesus names him one of the Twelve in 3:16. The Roman Empire knew him as *Peter* or as the Aramaic equivalent *Cephas* (1 Corinthians 9:5; 15:5; Galatians 1:18; 2:9, 11, 14), so Mark emphasises that he was a very different man at the start of his journey.

[12] Jesus puts the onus for our fruitfulness on himself when he promises literally, *"Come after me and I will turn you into fishers of men."* A fisherman is simply a pleasure-boater unless he returns with fish. Jesus enabled Peter to see 3,000 people saved as a result of a single sermon on the Day of Pentecost.

[13] The Greek word Mark uses for Peter's fishing partners *preparing* their nets in 1:19 is *katartizō*, the same word that Paul uses in Ephesians 4:11–12 to describe apostles *preparing* the Church for works of service.

Man of Woman Born
(1:21–39)

*He would not let the demons speak because they
knew who he was.*

(Mark 1:34)

In William Shakespeare's play, Macbeth is convinced that nobody can stand in the way of his desire to conquer Scotland. He has been told by a ghostly apparition to *"Be bloody, bold and resolute. Laugh to scorn the power of man, for none of woman born shall harm Macbeth."* He therefore confidently schemes and murders his way to the throne, telling his enemies that *"Thou wast born of woman. But swords I smile at, weapons laugh to scorn, brandished by man that's of a woman born."* One of the greatest moments in all of Shakespeare's plays is the point when Macbeth suddenly realises that his opponent was not born naturally like other men. *"Despair thy charm... Macduff was from his mother's womb untimely ripp'd,"* his enemy tells him before he dies.[1]

The end of Shakespeare's *Macbeth* is dramatic, but it is nothing compared to the start of Mark's gospel. Having told us very clearly in verse 13 that the Devil is real and determined, Mark now talks about the Devil's foot soldiers. He tells us that many demons were at work in first-century Galilee, convinced that nobody could ever challenge their control over many people in the region. Their surprise is palpable when Jesus suddenly bursts onto the scene. Peter may not yet fully grasp who Jesus is, but the demons are in no doubt. Mark wants us to

---

[1] Shakespeare wrote this in c. 1606 in his play *Macbeth* (4.1, 5.7 and 5.10).

experience these scenes with the same wide-eyed wonder as Peter. He wants to catch us up in the excitement of Jesus' story.

In verses 21–22, Mark describes how the crowds immediately sense something different about Jesus' teaching. There were many rabbis in the synagogues who taught about the Jewish Law, but there was nobody who spoke God's Word with such authority.[2] Matthew tells us that Jesus would often proclaim, *"You have heard that it was said... but I tell you...,"* according his own words the same authority as the Old Testament Scriptures, but he may have simply been repeating the words of verse 15: *"The time has come. The kingdom of God has come near."*[3] Whatever he said, it was like the moment when Macduff reveals his secret to Macbeth. Every human and every demon understood that Jesus was not like any other man of woman born.

Many twenty-first-century readers of Mark's gospel struggle to know what to do with his plain teaching that demons are real and active in the world. One of the most famous Bible commentators even writes that *"It may seem fantastic to us; but the ancient peoples believed implicitly in demons... even if there are no such things as demons."*[4] He pities Jesus for knowing less about the true state of Galileans than a newly qualified doctor today. Needless to say, the Devil is delighted with such an attitude. If he and his foot soldiers can continue their noxious work unseen, they may be able to resist the news that God's Kingdom has arrived. Jesus will have none of it. As soon as he opens his mouth, demons are quickly exposed and eliminated.

In verses 23–28, this happens to a man in the synagogue at Capernaum. Mark does not tell us how many times he had come to a service without feeling threatened by the teaching of the rabbis but, as soon as Jesus speaks, an evil spirit which

---

[2] Ezra founded an order of *teachers of the law* in the mid-fifth century BC, but later generations exchanged his anointed preaching for dreary manmade commentary.

[3] Matthew 5:21–22, 27–28, 31–32, 33–34, 38–39, 43–44.

[4] William Barclay writing in 1956 in his commentary on Matthew (8:28–34).

lives inside him starts to speak through him.[5] *"Have you come to destroy us?"* the demon shrieks, speaking for the many demons in the region and confessing that they all know the arrival of Jesus spells game-over for their plans. Peter and the rest of the Galileans in Capernaum may not be sure who Jesus is, but this demon is in no doubt: *"I know who you are – the Holy One of God."* Jesus only has to speak five words in Greek. He talks to the demon as a man talks to his dog. *"Be muzzled!"* he commands literally, *"and come out of him!"* The demon shrieks and flees. The crowds are overwhelmed that Jesus' authority extends beyond the words he preaches. He backs them up by freeing people from their oppressed by the Devil.

In verses 29–34, Mark turns the spotlight onto Peter. Will the fisherman take another step of faith deeper into Jesus' story? When the service at the synagogue ends, Peter invites Jesus to the home which he shares with his wife and his mother-in-law and his brother Andrew, telling Jesus that his mother-in-law is in bed with a fever.[6] Jesus touches her hand and rebukes the fever in the same way that he rebuked the demon in the synagogue.[7] Peter's mother-in-law is instantly healed![8] The synagogue service is over, but Mark uses the Greek word *episunagō* to tell us in verse 33 that the whole town *synagogued* at Peter's door. Peter may have lived in that house for many years, but he soon discovers that everything changes when we step into God's story. Jesus muzzles the demons again because they all know who he is, and then he wields authority like no

---

[5] Although some English translations talk about people being *demon-possessed*, the Bible never actually uses that phrase. Here, Mark simply talks about a man *with* an impure spirit and tells us it *came out of him*. In verse 32, he talks about people who are *demonised*.

[6] Mark's original readers knew Peter's wife (1 Corinthians 9:5), so this family detail was important to them.

[7] Mark focuses on the power of Jesus' touch. Luke 4:38–41 tells us that Jesus also rebuked the fever.

[8] Mark tells us that Peter's mother-in-law instantly started serving Jesus. She too stepped into his story.

one else of woman born. Everyone who comes to Peter's front door with sickness or with demons goes home healed because the Devil is no match for the Messiah.[9]

In verses 35–39, Mark tells us about the morning after. Peter wakes up to the sound of fresh crowds banging at his front door, but Jesus is nowhere to be found. He has crept out of the house under cover of darkness in order to spend time alone with his Father.[10] When Peter eventually finds him, Jesus has already moved on to the next step in his story. Peter's mind is focused on the needs of his friends and neighbours in Capernaum, but Jesus is consumed with a desire to extend God's Kingdom right across the region.[11] *"Let us go somewhere else – to the nearby villages – so that I can preach there also,"* he surprises Peter. *"That is why I have come."* Jesus carries amazing authority and power, but he also carries an amazingly clear sense of his life's mission.

Peter is faced with a fresh choice. Will he leave his wife and his mother-in-law and his friends and his neighbours behind in order to stay close to Jesus' agenda? Will he pick up on the clue which Jesus gives him when he says literally, *"That is why I have come **out**"*?[12] Will he grasp what the demons saw: that Jesus is the Holy One who has come down to earth from heaven? Peter looks at the facts and he decides to believe what he sees: Jesus is like no other man of woman born. Peter resolves to take another step deeper into the unfolding story. He hits the road with Jesus out of town.

---

[9] We should not read too much into Mark's statement that *many* of those who came were healed, as if Jesus was unable to heal some of them. Matthew 8:16 tells us that on this occasion *everyone* was healed.

[10] Mark's gospel will go on to teach us how to heal the sick and drive out demons, just like Jesus, but if we want to minister as he did, then we need to start by prioritising time with the Father as he did.

[11] Mark uses the word *kērussō* again in 1:38 and 1:39 to emphasise that Jesus *heralded* the Kingdom of God.

[12] Jesus uses the Greek word *exerchomai* because he is conscious that his true home is in heaven. He doesn't talk to Peter about why he came *into* the world, but about why he came *out of* heaven.

Where's the Line? (1:40–45)

Filled with compassion, Jesus reached out his hand and touched the man.

(Mark 1:41)

The singer Morrissey loves to explore the limitations of human love. In one of his most unpleasant songs, he turns on an ugly child and tells her: *"Sleep on and dream of love, because it's the closest you will get to love. Poor twisted child, so ugly, so ugly... a symbol of where mad, mad lovers must pause and draw the line."*[1]

Morrissey's lyrics may be particularly disturbing, but the truth is that we all have a point at which we draw the line on love. Human love and compassion always have their limits, so Peter was watching Jesus to see where he would draw his own line. Jesus had shown compassion to a worshipper in the synagogue, to Peter's mother-in-law (no jokes, please), and to Peter's friends and neighbours in the respectable Jewish town of Capernaum, but how far would his compassion go when they took to the road together? Peter didn't have to wait very long to find out.

Leprosy sufferers were the hideous outcasts of the ancient world. Pagans were so afraid of catching their incurable disease that they drove them out of town. Jews did the same but with an added twist. The Jewish Law decreed that anyone who touched a leper became ceremonially unclean – that is, unworthy to come to the Temple until they had meticulously purified themselves.[2] Furthermore, lepers were ugly. A modern leprosy doctor describes his patients:

---

[1] Morrissey in his song *November Spawned a Monster* (1990).

[2] Leviticus 13:45–46; Numbers 5:1–4.

The disease attacked the ears and nose, causing them to enlarge. Cartilage in the nose then collapsed. The eyes became inflamed and began to tear. Eyelids, lips and chin distended enormously... The whole face has a horrid appearance... Ulcers form on the metatarsal articulations of the fingers and toes, without any pain. The skin becomes gangrenous... by the slow progress of this terrible disease.[3]

So when a leper approaches Jesus on his travels, Peter expects him to draw the line. Lepers lived in groups to ease their loneliness, so this solitary leper must have been of the most hideous kind. Peter turns to Jesus. He has stepped into the Messiah's story but he isn't yet sure what the limits will be to Jesus' love. He is about to find out.

Peter has underestimated *Jesus' compassion*. Peter thinks like a first-century Jew. He refuses to eat non-kosher foods. He refuses to befriend non-Jews or to pay them a visit in their pagan homes.[4] But Jesus thinks differently. The Greek word Mark uses in verse 41 means literally that Jesus' *bowels went out* to the man. He looks at the leper's face and he feels gutted. He is filled with such compassion that he does not hesitate to touch him. The man has only dared to beg for a word of healing, but Jesus throws caution to the wind and steps forward to touch him. He confers great dignity on this outcast because, although a leper, he is still a human being loved by God.

Peter has underestimated *Jesus' mission*. Jesus has not come for the respectable. He has come for anyone who is humble enough to confess their sin, turn from their ungodly lifestyle and step into his story. First-century Jews linked leprosy to sinfulness, which is why the leper asks to be made clean rather

---

[3] Dr Edward Hoffman wrote this in 1866, quoted by John Tayman in *The Colony* (2006).

[4] Acts 10:9–15, 27–28; 11:4–9.

than simply to be healed.[5] He asks with such desperate faith that Jesus gladly embraces his life with the power of the Kingdom of God. Jesus heals him with one touch and sends him straight to the Temple – back into God's presence from which he has been excluded for so long. Jesus does more than simply heal the leper. He also fulfils his broader mission of bringing spiritual outcasts home to God.

Peter has underestimated *Jesus' character*. We do the same whenever we pray to God to heal a person *"if it is your will."* This is the only occasion in the gospels where somebody asks Jesus to heal *"if you are willing,"* and he reacts very strongly against it. *"I am willing,"* he shoots back. Of course he is. He is the God who revealed himself to Israel as *The-Lord-Who-Heals-You* (Exodus 15:26) and as the *God-Who-Saves-You-Out-Of-All-Your-Calamities-And-Distresses* (1 Samuel 10:19). To doubt that God longs for the diseased to be healthy is leprous theology, and it reveals a fundamental misunderstanding of his story. Although the name Jesus was common in first-century Israel (it is simply the Greek form of the Hebrew name Joshua), an angel gave this name to the Messiah because it means *The-Lord-Saves* or *The-Lord-Heals*.[6] Saving and healing people is integral to Jesus' character. When we pray, *"Jesus, if you are willing,"* it is an insulting contradiction in terms.

Peter has underestimated *Jesus' power*. He is thinking back to passages such as Haggai 2:11–13, which say that what is unclean defiles what is holy. He has not yet fully grasped the implications of the name he heard a demon attribute to Jesus in the synagogue in verse 24. Jesus isn't just holy. He is the Holy One of God. With him, contamination works the other way around. It only takes one touch from Jesus to make what is unclean clean and what is impure pure.

---

[5] The Jews had formed this view from passages such as Numbers 12:9–12, 2 Kings 5:20–27 and 2 Chronicles 26:16–21. Jesus says their thinking is too simplistic in John 9:2–3..

[6] Matthew 1:21. The Greek word *sōzō* is used for *healing* as well as saving in Mark's gospel.

So why doesn't Jesus heal everyone today? That's the natural question for us to ask when we grasp that Jesus is always willing to heal but often doesn't. What about cancer and HIV, the leprosy of our day? Where is Jesus when we need him to heal those things?

Mark admits there is some mystery in this. Jesus warns the man strongly not to tell the people of Galilee that he has been healed. We can tell from verse 45 that he says this because he does not want his healing ministry to restrict his preaching ministry, but the man is so confused by the warning that he ignores it.[7] Mark uses this to teach us that Jesus will not answer all of our questions about healing. Instead he simply commands us to trust and obey.

Jesus tells the man to go to the Temple and offer the sacrifices stipulated in Leviticus 14 in order to testify to the priests that the Messiah has come. We may still have questions but we can testify for sure that, when it comes to compassion towards the sick and hurting, Jesus never draws the line.

Last year at the church I lead in London, we saw two people healed of cancer. But I'll be honest. It's a big church, and we lost more people than we saw healed. I feel sorely tempted to respond to the disappointment by embracing the leprous theology of *"if you are willing."* I feel tempted to persuade myself that God is glorified through our sickness, despite the fact that 2:12 tells us plainly that he is far more glorified through our healing. But I refuse. I refuse to draw a line where Jesus will not draw one. I refuse to doubt that Jesus is the Healer, who sends nobody away. I am resolved to keep on stepping ever deeper into his story until I see as many people healed as Peter went on to see.

---

[7] Jesus did not perform healing miracles as a PR stunt to gain an audience for his teaching. Mark emphasises that he healed out of compassion for people, even when it would hinder his teaching ministry. Jesus was willing to be excluded from the towns in order that the leper might be restored to them.

Friends, Romans, Countrymen (2:1–12)

I want you to know that the Son of Man has authority on earth to forgive sins.

(Mark 2:10)

Jesus really knew how to offend friends, Romans and countrymen. He opened up a conflict on three fronts as soon as he returned to Capernaum. When the former leper's loose talk made it impossible for Jesus to tour the towns of Galilee without his preaching being drowned out by requests for instant healing, Jesus decided to travel back to Peter's house. Up to now he had been very popular, but the time had come for a bit of scandal.

First, he offended his friend Peter. Jesus did not own a house, so when Mark tells us in verse 1 that the Capernaum crowds *"heard that he had come home,"* he must be referring to the house he left in 1:35.[1] The people of Capernaum were still talking about their evening of miracles outside Peter's front door, and ever since Jesus left town the following morning they had been waiting for his return. They flocked to Peter's house in such large numbers that there was no place left to stand, either inside or outside the front door. Peter had not consulted his wife before leaving his fishing nets to follow Jesus in 1:18 and, as far as we know, he had not consulted her before going on tour with Jesus in 1:39. However understanding she was about this, her patience must have been tested when Jesus suddenly transformed her home into a crowded preaching station. Then

---

[1] Matthew 8:20; Luke 9:58.

it got worse. Four men dismantled the roof and ceiling in order to lower their paralysed friend down to Jesus. My children love this story. It's a family favourite. But it can't have been so popular with Peter's family. When Jesus brought the house down in Capernaum, the house was Peter's. Stepping into Jesus' story was proving very costly.

Next, Jesus offended his countrymen. His healings had made him very popular with the Jews, but he wanted to do far more than simply heal the sick among them. He had come to call them to repentance and confession of their sin.[2] He had come to deal with the heart of the human problem by dealing with the problem of the human heart. That's why, even though it was obvious to everyone why the paralysed man's friends had vandalised Peter's roof to lower him down, Jesus ignored the presenting problem. He was preaching and not healing when the overhead visitor interrupted him, so he carried on. Jesus looked at their faith – both that of the paralysed man and that of his friends – and decided that such faith warranted his opening up a conflict with the Jewish religious leaders. He turned to the paralysed man and told him, *"Son, your sins are forgiven."*

It is easy for us to miss how offensive this statement was to a first-century Jew. C.S. Lewis points out that

> *What this man said was, quite simply, the most shocking thing that has ever been uttered by human lips... I mean the claim to forgive sins: any sins. Now unless the speaker is God, this is really so preposterous as to be comic. We can all understand how a man forgives offences against himself. You tread on my toe and I forgive you, you steal my money and I forgive you. But what should we make of a man, himself unrobbed and untrodden on, who announced that he forgave you for treading on other*

---

[2] Jesus' early teaching closely echoed that of John the Baptist (see Matthew 3:2 and 4:17), so *"repent"* in 1:15 is meant to communicate to us that 1:4 is a summary of Jesus' early teaching too.

men's toes and stealing other men's money? Asinine fatuity is the kindest description we should give of his conduct. Yet this is what Jesus did. He told people that their sins were forgiven, and never waited to consult all the other people whom their sins had undoubtedly injured. He unhesitatingly behaved as if He was the party chiefly concerned, the person chiefly offended in all offences. This makes sense only if He really was the God whose laws are broken and whose love is wounded in every sin. In the mouth of any speaker who is not God, these words would imply what I can only regard as silliness and conceit unrivalled by any other character in history.[3]

We may fail to spot this, but the Jewish leaders didn't. Their instant response is *"He's blaspheming!"* In ancient Israel blasphemy was a crime bearing the death penalty, so they are not simply objecting to his message. For the first time they are plotting murder unless he retracts his teaching.[4] Jesus senses what they are thinking, but he refuses to backpedal. Instead he proves that he is able to do precisely what he says.[5] He performs a breathtaking miracle, which confirms that he possesses the authority to forgive sins. He can do what only God can do.

In doing so, Jesus also offends the Romans. He is careful how he does so because the Emperor Tiberius will not tolerate any rival to his rule, but his words are nonetheless a strong attack on Rome. One of Jesus' favourite titles for himself is *"the Son of Man."* He uses it fourteen times in Mark's gospel alone, and the first time that he uses it is here in verse 10. To

---

[3] C.S. Lewis in his book *Mere Christianity* (1952).

[4] Don't be surprised that this plotting began as early as the summer of 28 AD. Mark repeats this in 3:6.

[5] He does this by simply commanding the man, *"I tell you, get up."* He does not need to touch him or pray for him or rebuke his sickness. He commands him with authority to do what he cannot do, and he can.

an ignorant onlooker, it sounds like nothing more than a Jewish way of saying he is human, but not to anyone familiar with the prophecies of Daniel.[6]

Six hundred years earlier and six hundred miles away, Daniel had received a vision of the next four empires in world history. After watching the Babylonian, Persian and Macedonian Empires rise and fall, he had caught a glimpse of the mighty Roman Empire. At the height of Caesar's rule, he had witnessed the arrival of a very different king who built a very different kind of empire. He tells us in Daniel 7:13–14 that

> *I looked, and there before me was one like a son of man, coming with the clouds of heaven. He approached the Ancient of Days and was led into his presence. He was given authority, glory and sovereign power; all nations and peoples of every language worshipped him. His dominion is an everlasting dominion that will not pass away, and his kingdom is one that will never be destroyed.*

Jesus responds to this challenge to his authority by telling the crowds that he is this Son of Man, the glorious King about whom Daniel prophesied. As Mark's gospel progresses, he will explain that this means he is the Messiah and that he has authority to forgive sins, to end world history and to decide the eternal fate of every human being.[7]

Peter has every reason to be offended. His house has been vandalised, his rabbis have been scandalised, and his peace with Rome has been compromised. But Peter cannot argue with the

---

[6] Mark uses the phrase *"the sons of men"* in 3:28 to refer to humans in general, but he only ever uses the phrase *"the Son of Man"* to refer to the King whose reign is prophesied in Daniel 7:13–14.

[7] Mark 13:26 and 14:62. These verses make no sense unless Jesus is using the phrase *"the Son of Man"* to claim he is the King whose future reign Daniel saw. His enemies used this claim to convict him of blasphemy.

sight of this paralysed man leaping up and carrying his mat as he walks through the crowds to front door. *"We have never seen anything like this!"* the crowd exclaims in amazement, and Peter agrees.

No matter how offensive, no matter how dangerous and no matter how costly it may be, Peter decides to step deeper into the Messiah's story. He beckons us on in this journey of discovery, wherever Jesus may lead.

Runaway (2:13–17)

It is not the healthy who need a doctor, but those who are ill. I have not come to call the righteous, but sinners.

(Mark 2:17)

Levi was a runaway from God. He hadn't always been. His Jewish parents had such high hopes for him that they named him after the leader of the priestly tribe of Israel. The tribe of Levi had included Moses, the great Lawgiver, and his brother Aaron, the first high priest. It had included the worship leaders at the Temple who wrote many of the Psalms. Alphaeus and his wife therefore gave their son a name that proclaimed their strong desire that he would closely follow the God of Israel.

But as Levi grew up, he saw that godliness didn't pay as well as the Emperor Tiberius. He became a Roman tax collector, one of those treacherous quislings who collaborated with their nation's brutal conquerors. He became the worst kind of tax collector, one of those who sat in booths along the roadside and collected exaggerated custom duties from the people. Unlike the income tax collectors, these customs men were notoriously dishonest. They routinely overcharged their victims and pocketed the difference between the sum they collected and the tax they ought to charge. There is a reason Mark equates *tax collectors* with *sinners* in verse 15. Levi was the worst kind of spiritual runaway, hated by devout Jews along with the rest of his kind.

Peter had a history with Levi. Peter ran a fishing business out of Capernaum and had to pass Levi's tax booth whenever he took his catch along the Capernaum road. Peter must have been overcharged by Levi and his cronies countless times, so he was as surprised as anyone when Jesus stopped at the tax collector's booth and spoke the same words to Levi that he had spoken to Peter and his friends. *"Follow me,"* were the two simple words which Jesus said to the runaway. Levi leapt to his feet and left his tax-collecting career behind. The runaway was coming home. He was stepping back into God's story.

What happened to Levi mattered deeply to Peter because he had been a runaway too. Mark records Peter's journey of discovery, which explains why he emphasises Peter's faults and failures more than any other gospel writer. Despite his protestations to the contrary, Peter abandoned Jesus on the night of his arrest and ran away (14:50). When recognised and challenged, he denied three times that he knew Jesus (14:66–72). Peter knew exactly how it feels to have strayed far from God. Perhaps you do too. Many people who read Mark's gospel reflect on how far they have fallen away from their Christian faith in the past. They wonder if it is too late for them to step back into the story.

What happened to Levi also mattered deeply to Mark. He had been a runaway – more than once. He too had been with Jesus on the night of his arrest and, when the soldiers seized him, he had slipped out of his clothes and run home naked.[1] Eighteen years later, he had joined his cousin Barnabas and the apostle Paul on a missionary journey, but when things got tough on the journey he ran away again. He let the team down so severely that Paul later fell out with Barnabas rather than give a second chance to the runaway. Mark had walked the same road as Peter and many readers of his gospel. He had wondered

---

[1] Although Mark does not name himself in 14:51–52, most commentators agree that this strange piece of detail, which appears only in Mark's gospel, must have been included because it was autobiographical.

whether those who step out of God's story can ever step back in.[2]

That's why Mark is so delighted to record for us how Jesus treated the runaway tax collector Levi. Jesus came to dinner at his home and met all of his runaway friends so that he could invite them to step back into his story too. Jesus tells us in Matthew 18:17 just how dramatic an expression of acceptance this was in first-century Israel. No respectable Jew would ever dream of sharing food with a table full of grubby tax collectors. Nobody, that is, except for Jesus.

Enter the Pharisees for the first time in Mark's gospel. We have been trained to view them as the bad guys in the story but, remember, for Peter and Mark they were the ultimate good guys. Their name meant *"separatists"* in Hebrew, and they were leaders in the Jewish fight to resist the pagan influence of Rome. While the Sadducees controlled the Temple and fawned all over the governor, the Pharisees controlled the synagogues and made many converts to their radical Judaism. They were the greatest teachers of the law, preaching obedience to the Law of Moses, which they codified into 248 commands, 365 prohibitions and 1,521 amendments. The Pharisees were popular preachers who were doing everything humanly possible to bring the Jewish nation back to God. If Jesus should be sitting down to dinner with anyone then it was them, so they were appalled and asked Peter and his friends: *"Why does he eat with tax collectors and sinners?"*

Now comes the moment when Jesus answers our question. Is it ever too late for a runaway to step back into his story? Jesus points out to the Pharisees that a doctor's waiting room isn't full of healthy people, but of sick people. The Gospel is for those who confess their sins, who change their way of thinking and who recognise that their only hope lies in stepping into Jesus' story (1:4–5). This need not be more difficult for religious people, but

---

[2] Acts 12:25; 13:5, 13; 15:36–40.

it often proves harder for them to admit that their hard work has not made them righteous people. It has simply shown that, in spite of all of their best efforts, they are still sinners in need of a Saviour. Levi and his tax-collecting friends didn't have that problem. Spiritual runaways rarely do. Jesus announces that it is never too late for a humble person to run back home. The only thing that ever stops a person from stepping into Jesus' story is the spiritual pride that convinces them that they don't need to.

We discover in Matthew's gospel that Jesus gave Levi a new name, just as he gave a new name to Peter. He renamed him *Matthew*, which means *Gift-of-the-Lord*, as a reminder that forgiveness is a free gift from God. It is never earned. God turned the runaway Peter into his leading apostle. He turned the runaway Mark into his first gospel writer. He turned the runaway Levi into his second gospel writer.[3]

So if you are a spiritual runaway, don't fix your eyes on where you are now – on your sinful life or on your broken promises or on your sense of having betrayed the Lord. Fix your eyes instead on the Messiah who says he came to call the sick and not the healthy. Confess your sin and admit to Jesus that it is time for you to stop running and come back home. Tell him that from this moment on you are stepping back into his story.

---

[3] Matthew 9:9–13. We will see later that Mark probably wrote his gospel in the 50s AD. Matthew probably wrote his in c.60 AD, expanding on the brief and punchy text of Mark's gospel.

Black Cabs and Bales of Hay (2:18–3:6)

No one pours new wine into old wineskins... No, they pour new wine into new wineskins.

(Mark 2:22)

One of my friends is a London cabbie. Like all black cab drivers, he must abide by a number of strict rules. Some of them make sense and he would be fined heavily for breaking them. Others, rather less so.

Until quite recently, all London cabbies were required by law to carry a bale of hay. It was a throwback to the days of Queen Victoria when over 8,000 horse-drawn cabs crisscrossed the city. Still in force today is a law which requires my friend to check a dog for signs of rabies before it travels in his cab (despite the fact that rabies was eliminated from Britain in 1902) and another law which requires him to ask his passengers if they are afflicted by either smallpox or the plague (despite the fact that both diseases were eradicated from Britain many years ago). Naturally, my friend doesn't bother to observe these outdated laws. He knows no policeman would ever try to enforce Victorian horse-and-cart legislation in a modern megacity.

Hold that thought. Jesus tries to explain something similar to the Pharisees after they challenge him for having dinner with a group of tax collectors. Matthew, Mark and Luke all place this teaching about new wine and new wineskins immediately after Jesus' clash with the Pharisees over his friendship with Levi.[1]

41

---

[1] See Matthew 9:9–17 and Luke 5:27–39. These three are known as the *"synoptic"* gospels because, unlike John, they *"share a common perspective"* and a similar narrative structure.

Jesus did not ignore their concerns. He patiently explained that things had changed and that they needed to step into his story.

The first clash with the Pharisees is over fasting (2:18–22). The Pharisees used Old Testament verses to teach their followers that they needed to fast two days a week in order to attract the Lord's attention.[2] John the Baptist's disciples copied them, so they are surprised that Jesus does not teach his followers to do the same.[3] It's like black cabs and bales of hay, Jesus explains. It's an outdated way of thinking. The Messiah has come to earth as a bridegroom looking for a bride, so they already have the Lord's undivided attention![4] Striving for his favour now is inappropriate, like fasting at a wedding reception, like cutting up new and unshrunken cloth to patch an old coat, or like putting new wine into wineskins that are already bloated and worn with age. There will come a time for Jesus' followers to fast in order to lay hold of the Gospel as they continue his mission after his ascension.[5] But now it is time simply to sit back and enjoy his company. Stepping into the story of God's grace means stepping out of our old story of striving.

The second clash with the Pharisees is over the Sabbath (2:23–28). The Fourth Commandment instructed people to rest from sundown on Friday until sundown on Saturday, but the Pharisees had loaded this weekly day of rest with so many rules that observing it was more difficult than a workday. Moses had not forbidden Jesus' disciples from picking food to eat while they enjoyed a Sabbath walk across a field together, but the Pharisees treated it as farm work and as harvesting. Jesus has to remind them that the Sabbath was never about working hard to persuade God to bless us. It was always about downing tools

---

[2] See 1 Samuel 7:6, 2 Samuel 12:16, 1 Kings 21:27–29, Ezra 8:21–23, Nehemiah 1:4, Esther 4:16 and Luke 18:12.

[3] Matthew 9:14 says that John the Baptist's disciples initiated this conversation.

[4] The Church is described as the Bride of Christ in Ephesians 5:25–32 and in Revelation 19:7, 21:2 and 21:9.

[5] The command for Christians to fast in 2:20 is repeated in 9:29 and in Matthew 6:16–18.

to rest in the blessings which are already ours. The disciples were truly *Sabbathing* when they picked corn which the Lord had grown without them.

The Pharisees are not listening, so Jesus captures their attention. They boast that they are great Bible teachers, so Jesus offends their pride by asking, *"Have you never read what David did?"*[6] If God cared more about David's hungry followers than about the Tabernacle food laws, why are they so irritated that the Messiah's hungry followers are snacking as they enjoy a day of rest together? Jesus repeats the claim that he made at Peter's house. He is the Son of Man, which makes him Lord of the Sabbath too. He therefore declares that *"The Sabbath was made for man, not man for the Sabbath."*[7] The Sabbath isn't about burdening people; it's about setting them free.

The third clash with the Pharisees takes place on another Sabbath day (3:1–6). A man with a shrivelled hand attends their Sabbath services, but they have created a synagogue culture of burdening people with rules instead of setting them free. Jesus exposes their error by calling the man to stand at the front of the synagogue and by asking the Pharisees whether their Sabbath laws preclude him from bringing the Kingdom of God to bear on the man's life here and now. The Pharisees keep quiet and look down at their sandals because they know their laws consider healing to be part of Jesus' day job.[8] Jesus is furious that they refuse to repent. Mark tells us literally that he feels a mixture of *wrath* and *deep grief* over their *stony hearts*. He demonstrates his authority to correct their error by ordering the man to do the very thing he cannot do – stretch out his shrivelled hand. When Jesus

---

[6] Ahimelek was the high priest when David came to the Tabernacle in 1 Samuel 21, but his son Abiathar became high priest as a result of this event.

[7] The word *kurios* in 2:28 is the word used to translate *Yahweh*, or *the Lord*, throughout the Greek Old Testament. Jesus is telling the Pharisees that he is both Israel's Messiah and Israel's God.

[8] Incredibly, one synagogue ruler tells his congregation in Luke 13:14 that *"There are six days for work. So come and be healed on those days, not on the Sabbath."*

speaks, his words carry such authority that he neither needs to pray nor touch the man in order to overcome his physical deformity. When the man attempts to do what he cannot do, he discovers that he can. He *Sabbaths* by believing that God will do this work for him, and as a result he is completely healed.

Peter watches this scene as a Jew. He is accustomed to following the lead of the Pharisees. But when they storm out of the synagogue and join forces with the Herodians – the Jewish friends of Rome – he sees their separatist rules for what they are. They are not interested in entering into God's rest at all. They want to earn their own way to God by clinging to bale-of-hay rules in a black-cab world. Rather than accept Jesus' teaching about the Fourth Commandment, they break the Sixth Commandment by plotting how to murder him. Peter realises that stepping into Jesus' story means stepping out of theirs.

Mark wants his Gentile readers to watch this scene as closely as Peter. To help us, he omits much of the Jewish detail which appears in the parallel account in Matthew.[9] Mark wants to reassure us that stepping into Jesus' story doesn't mean embracing all the baggage of first-century Judaism. The Gospel does not burden us by telling us to pull an outdated hackney carriage. It tells us to stop striving for God's approval and invites us to enter into his rest. Jesus puts it this way in the parallel passage in Matthew:

> *Come to me, all you who are weary and burdened, and I will give you rest. Take my yoke upon you and learn from me, for I am gentle and humble in heart, and you will find rest for your souls. For my yoke is easy and my burden is light.*[10]

---

[9] Matthew 12:1–14 points out that the Jewish Law permitted priests to work on the Sabbath, and that even the Pharisees permitted basic care of livestock on the Sabbath. Matthew also includes quotes from Hosea 6:6 and states that Jesus is greater than the Jewish Temple.

[10] Matthew 11:28–30. Our chapter divisions were a medieval addition to the text. Matthew wants us to treat 11:28–30 as commentary on 12:1–14.

Quick Step (3:7–13)

Jesus went up on a mountainside and called to him
those he wanted, and they came to him.

(Mark 3:13)

Peter has come a long way since he took his first step on the journey of following Jesus. We are little more than two chapters into Mark's gospel, but its breathless flurry has already taken Peter from Jesus' baptism in the summer of 27 AD to the autumn of 28 AD.[1] Jesus is about to ask Peter to quicken his step by committing himself more deeply to his journey of discovery. In order to help him make this fresh decision, Jesus therefore gives him several signs to show that it is worth sacrificing everything to follow him.

In verse 7, Jesus shows Peter that he is *greater than the Pharisees*. The Jewish leaders have taken offence at Jesus' teaching and are plotting how to kill him. They will certainly not be inviting him back as a visiting speaker. But Jesus demonstrates that he needs neither their support nor their synagogues. He withdraws to Lake Galilee and sets up a new preaching centre of his own on the beach. Very quickly he gathers a large crowd of people from right across the whole region of Galilee. Matthew 23:15 tells us that the Pharisees had to work hard to win their converts one by one, but Jesus is far greater than the Pharisees. He can set up shop in the open air and expect the crowds to come.

In verse 8, Jesus shows Peter that he is *greater than King*

---

[1] Mark's gospel contains very few details that help us to mark the passage of time. We are forced to date these events from the time markers that are given by the other gospel writers.

Herod. Herod Antipas had been poised to rule over the whole of Israel after the death of Herod the Great, but his father doubled-crossed him on his deathbed by changing his will to make him heir to only a quarter of his kingdom. Although he called himself king, Herod Antipas was technically a tetrarch (literally a *quarter-ruler*) and he spent his entire reign trying to extend his lands beyond his little tetrarchy of Galilee and Perea.[2] Mark pointedly tells us that Jesus instantly draws large crowds from the other three tetrarchies too. He succeeds where the ambitious tetrarch failed. Jesus is the true King of the Jews.

In verse 9, Jesus shows Peter that he is *greater than any prophet*. John the Baptist had attracted massive crowds to hear his preaching at the River Jordan, but even he had not needed to preach from a boat because the crowds grew so large that they began to crush him.[3] Peter can tell from the crowds that are forming that he is watching the unfolding of Israel's greatest drama.

In verse 10, Jesus shows Peter that he is *the Son of Man*. As with the paralysed man at Peter's house and the man with the shrivelled hand in the synagogue, Jesus proves he is the King about whom Daniel prophesied by unleashing his authority to heal. The main reason Jesus needs a private boat from which to preach is that people keep bursting through the crowd because they know a single touch from the King will be enough to heal any of their diseases.[4] The boat helps minimise interruptions to Jesus' teaching about the Kingdom of God and allows him to choose when to demonstrate the truth of what he is proclaiming. Luke 6:19 records the same events and tells us that *"The people*

---

[2] The first-century Jewish historian Josephus recounts this in his *Antiquities of the Jews* (17.6.1 and 17.8.1). Mark 6:14 refers to *"King Herod"* for the sake of simplicity but Matthew and Luke both call him a tetrarch.

[3] The Greek word which Mark uses in 3:9 suggests that he asked for this boat to be on permanent standby. Mark 4:1 tells us that he used it again later, and Luke 5:3 suggests that the boat belonged to Peter.

[4] Mark 5:28; 6:56; 8:22; 10:13. Also Matthew 14:36 and 20:34.

all tried to touch him, because power was coming out from him and healing them all." Peter has worked his entire life in a boat on Lake Galilee but he has never shared a boat with anyone like Jesus.

In verse 11, Jesus shows Peter that he is *the Son of God*. Once again it is the demons who grasp Jesus' identity far more clearly than the Pharisees or his disciples. As soon as demonised people see Jesus, they fall down at his feet in abject surrender, crying out, *"You are the Son of God!"* Mark uses this to make a dangerous claim about Jesus. Since he wrote his gospel first and Matthew and Luke expanded on his words to write their own gospels, only 50 of the 661 verses in Mark are unique to his gospel. One of them is here in verse 11. Mark emphasises to his Roman readers that, although their emperors claim the title *divi filius* or *the son of a god*, no Caesar can compare with the power of Jesus. Anyone who comes to him in faith receives complete deliverance and healing.[5]

In verse 12, Jesus shows Peter that he is *inviting him to step out on a much longer journey*. One of the big characteristics of Mark's gospel is that he allows us to travel at the same pace as Peter on his journey of discovery. Jesus forbids demons to blurt out who he is (1:25, 34; 3:12). He forbids those he heals and delivers to shout too loudly about their experience of his power (1:44; 5:43; 7:36; 8:26). He hides away from the crowds (1:35, 45; 7:24; 9:30), and he tells his disciples to keep their growing revelation of his identity to themselves (8:30; 9:9). He is determined not to precipitate his crucifixion before he has prepared his followers to continue his story after he has returned to heaven. Verse 12 therefore reminds us that Peter's journey has barely started. He needs to quicken his step as he follows Jesus.

In verse 13, Jesus therefore makes the big ask of Peter.

---

[5] Although Mark tells us that Jesus healed *many*, emphasising that not everybody who was sick came to him, the parallel verse in Matthew 12:15 tells us that Jesus healed *everyone* who had the faith to come.

Up until now, he has simply been part of an informal band of followers, with the freedom to go with Jesus or to stay at home on any given day. Now is the moment when Jesus chooses twelve men from this informal group to become his permanent entourage. He asks Peter to become one of his dozen students and to make an up-front commitment to the rest of his unfolding story. Given what Peter has seen so far of Jesus, the wonder is not that he says yes but that Jesus ever gives him the option. When Jesus calls out the names of the twelve men he has decided to invite deeper into the journey with him, none of them is so ungrateful as to decline. They quicken their pace and take a big step deeper into the rest of Jesus' story.

We have seen enough of Jesus in these first few chapters of Mark's gospel for us to be able to do the same as Peter. If you are reading as a sceptic then Jesus asks you to let your guard down. If you are reading as a reluctant follower then Jesus asks you to run. He asks you to quicken your step by putting down this book and praying. Tell Jesus that you are committed to journeying much deeper with him, wherever he may lead you.

School of Rock (3:14–19)

He appointed twelve that they might be with him and that he might send them out.

(Mark 3:14)

Peter believed in Jesus but, before that, Jesus believed in Peter. He didn't just believe he should be part of his inner circle of twelve disciples. He believed he should become their leader. Every time the New Testament lists the disciples by name, it always lists Peter's name first.[1] Up until this point in his gospel, Mark has always referred to him by his birth name Simon, but from this point on he will use the new name which Jesus gave him. *Peter* in Greek and its equivalent *Cephas* in Aramaic both meant *Rock*.[2] Jesus told Peter that he believed in him and saw him as perfect building material for his Kingdom.

When Jesus spoke this new name over Peter on the first day he met him, Peter took him at his word and became intensely interested in Jesus.[3] He trusted Jesus to help him live up to this new name, and he left his nets behind on the beach at Galilee when Jesus promised to turn a fisherman into an apostle. Simon became Peter because he believed that Jesus would teach him how to become the man he said that he could be. When Jesus called Peter to become head boy in his school of twelve

---

[1] The disciples are listed four times – here and in Matthew 10:2–4, Luke 6:14–16 and Acts 1:13. The order in which their names are listed varies, but Simon Peter is always listed first.

[2] John 1:42; Galatians 2:9; 1 Corinthians 1:12; 3:22; 9:5; 15:5.

[3] Jesus gave Peter this name when he first met him in John 1:42. He explains why in Matthew 16:18. He was saying that Peter was a rock that he could build on.

disciples, Peter was elated. It meant that term-time had finally started in the School of Rock.[4]

Jesus would turn Peter into a rock he could build with if *he experienced God's Kingdom*. That meant spending lots of time with him. We live in a culture that generally feels too busy for serious Bible study, long time in prayer and commitment to Christian meetings. It's no coincidence that we also live in a culture that is severely lacking in its experience of God's Kingdom. Mark tells us that the first and greatest lesson in the School of Rock was very simple: Peter and his eleven friends needed to give up everything else *"that they might be with him."* The secret to successful Christian ministry is never a question of how, but always who. It all begins with a deep friendship connection with Jesus through time spent in regular prayer and fasting and worship. Jesus teaches us, as he taught Peter: *"If you remain in me and I in you, you will bear much fruit; apart from me you can do nothing."*[5]

Peter would experience the Kingdom as he left other things behind to spend time with Jesus, but he would also experience the Kingdom as he spent time sharing this journey with the other eleven disciples. It is helpful that Mark lists them here, because it reminds us just how difficult it must have been for Peter to spend the next two years with them. James and John were his fiery-tempered fishing partners (Jesus gave them the Aramaic name *Boanerges*, or *Sons of Thunder*, as a promise that he would turn their biggest vice into a virtue).[6] Andrew was his brother (never easy). Matthew had swindled him in the past and his brother James would naturally side with him if he clashed again with

---

[4] Some Greek manuscripts of 3:14 include the words *"naming them apostles."* Although these words were added to Mark later, the parallel Luke 6:13 affirms that Jesus formally named these twelve as his apostles.

[5] John 15:5. See Mark 9:29, Luke 24:52–53, Acts 1:14 and Matthew 14:33 and 28:16–17.

[6] *Boanêrges* can also be translated *Troublemakers*, and we catch a glimpse of their short tempers in Luke 9:51–56. Jesus would change them in the School of Rock and turn them into positive troublemakers for God.

Peter.[7] Bartholomew was a cynic and Thomas was a doubter.[8] Simon the Zealot was an angry young radical.[9] Judas Iscariot was a southerner and a future traitor.[10] Living in close proximity to these men for the next two years was going to be very difficult for Peter. But the New Testament cuts across the arrogant individualism of our culture when it tells us repeatedly that we will only fully experience God's Kingdom when we commit to working out our faith in Jesus in community with *"one another."*[11]

Jesus would turn Peter into a rock he could build with if *he listened to teaching about the Kingdom.* He wanted to send Peter out to preach the Gospel but, before he could do so, Peter had to learn what the Gospel actually is. The Greek word *euangelion* means literally the *good announcement,* so we are naïve if we think that God will use us if we fail to take the time to learn from him what we should be announcing! Peter was a man of action more than he was a man of study. As a result, Mark's gospel records a small fraction of all the preaching that appears in the other three gospels. Nevertheless, we are about to move into a whole chapter that records Jesus' teaching in detail. Peter would not be able to go out and preach until first he committed himself to listening.

Jesus would turn Peter into a rock he could build with if *he learned to speak out the message of the Kingdom.* Mark uses the Greek word *kērussō* again in verse 14 because he wants to

---

[7] Mark names James's father as Alphaeus in order to link back to 2:14 and tell us that there were three pairs of brothers among the Twelve: Peter and Andrew, James and John, Matthew and James.

[8] Bartholomew is called Nathanael in John 1:45–51. Thomas' character is seen in John 11:16 and 20:24–29.

[9] The Greek word *kananitēs* in 3:18 comes from the Hebrew word *qānā',* or *to be zealous.* Simon was part of the same radical sect which died trying to resist the Romans at Masada in 73 AD.

[10] Iscariot was not Judas' surname. It is a Greek transliteration of the Hebrew *Ish Keriōth,* meaning *Man From [the southern Judean town] of Kerioth.*

[11] Paul uses the Greek word for *one another* 40 times in his letters in order to emphasise that Christian community plays a vital role in how we experience God's Kingdom in our lives.

remind us that believers are heralds who proclaim the coming of heaven's King. It would make a massive difference to Peter's preaching if he were sent or if he merely went. Jesus invited him to invest in two years of intensive training in the School of Rock so that he could send Peter out to preach the kind of messages that would build a solid Church across the Roman Empire. If we find that our own proclamation of the Gospel is weak and lifeless, it is likely to reflect the fact that we are went-ones who have not taken enough time to listen to the words of Jesus and to become his sent-ones.

Jesus would turn Peter into a rock he could build with if *he learned to demonstrate the message of the Kingdom*. It wouldn't be enough for Peter to proclaim across the Roman Empire that heaven's King had come. It never is. In a world of copious gods and competing religions, Peter would only convince the world to step into God's story if he could demonstrate before their very eyes that the story is true. Jesus invited Peter to spend time with him so that he could teach him how to wield the same authority as he did over demons, over sickness and even over death. Peter said "yes". He stepped deeper into Jesus' story and committed to learning all he could in the School of Rock. As a result, he became everything Jesus said that he would be.

There are many good things in our lives, just as there were in Peter's life at Capernaum, but if we want to become rocks that Jesus can build with, we have to leave them behind in order to pursue what Peter did. If we devote ourselves to experiencing more and more of God's Kingdom by spending time alone with him, spending time with other Christians and spending time listening to his Word, then he will prepare us to be sent out to preach and demonstrate his Kingdom. We will allow him to speak over us what he spoke over Peter in Matthew 16:18:

> *I tell you that you are Rock, and on this rock I will build my church, and the gates of hell will not overcome it.*

Mad, Bad, God (3:20–35)

"He is out of his mind."... "He is possessed by Beelzebub."

(Mark 3:21–22)

In the Dan Brown novel and the Tom Hanks movie *The Da Vinci Code*, the heroes of the story pontificate on who they think Jesus may or may not have been. *"Almost everything our fathers taught us about Christ is false,"* claims one of them. *"Jesus was viewed by His followers as a mortal prophet... a great and powerful man, but a **man** nonetheless... Jesus' establishment as 'the Son of God' was officially proposed and voted on by the Council of Nicaea... A relatively close vote at that."*[1]

Sentiments like these are commonplace in our culture, 2,000 years after the events Peter experienced and Mark recorded. They make for an entertaining novel or a moneymaking film, but they don't make for anything that can be described as history. Mark refuses to allow us to project our own ideas about Jesus back onto him. He describes a discussion that took place shortly after he appointed his twelve disciples and which proves beyond a doubt who he really was and really is.[2]

Peter and his friends knew that becoming part of Jesus' inner circle would prove costly, and so it proves in the very first verse after they are appointed. Jesus is so popular that he has to escape the crowds at his preaching station on the beach by holing up nearby, probably in the house that belonged to Peter. But the

---

[1] Dan Brown in *The Da Vinci Code* (2003).
[2] Fewer than 10% of the verses in Mark are unique to Mark, but 3:21 is one of them. Mark records this in order to help us to consider the verdicts that were passed on Jesus by his contemporaries.

crowds know that front door. They are soon banging so hard that Jesus and his disciples have no time even to stop and make a meal. He is staggeringly popular and in demand. His mother and his brothers must be crazy to conclude that he is therefore mad. If it seems an odd conclusion when they turn up at the door and declare that *"He is out of his mind,"* consider that they are by no means the only ones to have argued this throughout history. Henry Havelock Ellis, one of the early campaigners for gay rights, argued that *"The whole religious complexion of the modern world is due to the absence, from Jerusalem, of a lunatic asylum."*[3]

A group of teachers of the law take a different view. They have heard what he did in the synagogue and they have travelled all the way from Jerusalem to see him. They do not try to argue that Jesus is mad – after all, no madman can heal people with a touch or command – but they argue instead that he must be in league with the Devil. The demons obey his commands because they recognise that he is working for the archdemon Beelzebub.[4] This is the Jewish leaders' normal way of trying to explain away Jesus' miracles in the gospel accounts, and they continue to argue in the Jewish Talmud that *"Jesus the Nazarene practised magic and deceived and led Israel astray."*[5] Whereas Jesus' family say he is mad, the Jewish leaders say he is bad.

Mark sees it as profoundly significant that these were the two main objections which people threw at Jesus during his three years of public ministry. It is easy for Dan Brown to sit at a desk in New Hampshire 2,000 years after the fact and argue that Jesus was simply a good human teacher who was misunderstood, but Mark's point is that nobody argued anything

---

[3] Henry Havelock Ellis in *Impressions and Comments, Volume 3* (1924).

[4] *Baal-Zebul (Lord-of-the-High-Place)* was a Philistine idol who is mentioned in 2 Kings 1:2. The Jews used its name to refer to Satan or to a powerful demon, changing it to *Beelzebub (Lord-of-the-Flies)* as an insult.

[5] Matthew 9:34; 10:25; 12:22–37; Luke 11:14–26; John 7:20; 8:48; 10:19–21. See also Peter Schäfer, *Jesus in the Talmud* (2007).

like this at the time. Nobody in the crowd said anything like "I'm not sure the leper was actually healed," or "Stop going on about the shrivelled hand; it's Jesus' moral teaching which really matters." They knew that they would be laughed out of town. Everybody knew that this man could heal sickness and drive out demons. He was either mad or he was bad or he was God. Those were the only options.

A few pages earlier, we looked at what C.S. Lewis said about Jesus' claim that he has the authority to forgive sins. Lewis continues:

> *I am trying to prevent anyone saying the really foolish thing that people often say about Him: "I'm ready to accept Jesus as a great moral teacher, but I don't accept His claim to be God." That is the one thing we must not say. A man who was merely a man and said the sort of things Jesus said would not be a great moral teacher. He would either be a lunatic – on a level with the man who says he is a poached egg – or he would be the Devil of Hell. You must make your choice. Either this man was, and is, the Son of God: or else a madman or something worse. You can shut Him up for a fool, you can spit at Him and kill Him as a demon; or you can fall at His feet and call Him Lord and God. But let us not come with any patronising nonsense about His being a great human teacher. He has not left that open to us. He did not intend to.*[6]

In verses 23–26, Jesus assures us that he is not bad. He points out that the Devil is not stupid enough to set demon against demon. If Satan's rule on earth is being replaced by God's rule, then it is utterly foolish to attribute it to Satan and not to God.

---

[6] C.S. Lewis in *Mere Christianity* (1952).

Jesus uses patient logic to convince us that anyone who fails to grasp this isn't lacking proof. They lack a willingness to see.

In verses 27–30, Jesus also assures us that he is not mad. No lunatic could ever make a healing tour of Galilee because sickness and demonisation are not simply psychological conditions. They are the very real work of a very real strongman, the Devil. Jesus has come to bring forgiveness, but if anybody attributes the power of the Holy Spirit to a lunatic spirit then *"they are guilty of an eternal sin"* – in other words, they have rejected the proof that is meant to lead them to accept his offer of eternal salvation.[7] By dismissing his story as the ravings of a madman, people condemn themselves to finishing the story of their lives in hell.

In verses 31–35, Jesus therefore assures us that he must be God. Although he honours his mother Mary and his brothers, Jesus does not stop teaching the crowd in order to go out and meet them.[8] Since God is his Father, he says that his true mother is the community of believers and that his true brothers and sisters are those who belong to it.[9] His family is anyone who opens their eyes to the proof that he is God and who steps into his story.

It is heavily ironic that Dan Brown makes his unhistorical speculations immediately after quoting the words of the great religious painter Leonardo da Vinci: *"Blinding ignorance does mislead us. O! Wretched mortals, open your eyes!"*[10] That's

---

[7] The New Testament letters clarify what Jesus means in 3:29. No sin is unforgiveable (1 John 1:9) except for the sin that causes us to reject God's message of salvation.

[8] Luke 8:19 tells us that his mother and brothers were unable to enter the house because of the huge crowd.

[9] This reassured any Roman reader who feared that Jewish tribalism might make a Gentile a second-rate follower of Jesus. However, it should disturb any Roman Catholic who venerates Mary and expects her to be able to save them. Mark presents her as decidedly flawed and human.

[10] The quote is from Section 1182 of Leonardo's *Notebooks*. Far from supporting Dan Brown's thesis, it comes directly after Section 1180: *"The*

precisely what we need to do as we consider who is standing before us in Mark's gospel. This miracle-worker cannot merely be a prophet or a moral teacher, since he is prophesying and teaching that he is God! He cannot be mad and he cannot be bad, for his actions leave no room for either possibility. The man who stands before us must truly be the living God. The Creator of the universe has stepped into the human story.

_____
greatest deception men suffer is from their own opinions."

How to Grow As a Believer (4:1–20)

> Others, like seed sown on good soil, hear the word,
> accept it, and produce a crop – some thirty, some
> sixty, some a hundred times what was sown.
>
> (Mark 4:20)

Every culture has its own prevailing story that answers the big questions of life. How did we get here? Where are we headed? What are we meant to be doing with our lives as a result? In our culture, the story is a particularly empty and depressing one. The British philosopher Bertrand Russell summarises:

> That Man is the product of causes which had no prevision
> of the end they were achieving; that his origin, his growth,
> his hopes and fears, his loves and his beliefs, are but the
> outcome of accidental collocations of atoms; that no
> fire, no heroism, no intensity of thought and feeling, can
> preserve an individual life beyond the grave; that all the
> labours of the ages, all the devotion, all the inspiration, all
> the noonday brightness of human genius, are destined to
> extinction in the vast death of the solar system, and that
> the whole temple of Man's achievement must inevitably
> be buried beneath the debris of a universe in ruins.[1]

Jesus wants to free us from this empty story, just as he wanted to free first-century Jews and Romans from their own culture's stories. Mark therefore does something quite unusual for

[1] Bertrand Russell in his essay *A Free Man's Worship* (1903).

his gospel. He breaks off from his fast-paced flurry of activity and gives us almost an entire chapter of Jesus' teaching.[2] He begins with the longest and most detailed parable in the whole of his gospel. The Parable of the Sower teaches us how to step into God's new story. It teaches us how to grow as believers in Jesus.

In verses 4 and 15, Jesus talks about those who respond to his story with a *hard heart*. He likens them to a first-century farmer sowing seed on the path instead of on the soil. If we resist Jesus' story by refusing to change our way of thinking about sin and forgiveness and baptism and obeying God, then the Devil will snatch the Gospel message away from us before it has any chance to take root in our hearts and change us. That's one of the reasons why Jesus told his parables at all. The word means a *comparison* or *illustration*, but he didn't just tell them to make his teaching more memorable for believers. Mark tells us in verses 10–12 that Jesus taught in parables in order to make his teaching more obscure for hard-hearted listeners so that they would reap the judgment they deserve.[3] Mark pleads with us not to allow the Devil to be like a crow and snatch away from us this life-changing account of what Peter saw and heard.

In verses 5–6 and 16–17, Jesus talks about those who respond to his story with a *superficial heart*. These people look promising. They *"hear the word and at once receive it with joy."* They look like some of the keenest and brightest followers of Jesus, but they have not learned what Jesus taught Peter in the School of Rock. They do not dig deep foundations for their walk with Jesus by studying Scripture, by talking to God in

---

[2] Depending on how we count them, there are eight parables in Mark's gospel, of which four are in this chapter. By way of contrast, there are 23 parables in Matthew and 24 in Luke.

[3] Mark's quotation in 4:12 from Isaiah 6:9–10 is his first Old Testament quotation since 1:2–3. He abbreviates and slightly changes the quotation because, even though his Roman readers are unfamiliar with it, it teaches us a vital principle. This is how God always responds to the hard-hearted (Daniel 12:10; Acts 28:24–28).

prayer or by devoting themselves to being an active member of a Christian community. Their grasp of Jesus and of his story is far too shallow to support them when trouble inevitably comes. Note what Jesus says in verse 17. He doesn't say *if* trouble and persecution comes; he says *when* trouble and persecution comes. Life is full of ups and downs, even as a child of God, and in many ways it gets harder when we start living according to a different story from the rest of the world.[4] If we fail to put down deep roots into Jesus' story then our faith will wither under pressure. If the story Mark is telling us is true, it is worth pursuing with everything we have.

In verses 7 and 18–19, Jesus talks about those who respond to his story with a *distracted heart*. These people start out well. They put down strong roots into Jesus' story, but they make the mistake of trying to squeeze following Jesus into the life they already have. Any gardener can tell you that plants need to be weeded out before there is any room for a new plant to grow. In the same way, Jesus describes the concerns of this life as thorns, which will choke us and stop us bearing fruit for his Kingdom. Jesus highlights as particular dangers *worry* and the *economic lie* that a little extra earning will satisfy us, but the truth is that most of the thorns in our lives are not sins. They are just *"desires for other things."* They are the hobbies and chores and social commitments which strangle our days and leave us no time to pursue what really matters.[5] It's pretty obvious that, if our lives are full before we step into Jesus' story, we are going to have to be ruthless with much of what we do in order to make time to follow him. Peter left his fishing nets and his busy life in Galilee

---

[4] This may have surprised Peter at the time, but it shouldn't surprise us. How could following a Messiah who was hated and betrayed and beaten and crucified ever be treated as the offer of an easy ride?

[5] Matthew 13:1 tells us that Jesus gave this teaching immediately after refusing to be distracted by his mother and brothers in Mark 3:31–35. Family are a blessing but not if we let them become a distraction.

behind. If we don't leave things behind to follow Jesus, we will never truly manage to follow him at all.

In verses 8 and 20, Jesus encourages us to be those who respond to his story with a *determined heart*. He assures us that anyone who leaves their old life behind and begins to live for his story alone will be massively fruitful. If we are quick to do everything he says, if we devote ourselves to pursuing our new relationship with him, and if we weed out from our lives anything that will distract us from his call, then there is no question whether he will transform us and use us to make a very real difference to the world. The only question is whether the fruit we bear in other people's lives will be thirty times, sixty times or a hundred times what Jesus sows into our own lives.[6]

We are almost a quarter of the way through Mark's gospel. We have charted the first year and a half of Peter's three-year journey of discovery with Jesus. This is a good time for us to take time out to consider which of these four types of soil most resembles our own heart. Are we still acting like spectators of someone else's story? Are we offering only a superficial or a half-hearted willingness to step into Jesus' story? Or are we willing to give up everything to follow him?

Jesus ends his parable with a reminder that we have no guarantee that we will be able to respond to his story on another day. He utters a solemn warning in verse 9 when he pleads with us to take this parable seriously: *"Whoever has ears to hear, let them hear."*[7]

---

[6] Jesus uses an agricultural parable because this fruit may take a long time to become visible. Luke 8:15 adds that we will only obtain it *"by persevering."* But, make no mistake, John 15:16 assures us it will come.

[7] Jesus repeats this phrase in 4:23 and seven times in Revelation 2–3. It is a reminder that we can only understand God's Word by God's grace. We need to respond to it straightaway if we understand, because we have no guarantee that we will understand equally clearly tomorrow.

How to Spread the Gospel
(4:21–34)

Night and day, whether he sleeps or gets up, the seed sprouts and grows, though he does not know how. All by itself the soil produces corn.

(Mark 4:27–28)

It's very moving to read how soldiers in the trenches of World War One felt just before they went over the top. *"I can still see the bewilderment and fear on the men's faces when we went over the top... I will never forget it,"* recalls one British soldier. *"They were both the longest and the shortest hours of my life. An infantryman in the front line feels the coldest, deepest fear,"* remembers another.[1] Unless we understand that this is how Peter and his friends were starting to feel, we will not understand this section of Mark's gospel.

We tend to think in terms of our own agenda, even after we respond to Jesus' call for us to step into his story. We expect his agenda to be all about us, but he surprises us by telling us that it is all about the world. Jesus told the Twelve in 3:15 that he had called them in order to teach them how *"to have authority to drive out demons,"* so Peter and his friends must have felt the same anticipation as a soldier in the trenches as they awaited being sent over the top in 6:7 to assert this *"authority over impure spirits."* There is nothing arbitrary about the parables and the events in Mark 4 and 5. Jesus is teaching his followers how to spread the message of his Kingdom.

---

[1] Quoted by Max Arthur in *Forgotten Voices of the Great War* (2002).

In verses 26–29, Jesus tells the only parable that is unique to Mark's gospel, so it deserves some particular attention. The Parable of the Growing Seed helps Peter and his friends not to feel weighed down by the pressure of being sent to share the Gospel with the world.[2] The Kingdom of God is like a farmer who scatters seed on the ground. A farmer does not stay up all night worrying about whether or not the seed will grow: *"Night and day, whether he sleeps or gets up, the seed sprouts and grows, though he does not know how."* Mark uses the Greek word *automatē*, which is the root of the English word *automatic*, when he adds that *"**all by itself** the soil produces corn."*[3] The disciples need not feel any pressure when they command people to submit to Jesus as their King, because they have no power to produce shoots of obedience themselves. Their job is to sow seed and to put the sickle in as soon as they spot that the harvest is ready. God will do the rest. We can almost hear Peter's sigh of relief. I can definitely hear my own.

That's one side of the equation. We sow seed, we look for a harvest and we leave the rest to God, knowing that only he can produce any Kingdom harvest from our message. Now for the other side of the equation. We cannot produce a Kingdom harvest, but we can certainly place limitations on its size. That's what Jesus addresses in the rest of these parables. How we cooperate with God at either end of the process makes a massive difference to whether our barns are full or empty.

In verses 21–23, Jesus tells us that we need to *go public about our faith in him.* If we do not sow, we will not reap. It stands to reason, so we need to make it very clear to those around us how much our lives have been transformed by stepping into

----

[2] It is unclear whether the teaching in 4:21–32 is addressed to the Twelve alone or to the wider crowd. Verse 21 suggests it is just for the Twelve, but verses 2 and 34 suggest it is for the wider crowd as well.

[3] The only other place in the Bible where this Greek word is used is when Peter is in prison as a result of preaching the Gospel. Acts 12:10 uses the same word to tell us that the prison door opened *"all by itself."*

Jesus' story. The Parable of the Lamp under a Bushel reminds us that God has made us bright lights in a world of darkness.[4] If we are embarrassed to go public about our faith in all we say and do, we are as foolish as a man who lights a lamp and hides it under a bed or basket instead of putting it on a stand to light up his home. Knowing that only God can save people must never become an excuse for laziness, or we will become like the fool in Proverbs 20:4: *"A sluggard does not plough in season; so at harvest time he looks but finds nothing."*

In verses 24–25, Jesus tells us that we need to *be generous about our faith in him.* If we sow the Gospel generously, we can expect to see a generous harvest, but if we sow it sparingly, we will forfeit whatever little fruit we think we have. We ought to live our lives with the same attitude as John Wesley, who taught his converts: *"Do all the good you can, by all the means you can, in all the ways you can, in all the places you can, at all the times you can, to all the people you can, as long as ever you can."* The Parable of the Sower delivers us from the naïve optimism that leads to discouragement when many people reject our Gospel message. Instead of complaining that there are three types of unfruitful seed, it spurs us on to sow all the more generously, knowing that the more we sow the more we will reap of the fourth type of seed.

In verses 30–32, Jesus tells us that we need to *be expectant about our faith in him.* We can place limits on our Gospel fruitfulness by sowing too little seed, but we can also place limits on it by looking out for too little harvest. The Parable of the Mustard Seed reminds us that the tiniest of seeds can become the largest plant in a garden.[5] If we fail to ask people

---

[4] Jesus told the same parables at different times to different crowds, and he explained its meaning more fully in the Sermon on the Mount in Matthew 5:14–16. He told his disciples, *"You are the light of the world."*

[5] The mustard plant grows much larger in the Middle East than in colder climes because it does not die back in winter. It grows very large for a garden plant – up to three metres tall. Note the link back to Daniel 4:12 and Ezekiel 31:6,

the kind of questions that reveal whether or not they are ready to respond to Jesus, we will miss many harvesting opportunities. Peter and his friends went shopping in a Samaritan village in John 4 without bothering to ask people questions because they were convinced that nobody was interested in stepping into God's story. Jesus asked a few simple questions which resulted in the entire village placing their faith in him, and he rebuked his disciples: *"Open your eyes and look at the fields! They are ripe for harvest."* The normal effect of sowing Gospel seed is a bumper harvest at the proper time. Unless we grasp this, we will experience a self-inflicted spiritual famine.

None of these parables was of purely academic interest for Peter and his friends. They were about to go over the top and into battle, proclaiming and demonstrating that God's Messiah had come to inaugurate God's Kingdom. They were nervous. They were dry-mouthed. But when they heard these parables they were reassured.[6] So long as they were faithful in proclaiming the news that heaven's King had come and were full of faith that their message carried power to save, then they could leave all of the pressure of extending the Kingdom of God to the Lord. Only he could make their message fruitful and he would make it fruitful *automatē* – all by itself. When the time came for them to go over the top, they could march together into battle unafraid.

---

which points out that the Kingdom of God easily outstrips the Babylonian and Assyrian empires.

[6] 4:33 tells us that Jesus would have reassured them more if they had been ready to hear more. John 16:12–14 tells us that our insight is not limited by God's willingness to share, but by our ability to hear.

The Perfect Storm
(4:35–41)

They were terrified and asked each other, "Who is this? Even the wind and the waves obey him!"

(Mark 4:41)

The ancient Chinese philosopher Xunzi taught his students to say, *"I hear and I forget; I see and I remember; I do and I understand."*[1] Jesus seems to agree. Having devoted almost an entire chapter to some of Jesus' classroom teaching, Mark returns to the flurry of activity which so distinguishes his gospel from the other three. To reinforce the classroom lessons of this chapter, Jesus takes the disciples into the perfect storm.

Jesus has been teaching the crowd on the beach from a boat in order to prevent them from interrupting him by surging forward to touch him and be healed.[2] As evening falls, he therefore closes his teaching and commands his disciples to sail his pulpit elsewhere. This gives his disciples an opportunity to demonstrate whether they have truly learned the lesson of these parables. Jesus has told them, *"Let us go over to the other side."* Do they truly believe that the word of Jesus is a seed, which carries power to bear fruit all by itself? Will they trust his word to do its work, even though they do not know how? Will they worry about the wind and the waves more than they trust in his word?

The sea was calm enough for Jesus to preach from a boat, but suddenly the disciples find themselves in a heavy storm.

---

[1] Xunzi wrote this in the third century BC in *The Teachings of the Ru* (8.11).

[2] Mark 3:9–10; 4:1. Luke 6:19.

Lake Galilee is only thirteen miles long and eight miles wide, but a fisherman like Peter knew how dangerous its waters could be. Two hundred metres below sea level, it is the lowest freshwater lake in the world and it is surrounded by high mountains which cause major temperature and pressure changes. Storms descend suddenly and, when they do, a small boat can easily sink and its occupants drown. Jesus is not worried about this, despite the water coming in over the sides. He is living out the Parable of the Growing Seed by lying fast asleep on a cushion in the stern of the boat, trusting his Father to be in control. Mark has used the word *eutheōs*, or *straightaway*, twenty times already in these first four chapters, so Jesus is exhausted enough to sleep through a storm so severe that even a seasoned boatman like Peter is convinced that they are about to die. But this event is about more than Jesus' tiredness as a human being. It is about putting his preaching in verse 27 into action. He trusts his Father to ensure that his life will end on the hill of Calvary and not at the bottom of Lake Galilee.

Peter and his friends do not share his confidence. Xunzi would say that they have heard and forgotten. Jesus brought them into this storm in order to give them an opportunity to see and remember. Peter and the other disciples wake up Jesus and ask him one of the most ridiculous questions in Mark's gospel. They ask him accusingly, *"Teacher, don't you care if we drown?"* Translated more literally, they ask him, *"Teacher, doesn't it matter to you that we are perishing?"*[3] They are talking to Jesus, the one who has come down to earth from heaven in order to bring salvation to the perishing, but the wind and the waves have caused them to forget his identity and his mission. They

---

[3] The Greek word *apollumi* is the same word that is used in John 3:16, when Jesus says that *"God so loved the world that he gave his one and only Son, that whoever believes in him shall not perish."*

need to learn to handle storms before they can start to play their own part in continuing his story.[4]

Jesus responds to their question by teaching them the power of his Word. He wants them to learn to sleep the trustful sleep of the farmer in the Parable of the Growing Seed. He addresses the wind and the waves in the same way he has addressed demons, confident that the world he created in the beginning with a command will not be able to resist his command now. He speaks two simple words in Greek, which men would normally say to their dogs: *"Shush! Be muzzled!"* Instantly the wind and waves die down and the lake becomes perfectly calm. That's the kind of seed we sow when we proclaim the words of Jesus to the world. We can be perfectly confident in the Lord's promise to us in Isaiah 55:10–11:

> *As the rain and the snow come down from heaven, and do not return to it without watering the earth and making it bud and flourish, so that it yields seed for the sower and bread for the eater, so is my word that goes out from my mouth: it will not return to me empty, but will accomplish what I desire and achieve the purpose for which I sent it.*

The disciples had heard and forgotten. They had now seen and could remember. But in order to play their part in Jesus' ongoing story they would have to do and understand. Jesus therefore rebukes them very strongly. He uses the same Greek words that are used in Revelation 21:8 to describe cowards and unbelievers being thrown into hell when he asks them in verse 40, *"Why are you such cowards? Have you still no faith?"* The disciples believe in Jesus more than they used to. They believe in Jesus more than

---

[4] Matthew 8:25 is much kinder to the disciples. It tells us that they asked, *"Lord, save us, we are perishing!"* Mark recounts the disciples' Aramaic words in their most unfavourable light in order to emphasise how much the disciples had yet to learn.

the teachers of the law. But they don't believe in him enough. Fair-weather faith is no faith at all if it disappears as soon as troubles come. Having heard and seen, they now need to learn to copy Jesus so that, when the next storm comes, they will be ready.

The tagline on the posters for the George Clooney movie *The Perfect Storm* stated that the problem for a fishing boat that sank off the coast of Massachusetts was simply that *"No one was prepared for this storm."* But you have been prepared. You have stepped into the story with Peter. You have heard Jesus' teaching and you have seen how you are to put it into practice when storm winds blow. When you are scared and lonely and lost and confused and nauseous and barely hanging onto life, you know the answer to the question the disciples ask in verse 41. Who is this man whose Word calls even the wind and waves to order? He is the God of Israel who has come down to earth to sail through the storms with you and me. If he says to us *"Let us go over to the other side,"* we can rest assured that we are already as good as there. We can sing with Reuben Morgan:

> *When the oceans rise and thunders roar,*
> *I will soar with You above the storm.*
> *Father, You are King over the flood.*
> *I will be still and know You are God.*[5]

_____

[5] Reuben Morgan's song "Still" is on the Hillsong album *Hope* (2003).

Too Strong (5:1–20)

This man lived in the tombs, and no one could bind him anymore, not even with a chain... No one was strong enough to subdue him.

(Mark 5:3–4)

When Leonidas and his 300 brave Spartans blocked the way for tens of thousands of Persian soldiers at the Battle of Thermopylae, he was defiant. When he was told that the Persians would rain down so many arrows on his tiny army that it would darken the sky, he replied, *"Good. We will fight them better in the shade."*[1] Nevertheless, after three days of fighting, all of his 300 men had died. Courage is no substitute for numerical odds. The Persian enemy was just too strong.

The storm has ended on Lake Galilee, but Jesus hasn't finished his practical demonstration of the lessons that he taught in chapter 4. The disciples realise that when Jesus said, *"Let us go over to the other side,"* he wasn't talking about sailing to one of the other towns in Galilee. He meant sailing to the Decapolis, the region east of the River Jordan, which was dominated by ten pagan cities.[2] They were about to set foot on foreign ground together. Mark's account of this visit is much longer than the account in Matthew or Luke, which is unusual, but he wants to show us how much the disciples were outside their comfort

---

[1] The ancient Greek historian Plutarch tells us that Leonidas gave this reply in his *Sayings of the Spartans* (51.6). It is therefore also a line in the movie *300* (Warner Brothers, 2007).

[2] *Decapolis* is Greek for *Ten Cities*. Although Galilee was home to many pagans as well as Jews (Matthew 4:15), these ten cities were majority pagan and aggressively so.

zone. They thought that Jesus was very brave to minister outside the Jewish enclave they called home, but they also thought the odds were stacked high against him. Everything about Jesus' first visit to the Decapolis cries out that the opposing forces are just too strong.

Mark fills these verses with detail that emphasises that we are now in pagan lands. They are farmed by people from the cities of Gerasa and Gadara (variations in the Greek text suggest that both cities laid claim to these fields). Jews were forbidden to eat the meat of pigs, but this is a region dominated by pig farming. Jews were forbidden from touching a grave and from mutilating their bodies, but here a wild man lives in a graveyard and cuts himself with stones.[3] *"Toto, I've a feeling we're not in Kansas anymore,"* Dorothy tells her dog in *The Wizard of Oz.* Peter and his friends must have felt the same.

Mark also fills these verses with detail that emphasises that these are difficult lands. It is human nature to think that Kingdom ministry is hardest wherever we are, but for the disciples it was actually true. This was a region where a man had proved too strong for any Jewish or pagan preacher. They had chained him hand and foot several times but he simply broke the chains with his bare hands because *"no one was strong enough to subdue him."*[4] The man tells Jesus that his name is Legion because so many demons live inside him. A Roman legion consisted of between 5,000–7,000 men and, since these demons later enter 2,000 pigs, this may not have been an exaggeration. Jesus is as outnumbered as Leonidas and his Spartans. He is very brave to have come here, but the enemy appears to be too strong.

Mark also fills these verses with detail that emphasises that Jesus' authority is under question in these lands. Jesus says,

---

[3] Numbers 19:16–20; Deuteronomy 14:1, 8; Isaiah 65:4. Luke 8:27 tells us he went naked too.

[4] Matthew 8:28–34 tells us that Jesus actually delivered two demonised men among the tombs. Mark focuses on the stronger of the two because he wants to show that nobody is ever too strong for Jesus.

"Come out of this man, you impure spirit!", and we read for the first time that the demons disobey. They start negotiating with Jesus over what they have to do after they leave. This must have shocked the disciples, who were used to seeing demons leave instantly in Galilee. Perhaps Satan has legitimate authority over these pig-farming pagans? Perhaps the Gospel seed which Jesus mentioned in his parables cannot grow in non-Jewish soil?

Jesus came to the Decapolis for this very reason. He made this short visit to demonstrate to the disciples that his Kingdom message is powerful everywhere and for everyone. Yes, the man is in the grip of a mighty army of demons, but the Word of God is even mightier. As soon as the man sees Jesus, he comes running and falls down on his knees like a humble subject before his king.[5] The demons shriek through the man, *"What do you want with me, Jesus, Son of the Most High God? In God's name don't torture me!"* They are in no doubt that Jesus has as much authority in their region as he does across the water in Galilee. In Matthew's account, the man says, *"Have you come here to torture us before the appointed time?"* Luke adds that *"they begged Jesus repeatedly not to order them to go into the Abyss."*[6] Mark tells us that they made no attempt to resist him by the power of Satan. They say literally, *"I adjure you by God!"* All of this is very telling. Every demon in the entire world knows that Jesus is King, that he will one day cast them into hell and that there is no way for them to resist the message of his Kingdom.

As for their negotiation, it is swift and entirely one-way. Jesus lets them go into the pigs, but only so that he can rid the area of unlawful farming. The 2,000 pigs drown in the lake and, by the time the farmers bring a group of locals to complain to Jesus, the man the disciples thought was too strong for the

---

[5] The Greek word *proskuneō* is a normally translated *to worship*. The man does not simply fall over at Jesus' feet. He prostrates himself as an expression of abject submission.

[6] Matthew 8:28–34; Luke 8:26–39. Matthew recalls the event out of order because he tends to group events by theme rather than by strict chronology.

message of God's Kingdom is *"sitting there, dressed and in his right mind."*

It's time for everyone to choose. Will they step into Jesus' story? The people of the Decapolis are afraid and they prefer to close the door on Jesus' message rather than to repent of their sin and follow him. They plead with him to leave their pagan lands and, even though he has just arrived, Jesus does as they ask. He takes his story back to Galilee.

The man who has been delivered of demons tells Jesus that he is making a different choice. No matter what it costs him, he is going to step into Jesus' story. He assumes this will require him to leave the Decapolis and travel back with Jesus to Jewish lands, but he is in for a surprise. Jesus will return to the Decapolis at the end of chapter 7, so he wants the man to play the role of John the Baptist to the pagans. Having told so many Galilean Jews to keep quiet about what he has done for them, he now commands this converted pagan to tell the Gentiles all that the God of Israel has done for him. Mark tells us that the man grasps the Gospel. He preaches to everyone that Jesus is the Lord.[7]

The disciples need to make a choice of their own as they get back into the boat and sail home to Galilee. Will they believe that the authority which Jesus gives them over demons and sickness is effective anywhere? Suddenly the parables that Jesus told them in chapter 4 become more real than ever. They understand that there is no place on earth where the odds stacked against Jesus can ever prove too strong.

---

[7] Jesus commands the man to *"tell your own people"* (that is, the Gentiles), what the Lord has done for him. The man shows his understanding by equating what *Yahweh* has done for him with what *Jesus* has done for him.

Twelve Add Twelve
(5:21–43)

A woman was there who had been subject to bleeding for twelve years... Immediately the girl stood up and began to walk around (she was twelve years old).

(Mark 5:25, 42)

There was nothing random about Jesus' decision to create an inner circle of twelve disciples. He had come to restore God's Kingdom to Israel, and Israel was a nation that consisted of twelve tribes. Jesus had chosen twelve apostles as a statement that he was reconstituting Israel under a dozen new patriarchs. Matthew wrote his gospel for Jewish readers, so it stands to reason that he states this most explicitly. Jesus says to his twelve disciples: *"At the renewal of all things, when the Son of Man sits on his glorious throne, you who have followed me will also sit on twelve thrones, judging the twelve tribes of Israel."*[1]

We should therefore be alert to the various occasions in Mark's gospel when he draws our attention to the number twelve. These are occasions when he highlights what Jesus imparted to the apostles at particular stages on their journey. Later, Jesus will send them to gather up twelve baskets of leftovers after feeding the five thousand, asking them, *"Do you*

---

[1] Matthew 19:28. This is why Judas' empty seat had to be filled in Acts 1. The parallel between the 12 apostles and the 12 tribal leaders of Israel is also seen in Luke 22:29–30 and in Revelation 4:4 and 21:12–14.

still not understand?"[2] He expects them to see the symbolism in what happens immediately after their return from the Decapolis to Galilee.

A synagogue ruler comes to meet Jesus at the beach. He is just about the last person the disciples might expect to respond to the Gospel message. He is almost certainly friends with the synagogue rulers who clashed with Jesus over the man with a shrivelled hand. He may even have been one of them.[3] But the disciples need to learn to write off nobody from responding to the message of God's Kingdom. Jairus falls at Jesus' feet and pleads with him: *"My little daughter is dying. Please come and put your hands on her so that she will be healed and live."*[4] Mark explains to us in verse 42 why this event is so significant. The man's daughter is twelve years old. She is an object lesson for the disciples in the power they wield as messengers of the Gospel.[5]

Jesus leaves his own makeshift synagogue on the beach in order to follow the synagogue ruler back to his home. The crowds decide to follow him and among them is a woman who needs healing. Her non-stop menstruation is more than a medical condition. It has placed her at the opposite end of the religious scale from Jairus. He is a synagogue ruler who leads the Jews in their Sabbath worship. Because of her unwanted blood flow, Leviticus 15:19–31 calls her unclean and forbids her from

---

[2] Mark 6:43; 8:19–21. We will see later that the number seven speaks about God's plan to save the Gentiles.

[3] Luke 13:14 gives us a window into how unpleasant synagogue rulers could be.

[4] Jairus is named after the judge *Jair* (Judges 10:3), and in Hebrew his name means *He-Enlightens*. Through a family tragedy, God enlightens the mind of one of the biggest opponents of his Son.

[5] Mark has no reason to tell us that the girl is aged 12 and the woman has been sick for 12 years unless it is for the same reason as in 6:43 and 8:19–21. This explains why, unusually, Mark's account of these two incidents is much longer and much more detailed than the parallel accounts in Matthew 9:18–26 and Luke 8:40–56.

even attending Sabbath worship. She has nothing in common with the synagogue ruler except for her desperate faith in Jesus and except for the number twelve. Mark tells us in verse 25 that she has been suffering from this menstrual problem for twelve years. She is another object lesson for the disciples in the power they wield as messengers of the Gospel.

The clock is ticking towards the moment in 6:7 when Jesus will send out the disciples to carry on his story by themselves. The question on all of their lips is the same as ours would be: *How can people like us ever do the same things as you?* That's why it helps that the woman is confused in her understanding of how the Messiah will fulfil his ministry. Although Mark does not mention Malachi 4:2, it appears that she has misread the fifth-from-last verse of the Old Testament, which talks about the Messiah and promises that *"the sun of righteousness will rise with healing in its rays."* The word translated "rays" was also used for the tassels on a rabbi's prayer shawl, so she assumes that the Messiah – the "sun of righteousness" – will heal her if she lays hold of one of his tassels.[6] Amazingly, when she reaches out as an expression of her very mixed-up faith, she is instantly healed.

Jesus stops the crowd and asks who has touched him. Peter and his friends are impatient. They want to get to the synagogue ruler's home because his daughter is dying. They protest that people bump into one another all the time in a crowd, but Jesus insists that somebody has touched him in a different way. Someone has laid hold of him with faith, and he knows it because he felt the power of the Holy Spirit go out of him through that touch. The woman comes forward, trembling with fear because she knows that she has broken the Jewish Law. She is an unclean woman who should not even be out in public and she has deliberately touched a rabbi. Numbers 19:20

---

[6] Matthew 9:20 and Luke 8:44 tell us that she particularly wanted to touch the *edge* of his cloak. Mark 6:56 tells us that, after this incident, crowds of other people started trying to touch his tassels too.

demands that she be cut off from the Jewish nation. Jesus looks at her tenderly and tells her, *"Daughter, your faith has healed you. Go in peace and be freed from your suffering."* Her twelve-year-old medical condition is instantly cured as a lesson for the twelve disciples. If Jesus can heal people with the tassels on his cloak, then he can also heal through them. If Jesus can heal when his attention is elsewhere, he can heal through them even when he is not with them. What matters is the woman's faith, the woman's flawed and fumbling faith. If they simply believe in the power of his Kingdom, they will do whatever he does.

Now for some discouragement. They are going to have plenty of discouragement when he sends them out to carry on his story. People come from the synagogue ruler's house to inform him that the twelve-year-old girl has died. The mourners laugh and sneer at Jesus when he assures them that a corpse is no harder for heaven's King to awaken than a sleeping child.[7] It is a big moment of truth for the disciples. Is Jesus only talking to Jairus, or is he talking to his disciples too, when he says, *"Don't be afraid; just believe"*?[8] Jesus invites Peter and his friends to step into the bedroom along with the girl's parents.[9] *"Talitha koum!"* he commands, using two simple Aramaic words which Mark translates for his Roman readers as *"Little girl, I say to you, get up!"* The twelve-year-old girl is instantly raised from the dead. It's a new type of miracle for Mark's gospel and it speaks volumes to the Twelve: Never underestimate God's Kingdom power when we speak in Jesus' name.

Twelve disciples. Twelve tribes of Israel. A twelve-year-old girl. A twelve-year-long medical condition. Twelve add twelve

---

[7] The Greek word *katagelaō* in 5:40 means more than *to laugh*. It means *to deride* or *laugh to scorn*.

[8] Jesus uses singular imperatives in Greek, so he is talking to Jairus, but it is also for the benefit of the Twelve.

[9] Peter, James and John were an inner circle of three within the inner circle of twelve. 5:43 tells us that Jesus performed this miracle in private so that news of it would not impede his teaching ministry still further.

add twelve add twelve equals one. It all amounts to one clear message for the disciples as Jesus prepares to send them out to carry on his story. It tells them that no Pharisee can resist them, that no doctor can contradict them and that no amount of cynical laughter should dissuade them because death itself cannot resist them. The message of the Kingdom of God is indeed like a growing seed. All by itself it bears fruit, even if they do not know how.

Compartments (5:21–43)

Daughter, your faith has healed you. Go in peace and
be freed from your suffering.

(Mark 5:34)

Just before midnight on 14th April 1912, the *Titanic* hit an
iceberg at high speed in the North Atlantic Ocean. She was the
largest ship in the world, but she sank in less than three hours
because of a problem with the compartments in her hull. A
ship's hull is divided into watertight sections so that damage
is limited if it is holed beneath the waterline. The *Titanic* hit
an iceberg so large that it holed five of sixteen compartments,
and the captain discovered too late that those compartments
were not watertight at all. The seawater spread throughout the
entire hull, and you know the rest of the story. The world's most
invincible ship became the world's most famous shipwreck.

The Devil is like the captain of the *Titanic*. He knows he has
to play at damage limitation whenever he comes into contact
with the iceberg of the Kingdom of God. We saw this when the
demons begged for permission to enter a herd of pigs instead
of leaving the region entirely.[1] We also saw it when Jairus'
friends from the synagogue laughed at Jesus for suggesting that
the Gospel is about miracles as well as mercy. The Devil wants
to limit our understanding of the message of the Kingdom, and
Mark is determined not to let him. He uses these two encounters
to show us that the Gospel delivers us from all of the Devil's work

---

[1] The Devil always tries to play the game of damage limitation. For another
example, see Exodus 8:25–28, 10:8–11 and 10:24. Because Moses was firm in
Exodus 10:26, Pharaoh finally surrendered in 12:31–32.

in our lives. The Kingdom doesn't just deal with our sin. It deals also with our sickness, our suffering and any other limitation which the Devil tries to place upon our lives.

Mark tells us that the message of the Kingdom *means that God heals bodies*. He has no time for the prevailing Roman view that spiritual things matter more than physical things, a view which the first-century philosopher Epictetus summarised as *"You are a little soul, burdened with a corpse."*[2] Mark takes the Greek word *sōzō*, which means *to save*, and he uses it in these verses to describe what Jesus does for the woman and for Jairus' daughter. In a literal translation, Jairus asks Jesus to *save* his daughter, the woman believes that touching Jesus will *save* her, and Jesus tells her that her faith has *saved* her. Salvation is as much about our bodies as it is about our souls.[3]

Many twenty-first-century Westerners struggle with this. We are deeply infected by the compartmentalising lie that God is more interested in our souls than he is in our bodies. Peter fought against this the first time he preached the Gospel to a group of Romans, telling them in Acts 10:36–38 that Jesus preached the Kingdom by bringing peace to every aspect of people's lives: *"He went around doing good and healing all who were under the power of the devil, because God was with him."* Jesus emphasises it here in verse 34 when he tells the woman to *"go in peace"* and commands her to be *hugiēs*, or *whole*. The Hebrew word for peace is *shalōm*, and it carries a far greater meaning than simply the absence of conflict. It means wholeness, completeness, restoration in all things.

Mark tells us that the message of the Kingdom *means that God helps us in our suffering*. Many people grasp at this as a way of reinforcing the Devil's compartmentalisation of

---

[2] Epictetus was a Stoic philosopher based in Rome. This quotation comes from his "Fragment 26".

[3] Mark uses the word *sōzō* in 5:23, 5:28 and 5:34. He also uses it for those who copy the woman's faith in 6:56. The normal Greek word for *to heal* is either *therapeuō* or *iaomai*, so Mark's choice of words here is deliberate.

the Gospel, pointing out that surely this is why we should not expect automatic and instant healing. I have even heard people argue from this very passage that God wants us to be sick so that we can glorify him, since the noun Mark uses to describe the woman's *affliction* in verses 29 and 34 comes from the same verb that is used in Hebrews 12:6 to encourage us that *"The Lord disciplines the one he loves."*[4]

Of course healing is not automatic and it may not be instant (as Jesus demonstrates in 8:22–26), but we must be very careful not to twist Mark's words to mean the very opposite of what he is saying. We must be careful not to talk about sickness as a friend when Jesus treats it in this passage as a terrible enemy.[5] He does not tell the woman to go home and rejoice that her constant flow of menstrual blood is a gift from the Lord to sanctify her. He heals her! Nor, despite the fact that he is constantly surrounded by crowds of sick people, does he ever teach that God might want some of them to stay that way to glorify him. Instead, he tells the woman, *"Daughter, your faith has healed you. Go in peace and be freed from your suffering."* The Lord wants to comfort us in our troubles, sometimes by delivering us from them and sometimes by carrying us through them. But when it comes to physical sickness, the Lord wants us to believe and to be healed.[6]

Mark tells us that the message of the Kingdom *means that God wants to set us free from every other limitation which the Devil tries to place upon our lives.* Whatever the Devil does to harm us and to rob us of God's blessing, Jesus reverses it through the message of his Kingdom. Satan has no greater

---

[4] Mark also uses this same word to describe people's *diseases* in 3:10.

[5] In 3:1–6, Jesus is furious at the Pharisees' failure to fight sickness as an enemy. Mark tells us in 2:12 that God is far more glorified through our being healed than he is through our continuing to be sick.

[6] Jesus often tells the crowds that suffering is part and parcel of following him, but never once does he tell them that sickness is – despite the fact that he is constantly surrounded by crowds of sick people!

weapon than death, so Jesus demonstrates this to Peter and his friends by reversing under their noses even the power of death. John was in the room and he wrote later in 1 John 3:8 that *"The reason the Son of God appeared was to destroy the devil's work."* It is very easy to become like Jairus' friends in verse 35 and tell people not to bother Jesus with the troubles they are facing. It is very easy to become like the mourners in verse 40, quick to weep with people in their troubles but slow to believe that Jesus wants to put an end to them. If Jesus can raise a dead girl back to life then there is no limitation the Devil can possibly put in our way that Jesus cannot demolish with just one word. Jesus tells us in verse 36, *"Don't be afraid; just believe."*

This is why the message of God's Kingdom is known as *the Good News.* Forgiving our sins would be mercy enough, but Mark insists that the Gospel message also offers us so much more. Don't fall for the Devil's damage limitation, fooling you that God is interested in the spiritual condition of your soul but not in the physical condition of your body or in the healthy condition of your life as a whole.[7] Don't compartmentalise the Gospel, or you will be left with something less than the Gospel.

Don't let the Devil rob you of anything that is yours as a result of the good news that Jesus is King. Satan's ship has been holed by the towering magnificence of the Gospel iceberg. Don't be party to his attempts to stop his entire ship from going down.

---

[7] Mark also emphasises this by recording that, while the girl's parents were busy celebrating the fact that she had come back to life, Jesus pointed out that somebody ought to make her a meal.

When Jesus Couldn't Heal (6:1–6)

He could not do any miracles there, except lay his hands on a few people who were ill and heal them.

(Mark 6:5)

In the TV drama *The West Wing*, President Bartlet has just failed and failed big-time. He is about to go on live television to address the nation's schoolchildren and to use NASA's landing of the *Galileo V* space probe on Mars as a chance to lecture them about the greatness of the American Dream. His problem is that *Galileo V* has just burned up on entry. His government has wasted millions of dollars in return for nothing. When he gathers his staff team in the Oval Office to discuss how best to extricate himself from the television broadcast, his press secretary suddenly has a different idea:

> We have at our disposal a captive audience of schoolchildren. Some of them don't go to the blackboard or raise their hand because they think they're going to be wrong. I think you should say to these kids, "You think **you** get it wrong sometimes? You should come down here and see how the big boys do it." I think you should tell them you haven't given up hope and that it may turn up but, in the meantime, you want NASA to put its best people in the room and you want them to start building *Galileo VI*. Some of them will laugh and most of them

won't care but, for some, they might honestly see that it's
about going to the blackboard and raising your hand.[1]

Jesus understood this. He was about to send out Peter and the other disciples to have a go at continuing his story by themselves. He knew they needed one more gift from him before they would be ready. They needed to see him unable to do something so that he could reassure them that all he wanted them to do this time around was go to the blackboard and raise their hand. So Jesus looked for the place where he knew that it would be most difficult for him to proclaim the message of the Kingdom. He took the disciples to his hometown of Nazareth and offered himself as a visiting preacher at their synagogue.

Nazareth was where Jesus had grown up. He must have attended this synagogue as a child. The people there remembered him as a gangly teenager and as a grubby carpenter. Many of them probably viewed him with suspicion because he was an unmarried 32-year-old in a culture where everyone was expected to be married by that age. Whatever spirit inspired Hollywood to produce the mocking Steve Carrell movie *The 40-Year-Old Virgin*, that spirit was alive and well in Nazareth. As for preaching in a synagogue, the last time Jesus did that the leaders had stormed out and started plotting how to kill him.[2] Jesus therefore chose the one place where he was least likely to succeed as a preacher of God's Kingdom, because he wanted his disciples to watch him struggle.

In verses 1–3, Jesus reassures his disciples that a lot of our failure is simply due to *people's prejudice*. Jesus preaches every bit as well at the synagogue in Nazareth as at his makeshift synagogue on the beach at Capernaum, but the people dismiss

---

[1] C.J. Cregg says this in *The West Wing*, Season 2, Episode 9 – "Galileo" (2000).

[2] Luke 4:16–30 also tells us of an earlier occasion, not mentioned in Mark's gospel, when Jesus preached in this same synagogue and was almost lynched. Going back to it was courting almost certain failure.

the possibility that he may be the Messiah because he is a manual labourer, because they remember him hanging a door for them,[3] because they know his mum or because they went to school with one of his sisters.[4] None of these is a good reason for them to ignore his message. It reflects their own shortcomings and not his. While we tend to beat ourselves up over the fact that people are not receptive when we share the Gospel, Jesus simply remembers the Parable of the Sower. Some people will be hard-hearted. That's just the way it is. That doesn't make us failures. We only fail if we allow our fears and discouragements to stop us from proclaiming that Jesus is the world's true King at all.

In verse 2, Jesus reassures his disciples that a lot of our failure is simply due to *people's stubborn rebellion*. The people of Nazareth admit that Jesus preaches with such unparalleled wisdom that his words can only have been given to him by God. They admit he performs such remarkable miracles that there must be a divine explanation. The fact they know that his miracle-working hands are the same hands that used to fix their furniture makes them guiltier than the rest of Galilee if they fail to follow logic where it leads. It is easy for us to think that we would see more fruit in sharing the Gospel if we were better at backing up our words with demonstrations of God's power. Although that is undoubtedly true, Jesus shows us that it isn't the whole picture. Sometimes we can be doing everything right, but the listener's unwillingness to submit to God's authority is all wrong.

In verses 4–6, Jesus reassures his disciples that a lot of our failure is simply due to *people's failure to believe*. The first half

---

[3] The Greek word *tektōn* in 6:3 means any *worker in wood*. Jesus' job as a carpenter may have involved as much work on a building site as it did in a workshop as a furniture maker.

[4] Joseph is not mentioned, so it appears that he was dead. Although Jesus' brothers thought he was mad at this stage (3:21), James and Jude would later go on to become writers of books in the New Testament.

of verse 5 is one of the most remarkable statements in Mark's gospel: *"Jesus could not do any miracles there."* Read that again. Mark says that Jesus, the God who created the universe in six days and who drives out thousands of demons with a simple command, was not able to do any miracles in Nazareth because of *"their lack of faith."*[5] Peter and his friends needed to witness this before they tried to continue his story throughout the towns of Galilee. There are many reasons why a person may not be healed when we minister to them, and we need to know that not all of them are things for which we bear the burden of responsibility.

Jesus did not fail in Nazareth. He succeeded in teaching the Twelve the final lesson they needed before they could try to carry on his story by themselves. In fact, he succeeded even more than that. Although Mark tells us that he was unable to heal as many people in Nazareth as in Capernaum, he deliberately lets slip in verse 5 that the problem was not that he prayed for lots of people and few were healed, but that few people asked for healing at all. When he did pray for them, they were healed just as easily as in Capernaum. It does not matter if we are working in a place where there is an atmosphere of dead religion (2:6–7), of stubbornness and anger (3:5), of past failure (5:4,26) or of mocking laughter (5:40).[6] The message of the Kingdom is just as powerful to transform the life of anyone who believes.

It remains the good news that Jesus is the King of heaven and that he has defeated the power of Satan in the world. It remains the good news that he has given us authority to assert his reign as King any time, any place and anywhere.

---

[5] Matthew 13:58 puts it more gently: *"He did not do many miracles there."* Mark puts it starkly because he wants us to learn the same lesson as Peter and his friends. Failure to see healing isn't always our fault.

[6] Lack of faith among the Nazarenes made fewer people ask for healing. It did not make it harder for Jesus to heal those who did. After all, Jairus' daughter was dead and therefore had no faith at all!

What to Expect When You're Expecting (6:6–29)

Calling the Twelve to him, he began to send them out two by two and gave them authority over impure spirits. These were his instructions...

(Mark 6:7–8)

The moment had finally arrived. It was time for Peter and his friends to take another giant leap for all mankind. Jesus was about to send them over the top of the trenches to become the first people in history to proclaim the Christian Gospel by themselves. They would begin a new chapter in his story which still continues today whenever we go out in expectant faith that God will use us to extend his Kingdom. Mark therefore invites us to read these verses slowly. They tell us what to expect when we're expecting God to use us.

In verses 7–9, Mark tells us to expect *God to be with us*. Jesus tells the disciples not to worry about what they will eat, what they will wear or how they will pay their way, because the Lord has sent us on this mission and he knows precisely what we need before we go. Jesus sends the disciples out in pairs because faith for finance is easier as part of a team than it is on our own. The British missionary pioneer Hudson Taylor had very little money when he launched a team of evangelists upon an unsuspecting China, but together they discovered that God was more committed than they were to funding their plans to reach a nation which represented a quarter of the world's population. He recorded in his diary his conviction that

*My God shall supply **all** my need; to Him be all the glory. I would not, if I could, be otherwise than I am – entirely dependent myself upon the Lord, and used as a channel of help to others... Oh, it is sweet to live thus directly dependent upon the Lord, who never fails us... being assured that it was the Lord's work and that the Lord would provide.*[1]

In verses 10–11, Mark tells us to expect *God to open doors for us*. Jesus warns the Twelve that some towns will refuse to listen to their message and that they will need to wipe the soil off their feet as a warning that they want no share in the judgment which will come on any town which rejects heaven's King.[2] However, he also reassures them that they will find particular households in many towns which will start an embryonic church in that community. Our goal is very simple. It is not to flit from house to house in an endless succession of cold-contact conversations. It is to find a person who is open to the Gospel, to disciple them thoroughly and to equip them to reach the rest of their community. Jesus reached the crowds by investing his life in the Twelve, and he expects us to follow this same principle.

In verses 12–13, Mark tells us to expect *God to back up our message*. He tells us that when Jesus gave his disciples authority over impure spirits, they truly found that demons were forced to obey them as much as they obeyed Jesus himself. The disciples anointed sick people with oil as an outward sign that they were relying on the Holy Spirit to do the healing and, as a result, they discovered that demons and sickness fled before them. We need to believe that we have not been sent on a fool's errand. We have been sent as ambassadors for the King. Hudson Taylor discovered

---

[1] He wrote this at the end of 1857. He quotes it in his autobiography, *A Retrospect* (1894).

[2] This is also good advice on how to handle discouragements along the way. Don't make them part of your spiritual baggage. Brush them off and share with someone else who is willing to listen.

this and, in spite of all the trials and setbacks he suffered, by the time he died the missionary agency he founded was the largest in the world. The historian Kenneth Latourette concludes that *"Hudson Taylor was... one of the greatest missionaries of all time, and... one of the four or five most influential foreigners who came to China in the nineteenth century for any purpose."*[3]

In verses 14–29, however, Mark warns us to expect *intense persecution.* If we are under the delusion that the Gospel message is the news that God wants to step into our story, then this seems odd, but Mark has already shown us that this is a false gospel. The message of the Kingdom is the news that Jesus has a story of his own and that unless we give up everything to step into it he will punish our rebellion. Mark does not tell us in verse 12 that the disciples asked people to "invite Jesus into their life". He tells us that they commanded people to repent. This won them fervent friends but it also made them many bitter enemies. The Gospel always does.[4]

Matthew and Luke refer to the ruler of Galilee by his real name: "Herod the tetrarch". Mark wants to emphasise how offensive our message is, so he uses the ruler's self-styled name instead: "King Herod". Having already told us in 1:14 that Herod imprisoned John the Baptist, Mark now chooses this moment to inform us what he did to him in prison. Like many twenty-first-century Westerners, Herod took offence at the notion that Jesus is King and that he therefore needed to bow the knee to God's agenda or face the deadly consequences. He was particularly outraged that Jesus' followers dared to question his sexual activity. Mark tells us in verse 20 that Herod knew that John was *"a righteous and holy man."* There was nothing wrong with

---

[3] Kenneth Scott Latourette in *A History of Christian Missions in China* (1929).

[4] Although his gospel is shorter than Matthew and Luke's, Mark devotes more space to John the Baptist's death than they do. He particularly wants to emphasise the necessity of suffering for the Gospel.

John's preaching except for the fact that his message was not what Herod wanted to hear.

Mark is writing for Roman readers so he uses their Emperor's man in Galilee to warn them that proclaiming Jesus is King will not be universally popular in Caesar's city. Rulers will be sinful (everybody knew that Herod was wrong to steal his brother's wife). Rulers will be perverted (everybody knew that Herod should not have asked his stepdaughter to dance seductively to indulge his lust towards her teenaged body). Rulers will be manipulated by evil people (readers would laugh at Herodias as the domineering wife who often appeared in their Roman stage plays). Rulers will be governed by their foolish pride (Herod is more concerned about his dinner guests than he is about truth or justice).[5] Mark reminds us that those who want to act like little kings will not always take kindly to the news that Jesus is King and that they therefore are not.

Admiring Hudson Taylor's fruitfulness is easy, but copying him is costly. When the full force of the Chinese Boxer Rebellion struck his missionaries in 1900, fifty-eight of his adults and twenty-one of his children were murdered. Proclaiming that Jesus was the true King of China won many converts and it also created many enemies. But Hudson Taylor had known what to expect when he set out on his mission. He wrote home during his early days in China and declared defiantly:

> *If I had a thousand pounds, China should have it. If I had a thousand lives, China should have them. No! not China, but Christ. Can we do too much for Him? Can we do enough for such a precious Saviour?*[6]

---

[5] This distain for justice would be one of the reasons why the Emperor Caligula deposed and exiled Herod Antipas in 39 AD.

[6] He wrote this in a letter home to his sister on 14th February 1860.

Send Them Away (6:30–44)

"This is a remote place," they said, "and it's already very late. Send the people away."

(Mark 6:35–36)

You probably know the story about the three tortoises that go for a picnic in a field. They realise that they have forgotten to bring drinks so one of them volunteers to go to the shop, just so long as the other two promise not to eat his sandwiches while he is gone. They wait. They wait a bit longer. They wait for two whole days but their slow friend still does not return. Finally, one of them suggests to the other that they should eat the remaining sandwiches because their friend is taking too long. Suddenly they hear a voice which comes from the gate to the field, only 200 metres away, and which threatens: *"If you're going to talk like that, I'm not going to go!"*

The disciples were excited when they came back from preaching throughout the towns of Galilee. They thought they had just completed the marathon of a lifetime. Jesus had to explain to them that they had not yet even reached the gate out of the field. This was just a taster for a lifetime of adventure. Jesus teaches the disciples that their short-term ministry trip was simply the beginning of a new chapter in his story.

In verses 30–31, the disciples return to Jesus exhilarated but exhausted. They can't wait to share their stories about all they did and said in the towns of Galilee.[1] But there is a

---

[1] Note that the Twelve talk about what they have *done* and *taught*, in that order. If we proclaim the Kingdom without demonstrating the Kingdom, our balance is all wrong.

problem. The crowds do not realise that this is their own time and that they are now off duty. So many people crowd around Jesus that they have no time to eat, let alone to relax and debrief together.[2] Jesus tells them to get into the boat: *"Come with me by yourselves to a quiet place and get some rest."* He can see that they are more than exhausted. They are also getting impatient and frustrated with the crowds.

In verses 32–34, the disciples discover that things are no better on the other side of the water. Their quiet place is not quiet for very long.[3] The crowds can't take a hint and have run around Lake Galilee to follow them. Can't the people see that they are tired and hungry and in need of some time alone with Jesus? Note the difference in Jesus' attitude towards the crowds, however: *"He had compassion on them, because they were like sheep without a shepherd. So he began teaching them many things."*[4] Jesus does not have a clock-in, clock-out mentality when it comes to Kingdom ministry. The disciples have not finished their mission. They have barely reached the gate out of the field.[5]

In verses 35–36, the disciples can no longer conceal their frustration. It is late in the day and they are beginning to resent the crowds. Peter and his friends tell Jesus to *"Send the people away so that they can go to the surrounding countryside and*

---

[2] Eating is a very legitimate need! Jesus is not saying that our needs do not matter, but that our needs will be far better filled if we deny ourselves to serve the crowds (John 4:31–34).

[3] Mark calls the place literally a *desert* in order to make a link between this miracle and God's provision of manna for Israel in the desert. Mark's words in 6:34 also make a deliberate link back to Numbers 27:17 and to Moses' prayer that God would care for his People by appointing *Joshua* (in Greek, *Jesus*) to rule over them.

[4] Mark 6:34 tells us that Jesus had compassion and *taught* the crowd. Matthew 14:14 says he had compassion and *healed* the crowd. Luke 9:11 says both. For Jesus, Kingdom ministry always meant both word and deed.

[5] Jesus had even more reason than the Twelve to demand some time alone. Matthew 14:12–14 tells us that he had just heard the news that John the Baptist had been killed.

villages and buy themselves something to eat."[6] Jesus has a different idea, one that requires them to see their short-term ministry trip as the start of a whole new lifestyle: *"You give them something to eat."*

In verses 37–38, the disciples show that they have not yet learned what to expect when they're expecting. They do not think in terms of God's provision. They think in terms of human mathematics and of catering bills. There are 5,000 men, plus women and children, so this event should really be called the feeding of the ten thousand or more. The disciples are appalled that the total food bill will be the equivalent price of a brand new car today. Their focus is entirely on the size of the need. They are not focused on the resources God has placed at their disposal, so Jesus asks them, *"How many loaves do you have? Go and see."* They return with the news that they have five small loaves of bread and two fish. There is hardly enough to feed the Twelve, let alone the crowds.

In verses 39–42, Jesus teaches the disciples to make Kingdom ministry their daily lifestyle instead of treating it as an occasional adventure. He can see that they are tired and hungry and frustrated and increasingly impatient. Yet instead of feeding the crowds without them (let's face it, the one who could multiply loaves and fishes could also distribute them without the help of the disciples), he intentionally brings the disciples right into the heart of his miracle. He tells them to make the people sit down in groups of fifty or a hundred on the green grass.[7] He gives thanks to his Father and then gives them the bread to distribute to the hungry crowds.[8] By the time they

---

[6] This is not a one-off attitude for the disciples. See also Matthew 15:23 and Mark 10:13–14.

[7] Mark is the only gospel writer to add the eyewitness detail that the grass was *green*. This event was clearly still very vivid in Peter's mind. Since grass is only green during springtime underneath the fierce sunshine of Israel, this pinpoints the date of this miracle to around March 29 AD.

[8] Jesus does not pray for the bread to multiply. He simply blesses it. His authority is such that heaven's power lines up to bless whatever Jesus blesses.

return, he has also broken the fish into pieces and sends them back among the crowds. The disciples are astonished. They find that five loaves and two fish are able to feed and satisfy thousands of people. Jesus has made them waiters at one of the most famous meals in history. Suddenly they aren't feeling tired any more.

In verses 43–44, Jesus sends the disciples to pick up twelve baskets of leftover food. As we saw earlier, the number twelve is very significant whenever Jesus teaches his disciples. Every disciple fills his basket and discovers that his needs are better fulfilled by serving Jesus and the crowds than they are by serving self alone. If we act as if the Gospel is an offer from Jesus to step into our story, we will never be satisfied by our self-centred faith. But if we grasp that the Gospel is a command to step out of our own lives and into Jesus' story, we will be truly satisfied. Jesus stepped into our world in order to lay down his life for us, and the Gospel invites us to step into his story and to lay down our lives for him and for other people. It's an extremely radical new way of living.

The disciples have completed a short-term ministry trip to the villages of Galilee. Six pairs of disciples, each going to a maximum of five towns – they had only managed to impact thirty Galilean communities. But if they turn their short-term mission trip into a lifestyle, even when it's least convenient – perhaps *especially* when it's least convenient – then Jesus promises that he will use them to satisfy the hunger of the entire world.

So don't be a tortoise. Don't think that you have made it in the Christian life when you have barely reached the gate out of the field. Step into this new chapter in the story. Tell Jesus that you know it's true: the more you keep your life to yourself, the less you will be satisfied, but the more you give your life away for others, the more you will find it and find it by the basketful.[9]

This miracle echoes the one in 2 Kings 4:42–44.

[9] Jesus explains the message behind this miracle in 8:34–35.

Refuel (6:45–56)

After leaving them, he went up on a mountainside to pray.

(Mark 6:46)

General Bernard Montgomery knew that he would never be able to defeat his German counterpart by conventional means. Erwin Rommel was the undisputed master of tank warfare. The Germans would easily win a fair fight in North Africa, so Montgomery decided to wage an unfair one instead. He targeted the German tank commander's fuel supply.

In September and October 1942, the British managed to sink two-thirds of the fuel tankers on which the German Panzer divisions so heavily relied. When Rommel received news that the RAF had sunk the oil tankers *Tergestea* and *Proserpina*, he wrote dejectedly in his diary that without fuel the battle was already as good as lost. Sure enough, Montgomery routed Rommel at the Second Battle of El Alamein. Rommel lost 500 tanks in the battle, many of them simply because they ran out of fuel and had to be abandoned. The British Prime Minister Winston Churchill reflected later that *"It may almost be said, 'Before Alamein we never had a victory. After Alamein we never had defeat.'"*[1] The Germans lost the whole war in North Africa because their tanks ran out of fuel.

Jesus understood this. He was determined not to let the Devil win the battle by cutting off his fuel supply. We saw this earlier, after a tiring evening healing the crowds outside Peter's

[1] Winston Churchill in volume 4 of his World War Two Memoirs, *The Hinge of Fate* (1951).

house in Capernaum. While Peter slept soundly, Mark 1:35 tells us that *"Very early in the morning, while it was still dark, Jesus got up, left the house and went off to a solitary place, where he prayed."* Jesus pursues the same priority again after feeding the five thousand. He tells his disciples to cross Lake Galilee in their boat, and *"after leaving them, he went up on a mountainside to pray."*

Jesus is exhausted. He is emotionally spent from having just heard about John the Baptist's execution and from having been constantly hounded and pressed and manhandled by the needy crowds.[2] The thought of the cushion in the stern of the boat must have been enormously attractive, but Jesus is determined to refuel. He dismisses the crowd and then prays until *"shortly before dawn"* – in other words, for nine or ten straight hours.[3] He puts himself in an awkward position. By staying behind, he now needs to perform another miracle by walking on the waters of Lake Galilee. Jesus would rather be in an awkward position with fuel than in a comfortable one without.

Mark teaches us in verses 47–48 that unless we refuel ourselves through prayer, *we will labour to little purpose.* Lake Galilee is only thirteen miles across at its widest point, but the disciples only manage to reach the middle after ten straight hours of rowing.[4] That's the problem. They are in a sailboat but *"the wind was against them."* Without divine help, they had been reduced to *"straining at the oars."* If your Christian life feels a lot more like heavy rowing than water walking, don't be surprised.[5]

---

[2] Matthew 14:12–14. Jesus did not feed the 5,000 in order to carry on preaching longer. He did it out of compassion for their bellies before he dismissed them. God is as interested in our bodies as he is in our souls.

[3] Mark 6:48 tells us literally that he set out *"about the fourth watch of the night"* – in other words, somewhere between 3 a.m. and 6 a.m.

[4] Mark says they set off for Bethsaida. John 6:17 says they set off for Capernaum. Both were in a northerly direction. Mark tells us that Jesus eventually let them anchor at Gennesaret, which was closer than either.

[5] Surprisingly, Mark's account of Peter's story does not tell us that Peter also walked on the water (Matthew 14:22–34). Perhaps Peter did not want to boast about his own faith to defy the laws of physics alongside Jesus. Perhaps he

Mark says this will always be the case if we neglect fellowship with the Holy Spirit who alone can fill our sails. Prayer in private is the source of our power in public. Don't become all tank and no fuel.

Mark teaches us in verses 49–52 that unless we refuel ourselves through prayer, *we will never become the people that we truly are*. Jesus is about to pass the disciples by, but they start screaming at the sight of a man walking on the water.[6] They think it must be the ghost of the lake. The significance of his reply is lost in most English translations. He tells them, *"Take courage! I AM. Don't be afraid."* The time he has spent with his Father has left him in no doubt over his identity. He is the God of the Old Testament, the one who revealed himself to Moses as *Yahweh*, the great *I AM*. Jesus simply climbs into the boat and asserts his identity over the wind and the waves, because he knows who he is. Mark reminds us that we have a new identity too. He says the disciples' problem was that *"they had not understood about the loaves; their hearts were hardened."* In other words, they had not realised that God had an individual basket set aside with their name on it. They were apostles. They were chosen ones. They had been appointed to bear fruit that would last. They didn't have to strain and worry and scream and struggle. They could simply come to God as children and receive their Father's power.[7]

Mark teaches us in verses 53–56 that unless we refuel ourselves through prayer, *we will always struggle to attract a crowd*. Think of all the Christian energy that is expended on creating websites and flyers and press releases and evangelistic campaigns. Jesus does none of this. He simply emerges from the presence of his Father with such power that crowds form

---

simply wanted to amplify the contrast between Jesus' power and that of his disciples.

[6] The Lord sometimes pretends to pass us by in order to stir our passion to spend time with him (Luke 24:28).

[7] The "lesson of the loaves" was also that Jesus is the same Yahweh who provided manna for Israel in the desert (John 6:48–51).

naturally wherever he goes. Mark tells us intriguingly in 5:30 that Jesus felt power going out from him when he healed people. Presumably then, he also felt power going back into him during his prayer times. We will search the gospels in vain for a formula or technique for healing people. Is it touching or commanding or blessing or casting out demons? It is all of those things and none. How we minister the power God gives us is of secondary importance. What really matters is whether we have received his power at all. *"You will receive power when the Holy Spirit comes on you,"* Jesus promises in Acts 1:8. The place in which that happens is the place of prayer.

Mark emphasises this in verse 56 by ending this chapter with one of the strangest verses in his entire gospel. He tells us that Jesus healed everyone who touched the tassels on his prayer shawl, placing their faith in the same misinterpretation of Malachi 4:2 as the woman with the menstrual problem. What is more, in the Greek text Mark is deliberately ambiguous as to whether Jesus was even wearing the shawl at the time. Some commentators suggest that he went to bed and left his shawl outside for the crowds to touch in faith while he had a sleep inside.[8] Whatever the exact detail, Mark is assuring us that if we refuel regularly in prayer, there is no limit to what the Holy Spirit will do through our ordinary lives.

Erwin Rommel wrote in June 1941, *"We knew that our moves would be decided more by the petrol gauge than by tactical requirements."*[9] He knew it, but still he allowed his enemy to stop him from refuelling. Don't fall for the Devil's desire to keep you from praying. Remember what Mark told us in 3:14–15: *"Jesus appointed twelve that **they might be with him** and that he might send them out to preach and to have authority to drive out demons."*

---

[8] Mark 6:56 and the parallel Matthew 14:36 are both ambiguous in Greek as to whether the crowds touched *him* or *it*. Luke is unambiguous, however, when he talks about Paul healing people this way in Acts 19:11–12.

[9] Included by B.H. Liddell-Hart in *The Rommel Papers* (1953).

Goodbye, Galilee (7:1–23)

Jesus left that place and went to the vicinity of Tyre.

(Mark 7:24)

If John's gospel reads like a travel documentary, then Mark's gospel is like a stage show. John presents Jesus as a man who is constantly on the road, shuttling back and forth between Galilee and Jerusalem,[1] whereas Mark's gospel moves along at a much faster pace but changes the scenery much less often. There are only three main locations for the whole of Mark's gospel and Jesus stays in each one of them for many chapters at a time. The whole of Mark 1:1–7:23 takes place in Galilee. The whole of Mark 7:24–9:50 takes place in the majority-pagan lands to the north and east of Galilee.[2] Jesus then takes the road to Jerusalem in Mark 10 and spends the whole of Mark 11–16 in the capital of Judea. There are only three scenes in Mark's gospel, and Jesus is about to exit the first of them.

It is appropriate that Jesus ends his twenty-one months in Galilee with a showdown with the Pharisees who dominate the region's synagogues.[3] Jesus has been almost universally popular in this first part of Mark's gospel. The exceptions have been his clashes with the Pharisees in the synagogue in

---

[1] John tells us about Jesus' frequent trips to Jerusalem to celebrate Jewish feasts at the Temple, and these trips are our main way of dating the events which take place in the other three gospels.

[2] Jesus takes a day trip to the Decapolis in 5:1–20 and another day trip back to Galilee in 8:13–26, but these day trips only serve to reinforce what he is teaching his disciples on the main stage.

[3] These Galilean Pharisees called in support from some leading teachers of the law who came from Jerusalem, but their power base was not in the Jerusalem Temple. It was in the provincial synagogues.

3:1-6 and with the Nazarenes in the synagogue in 6:1-6. Mark therefore ends part one of his gospel by using another clash to teach us an important lesson. The opportunity to step into God's story will not be open to us forever. Galilee has had its chance and Jesus is about to take his story elsewhere.

Mark also wants to use this final event in Jesus' Galilean ministry to answer one of the biggest objections that the Romans raised when considering the Gospel: *How can Jesus truly be the Jewish Messiah if we know that the majority of Jews have rejected him?* It was a good question, so Mark gives it a good answer.[4]

In verses 1-5, Mark exposes the polluted spirit behind first-century Judaism. The Pharisees had meant well when they set out to codify and amplify the Law of Moses. They had hoped that, if they tightened its regulations, they would strengthen the distinctions between the Jews and the pagans and the Herodians who were neither one nor the other.[5] This is one of the reasons why they were so offended when Jesus shrugged off the extra rules which they taught in all their synagogues. He obeyed the Torah perfectly but he largely ignored their additional laws about washing hands and plates and pots and pans.[6] They were so consumed with their legal textbooks that they weren't there to see him multiply loaves in order to give bread in the desert to a new generation of Israelites. As a result, they were unaware that Jesus was the true fulfilment of the Law of Moses.[7]

In verses 6-13, Jesus commands them to repent of the

---

[4] Mark patiently explains Jewish customs for his Roman readers in 7:3-4. Matthew never has to do this for his Jewish readers.

[5] The followers of Herod were some of the most Romanised Jews in the land, which is why the alliance formed in 3:6 demonstrated how little the Pharisees' outward rule-keeping had actually purified them.

[6] It is significant that the only complaint which the Pharisees could level at Jesus was that he failed to obey their supplementary laws. This was a tacit admission that he perfectly obeyed the entire Law of Moses.

[7] The Pharisees complain literally in 7:2 and 5 that the disciples are eating *bread* without washing their hands. Mark is making a link between their polluted religion and their failure to submit to the lesson of 6:30-44.

shortcomings of first-century Judaism. The Greek word Mark uses for *washing* in verse 4 is *baptismos*, which is ironic because responding to the humbling message of John the Baptist would have prepared them to receive Jesus as their Messiah. So far in his gospel, Mark has only quoted three times from the Old Testament, but here he records three verses that Jesus used to confront the error of the Pharisees. In verses 6–7, Jesus uses Isaiah 29:13 as a reminder that God is not interested in manmade rules. He wants our heartfelt submission. In verse 10, he quotes from Exodus 20:12 and 21:17 to expose the fact that their manmade rules actually contradict the Law of Moses.[8] He isn't a lawbreaker because he fails to adhere to their rules for ritual washing. They are the real lawbreakers![9] Mark's Roman readers need to understand that the reason many Jews reject Jesus as Messiah is that their nation has corrupted the faith of Moses.

In verses 14–23, Jesus turns to the crowd of Galileans and appeals to them to distance themselves from the shortcomings of first-century Judaism. The error of the Pharisees has been to assume that people can cleanse their sinful hearts by observing rules on the outside. This is not the Gospel in either the Old or New Testament, as he explains to his disciples later. The Torah described ways for the Jews to celebrate the fact that God had changed them on the inside and was causing his internal righteousness to flow out from them through the Holy Spirit. The true marker of whether or not somebody is part of the People of God has never been their adherence to ritual washing or to food laws. It has only ever been the way that their heart is

---

[8] The Torah repeats itself, so in 7:10 Jesus could just as easily be quoting Deuteronomy 5:16 as Leviticus 20:9.

[9] The Hebrew word *qorbān* is used 82 times in the Old Testament, 78 of which are in the Torah. Mark translates it for his Roman readers as a *gift* or *offering* to God. The Lord wants our heartfelt obedience far more than he wants our external sacrifices (1 Samuel 15:22).

being changed by the Holy Spirit to produce character like that of Jesus.

Mark has answered lots of Roman questions. With tragic irony, he has explained that many Jews reject Jesus as Messiah because the Devil has polluted their ancient faith and persuaded them to rely on empty acts of ritual cleansing. Put more positively, he has told them that their reservations about first-century Judaism need not become a barrier to their stepping into Jesus' story themselves. God finds the faith of the Pharisees every bit as unattractive as they do. They can respond to Jesus without embracing polluted rules for cleansing or futile attempts to earn God's forgiveness.

But Mark has also raised a question for the Romans. What are they going to do at the end of part one of Jesus' story? If the Devil can dupe Jews into forfeiting their birthright, he can certainly dupe pagans too. If Jesus eventually called time on the Galileans and took his story elsewhere, then they do not have forever to make their own decision about eternity. Even as Mark demolishes Roman objections to the Gospel by stating clearly that followers of Jesus do not need to follow Jewish food laws, he appeals for his Gentile readers to be made clean through the Gospel.[10] God will accept them if they ask him, but time is running out for them just as it ran out for the Galileans.

Time is running out for us too. As we come to the end of part one of Mark's gospel, it is time for us to decide. We know enough now to be as guilty as any Galilean synagogue ruler if we do not lay hold of the message of God's Kingdom with both hands. So before you read further, take time to confess your sin and to tell Jesus that you want to be forgiven and to follow him. Take time to tell Jesus that you are committing yourself to him. Tell him that, with all your heart, you are determined to step into his story.

---

[10] Mark is the only gospel writer to spell this out explicitly (7:19). Peter had fought hard for this message in Acts 10–11 and 15. So had Paul, the converted Pharisee, who was also known to many Roman readers.

Part Two:

The World's Story

(Mark 7:24–9:29)

Breadcrumbs (7:24–30)

"Lord," she replied, *"even the dogs under the table eat the children's crumbs."*

(Mark 7:28)

Gentiles. Pagans. Heathens. The uncircumcised. Dogs. Goyim. Shgatzim. Shiksas. Jewish people have used many names throughout history to describe a person who is not a fellow Jew. Mark's Roman readers knew that Jewish people called them names behind their backs, and they no doubt called the Jews some names of their own. Mark strongly attacks the sin of racism in part two of his gospel. He makes it clear to his readers that the Gospel isn't just the Messiah's story; it is also the whole world's story.

Jesus has left Galilee. He has started a tour of the four mixed-race regions of Palestine: Syro-Phoenicia, Abilene, Trachonitis and the Decapolis. His first stop is the port-city of Tyre, once the mighty trading metropolis of the Phoenicians but now dominated by the Syrians.[1] Mark tells us that *"He entered a house and did not want anyone to know it."* Perhaps he wanted to find some time alone to pray and plan this new tour of duty. Whatever his intentions, *"he could not keep his presence secret."* He was far too famous as a miracle-worker, even in a largely pagan city. A Greek woman comes and begs Jesus to cast a demon out of her little daughter. Part two of Mark's gospel has just begun.

---

[1] Matthew 15:22 calls her a *Canaanite* and Mark calls her a *Greek* because the people of Tyre were Canaanite Phoenicians who had been Hellenised by Alexander the Great and his Seleucid successors.

Jesus appears to be rude to the woman. There is no other way of putting it.[2] He treats her with the brusque and aloof manner which Jewish rabbis tended to use whenever they were unable to avoid talking to Gentile women.[3] But his apparent rudeness is a ruse. It is only a way to draw out what is in her heart and in the hearts of his disciples.

What Peter was thinking wasn't pretty. Later, when he became the first Christian in history ever to preach to a roomful of Romans, he confessed to them that he used to be as revolted by the thought of friendship with a pagan as he was by the thought of eating ham and bacon pie. He confessed that *"You are well aware that it is against our law for a Jew to associate with or visit a Gentile. But God has shown me that I should not call anyone impure or unclean."*[4] It had taken Peter over ten years to grasp fully what Jesus taught him in a house in Tyre shortly after he left Galilee. This is probably why Mark records the fact that Jesus had to rebuke him and his friends in 7:18 for clinging to their stubborn prejudices, asking them, *"Are you so dull?"*[5] As a result of their prejudices, Peter and his friends must have nodded approvingly at the way in which Jesus repelled this pagan invader: *"First let the children eat all they want, for it is not right to take the children's bread and toss it to the dogs."*[6] Quite right, Jesus. You tell her, Jesus. "Dogs" was one of the politer ways that

---

[2] Matthew 15:21–28 tells us that he actually refused her request twice, not just once.

[3] We tend to be shocked by Jesus' offhand manner here. John 4:9 and 4:27 remind us that, in the first century, it was shocking for a Jewish rabbi to be willing to talk to a Gentile woman at all.

[4] Acts 10:9–16, 27–29, 34–35, 44–46; 11:1–18.

[5] Ironically, the Greek word *asunetos*, or *stupid*, which Jesus uses in 7:18, is the very same word God uses in the Greek Old Testament to describe the salvation of senseless pagans in Deuteronomy 32:21.

[6] This is wonderful news for Christians who need God's healing. Jesus does not merely heal as a PR exercise to win over non-Christians (in fact, it causes PR problems throughout Mark). He heals out of compassion and he heals Christians even more than he heals non-Christians. Healing is the children's bread.

Jews referred to pagans behind their backs, so it was about time that a rabbi dared to say it to one of their faces.[7]

The thoughts of the foreign woman's heart are as beautiful as the disciples' thoughts are ugly. *"Lord,"* she replies, using the Greek word *kurios*, which can just mean "sir" but which is also the word used to translate the name *Yahweh* in the Greek Old Testament. *"Lord, even the dogs under the table eat the children's crumbs."* She admits she is completely unworthy to have a share in God's Kingdom, but she tells Jesus that she is nevertheless desperate for a taste of the bread he has come to offer to Israel. Don't miss the way that this event is sandwiched (excuse the pun) between the feeding of 5,000 Jews in 6:30–44 and the feeding of 4,000 foreigners in 8:1–10. The Pharisees ignored the way Jesus provided miraculous bread for people in the desert and, instead, complained that his followers ate their bread with unclean hands. They despised the Bread of Life, but this woman is willing to grovel on the floor to get a share.

Whatever else Peter and his friends might have expected Jesus to say to this foreigner, they did not expect him to say, *"For such a reply, you may go; the demon has left your daughter."* They came from a culture which taught that foreigners had no right to receive God's help (it was *"the **children's** bread"*) because they had deliberately given themselves over to the worship of demon idols (after all, 1 Kings 16:31 tells us that this region was home to the evil Queen Jezebel). Jesus demolishes this wrong thinking by delivering her daughter from the demon as easily as if she had been a Jewish worshipper in the synagogue at Nazareth – perhaps more easily. The message of the Kingdom is not just God's story for Israel. It is God's story for the entire world.

Peter would not understand this fully until over ten years later, until partway through his sermon to a roomful of Romans at the house of the centurion Cornelius. He did not pray for

---

[7] Paul picks up on this racist insult and uses it against the Judaisers in Philippians 3:2.

them to receive the Holy Spirit any more than Jesus prayed for the foreign woman's daughter to be delivered. He simply issued the Gospel proclamation that Jesus is King and the Holy Spirit fell. Luke, himself a pagan convert from Syria, tells us in Acts 10 that *"The circumcised believers who had come with Peter were astonished that the gift of the Holy Spirit had been poured out even on Gentiles... Then Peter said, 'Surely no one can stand in the way of their being baptised with water. They have received the Holy Spirit just as we have.'"*

This event in Tyre was therefore the beginning of a new chapter in the understanding of Peter and his friends. It was also of vital importance to Mark's original Roman readers. But it is also of vital importance for you and me. We must not miss the message for us behind this story.

It tells us that God has made all races and hates all forms of racism. It tells us that he invites people from every single ethnic group on earth to step into his story. It tells us that we must not write anybody out of God's story because of their location or their background or their culture. Not the Buddhist next to you on the bus, not the Muslim in your office, not the Hindu who has just moved in next door. Not the person who lives in the so-called "Muslim world" or who lives in a notoriously hard-to-reach nation. Not the person who lives under the government of somebody like Herod the tetrarch, who wants to deny them the right to hear the news that Jesus is King.

No. Jesus uses his visit to Tyre to proclaim that his Kingdom on earth is a Kingdom without borders. He starts a new chapter in his story by proclaiming the truth of Psalm 24:1: *"The earth is the Lord's, and everything in it, the world, and all who live in it."*

Spit on a Foreigner
(7:31–37)

Jesus put his fingers into the man's ears. Then he
spat and touched the man's tongue.

(Mark 7:33)

A French doctor named Étienne Perlin, living in London in 1553, complained about the everyday racism of Tudor England: *"The common people are proud... These villains hate all sorts of foreigners and... spit in our faces."* I have never met anyone who disagrees with Étienne Perlin that it is very wrong to spit on a foreigner. I know that. You know that. Jesus knows that too. That's why it's so surprising what he does next as he continues his tour of the mixed-race borderlands of Palestine. When he meets a deaf foreigner, he decides that the only right thing to do is to wipe his spit on him.

Jesus has gone north from Tyre to Sidon, completing his tour of the major cities of Syro-Phoenicia. He has then taken a boat trip across Lake Galilee to the second of the region's four majority-pagan regions. He is back in the Decapolis, the region where he delivered a man from a legion of demons in chapter 5. The man has been obedient to his parting instructions and has told everyone about Jesus. A large crowd starts to gather, and among the first arrivals is a man who is deaf and can barely talk.[1] His friends beg Jesus to place his hands on him because they believe that he can heal with his touch and with his tassels.

---

[1] Never underestimate the power of one person's diligent evangelism. Last time, the Decapolis crowds begged Jesus to leave. Because of one man's preaching, they now hang on his every word.

Matthew 15:29–31 tells us that this crowd *"praised the God of Israel"* – in other words, they were pagans who celebrated the fact that were being granted a share in the Jewish story. Mark homes in on this one man because Jesus takes him away from the crowds – not, as some suggest, because he is unable to heal in an atmosphere of pagan disbelief. Jesus raises Lazarus from the dead in John 11 despite the widespread disbelief in Bethany and besides, Matthew 15:29–31 tells us there was as much faith in the Decapolis as there was in any of the towns in Galilee. The most plausible explanation, therefore, seems to be that Jesus wants to ensure that Peter and the other disciples do not miss this lesson amidst the blur of the crowd. He takes them to one side because what he is about to do marks a crucial milestone in their journey of discovery.

In 1787, when British racism had sunk to far worse depths than in the days of Étienne Perlin, the English pottery manufacturer Josiah Wedgwood decided to do something very brave. He started producing ceramic medallions that bore the image of one of the many thousands of black slaves who were being transported in British ships across the Atlantic, and which asked the radical question: *"Am I not a man and a brother?"* His medallions became a popular fashion accessory and played a major role in the abolition of the British slave trade twenty years later, but he took a terrible risk in producing them. He was as revolutionary as the French across the Channel two years later.

Jesus does something very similar when he takes the deaf and mute man to one side in the Decapolis. He ignores the many reasons why he should not help him. He is a Jew and the man is a Gentile. He came to the Decapolis a few months earlier and was asked to leave by this man's neighbours because they cared more about bacon prices than they did about the arrival of the Messiah. If word gets out that he is healing Gentiles, it will make a hard job even harder for him when he finally goes south to

Jerusalem. There are lots of good reasons for Jesus to say no, but he ignores every one of them.

Jesus decides to demonstrate that this deaf and mute foreigner is a friend and a brother. Has he a problem inside his ears? Then I shall put my clean Jewish fingers into his dirty pagan ears to demonstrate my willingness to bear the problem of his deafness. Has he a problem with his tongue? Then I shall spit on this foreigner. I will mix my pure Jewish saliva with his unclean pagan spit to demonstrate my willingness to bear the problem of his muteness. Does his heart break daily over the misery of his affliction? Then I will groan deeply in my own heart and look up to heaven as a sign to my Father that I am willing to bear his suffering.[2] I will cry out *"Ephphatha!"* – Mark translates the Aramaic word for his Roman readers as *"Be opened!"* – as a demonstration of my willingness to use my Messianic authority to save this lost and sinful pagan.

Jesus is teaching the disciples that he is as much the Messiah of the Decapolis as he is the Messiah of Galilee. The word Mark uses in 7:32 to describe the man as *mute* is very unusual. The word *mogilalos* means *having difficulty speaking*, and it is so rare that this is the only time it is used in the New Testament and it is only used one time in the whole of the Greek Old Testament. It is used in Isaiah 35:5–6 in one of the greatest Old Testament prophecies about the future ministry of the Messiah: *"Then will the eyes of the blind be opened and the ears of the deaf unstopped. Then will the lame leap like a deer, and the mute tongue shout for joy. Water will gush forth in the wilderness and streams in the desert."*

This ancient prophecy about the Messiah is instantly fulfilled while Peter and the other disciples look on in wonder. Mark echoes its wording when he tells us that *"the man's ears were opened, his tongue was loosed and he began to speak*

---

[2] The Greek word *stenazō* in 7:34 normally means *to groan*, but it literally means *to be in distress*. Jesus was willing to feel this man's pain.

plainly."[3] Mark tells us literally that *"the chain of his tongue was loosed."* In other words, he was set free from his affliction like one of Josiah Wedgwood's slaves.[4] Unlike the man Jesus delivered from a legion of demons, he is forbidden to tell anyone the details of this miracle. Jesus has quite enough crowds already, and he wants to be received as King rather than just as a worker of Kingdom miracles. Nevertheless, the crowd don't need to be told all of the details in order to understand the meaning of the miracle. They echo the words of Isaiah 35 as they marvel at his healing ministry. They now know that God's Messiah is the Saviour of the whole world.

No wonder Matthew 15:31 describes this same event by telling us that *"The people were amazed when they saw the mute speaking... and they praised the God of Israel."* They now knew that God had sent his Messiah to the Decapolis as much as he had sent him to Galilee and Judea. They now knew that the pagan world had been included in God's invitation to step into the Messiah's story.

---

[3] This foreigner listens better than some of the Galileans in 6:11 and he speaks better than the Pharisees in 3:4. What matters is not a person's ethnicity, but a person's faith.

[4] As in 9:25, Jesus may be saying that this physical problem was the outward evidence of demonic oppression. He describes a woman's crippling back problems in a similar way in Luke 13:16.

Déjà Vu (8:1–10)

*His disciples answered, "But where in this remote
place can anyone get enough bread to feed them?"*

(Mark 8:4)

In the science-fiction movie *Déjà Vu*, Denzel Washington manages
to save the city of New Orleans from a major terrorist attack
because he has seen it all before and therefore knows what he
should do. He has quite literally seen it all before. He works for a
government agency that is pioneering crime detection through
time travel. Denzel Washington knows that attempting time
travel may well cost him his life, but he is willing to take the
risk in order to prevent the terrorist attack before it happens.
He explains: *"For all of my career, I've been trying to catch people
after they do something horrible. For once in my life, I'd like to
catch somebody before they do something horrible."*[1]

The disciples are about to have a déjà vu moment of their
own, and they are not as clear-witted as Denzel Washington.
Mark told us in 6:52 that *"they had not understood about the
loaves; their hearts were hardened,"* and in 7:18 that Jesus asked
them, *"Are you so dull?"* Peter and his friends are about to have
a déjà vu experience, and they are about to prove every bit as
unready as they were the first time around.

Mark gives us several clues as to what is happening in the
Decapolis during the first ten verses of chapter 8. He tells us
that *"another large crowd gathered"* – in other words, another

---

[1] *Déjà Vu* (Buena Vista Pictures, 2006).

large crowd like the last one which he mentioned in 6:34.[2] Jesus tells the disciples that *"I have compassion for these people"* – just as Mark told us *"he had compassion"* on the previous crowd in 6:34.[3] When Jesus asks the disciples how they think he should feed the crowd, they point out that they are in a *remote place* – literally, a *desert*, just like the one where Jesus fed 5,000 Jewish men in 6:35. If you feel as though you are experiencing déjà vu as you read these verses, it's because you are. Mark wants us to recognise that we have been here before.

It is obvious to Jesus what they should do. It may be obvious to us as well, but it certainly isn't obvious to the disciples. Even as they reply to Jesus, they do not understand the significance of their own words. They ask him how they could ever feed these people *"bread in the desert."* Their own words should make them recall the miraculous manna with which God fed the Israelites for forty years in the desert. It should remind them of the way in which Jesus re-enacted that miracle in chapter 6 to demonstrate that he is the Bread of Heaven.[4] It should make them recall the conversations which have taken place since the feeding of the five thousand. The Pharisees complained that the disciples were eating *bread* without washing their hands, prompting Jesus to say goodbye to Galilee and sail to mixed-race lands.[5] The Syro-Phoenician woman asked Jesus for the children's *bread* and told him that she would be satisfied even with a few of their

---

[2] Jesus says in 8:3 that many people in the crowd have come a long distance to listen to him. We are meant to understand that this is a crowd of foreigners from the whole of the Decapolis and beyond.

[3] Mark uses the same Greek word *splangchnizomai* in 8:2 that he used in 1:41 and 6:34. Literally, Jesus *was moved in his bowels towards them*, or *was gutted for them*. As with the 5,000, Jesus did not perform this miracle in order to be able to preach longer. He performed it out of compassion and then dismissed the crowd.

[4] It is so important that we grasp this that, unusually, all four gospel writers record the feeding of the 5,000. John 6:30–58 spells out its meaning and Matthew 15:32–38 also records the feeding of the 4,000.

[5] Although some English translations simply talk about *food* in 7:2 and 7:5, it is very significant that Mark's Greek text talks literally about *bread*.

breadcrumbs. Those conversations are sandwiched between the bread of chapter 6 and the bread of chapter 8 for a reason. Jesus is saying that the Bread of Life is for foreigners too.

The disciples just don't get it. They do not see the link between what Jesus did for a Jewish crowd and what he might do for this largely pagan crowd in the Decapolis. What did that re-enactment of Israelite history have to do with these uncircumcised Gentiles? What did twelve baskets and twelve disciples and twelve Israelite tribes have to do with the Greek cities of the Decapolis? This pagan crowd is more like the seven foreign nations that the Lord destroyed on both sides of the River Jordan in order to give the Promised Land to the Israelites. The disciples assume that this crowd has no share in Israel's story. Jesus sees that he needs to re-enact his previous miracle on foreign soil.

"How many loaves of bread do you have?" Jesus asks them. *"Seven,"* they reply. That's very interesting because, even though Mark does not tell us how many fish Jesus multiplied, three times in this short miracle he uses the number seven. Jesus makes the foreigners sit down on the ground, just as he did the Jews two chapters earlier, praying over the loaves and asking his disciples to distribute them in the same way. When the 4,000 men, plus women and children, are fully satisfied, Jesus sends the disciples to collect the broken pieces of bread that are left over. The Greek word Mark uses for the twelve baskets in chapter 6 is *kophinos*, meaning normal-sized baskets, but the word he uses for the seven baskets in this miracle is *spuris*, such large baskets that Paul could be lowered from the walls of Damascus while hiding in a *spuris* in Acts 9:25. The difference is therefore not in the quantity of bread but in the quantity of baskets. These seven basketfuls are as laden with meaning as the twelve basketfuls in chapter 6.

Mark does not spell out for us the significance of the number seven, but it is meant to remind us of God's charge to

Israel concerning the foreigners who lived in the Promised Land. He told them to drive out *"the Hittites, Girgashites, Amorites, Canaanites, Perizzites, Hivites and Jebusites, **seven nations** larger and stronger than you."*[6] We are therefore meant to understand that those who were driven out of God's Kingdom by Joshua are now embraced into God's Kingdom by the Messiah. The feeding of the five thousand produced twelve basketfuls of leftovers and demonstrated God's desire to grant the Bread of Heaven to the twelve tribes of Israel. The feeding of the four thousand produced seven basketfuls of leftovers and demonstrated God's desire to grant the Bread of Heaven to every nation of the world. Jesus warns us in verses 19–21 not to miss this because it is very significant. People from every nation can step into his story.[7]

The disciples still fail to understand, so there is only one thing for it. Jesus will have to take them on a quick sortie back to Galilee in order to contrast the way in which the Jews despise the Bread of Heaven and the way in which the Gentile dogs long to eat the breadcrumbs from the Jewish table. Jesus sails across the lake to Dalmanutha (also known as Magadan or Magdala, home to Mary Magdalene) on the western shore of Galilee.

Don't be as slow as the disciples to grasp the significance of this déjà vu moment. Praise Jesus that the Messiah's story is also a story for the entire world.

---

[6] Deuteronomy 7:1; Joshua 24:11. Acts 13:19 also affirms that we should treat the number seven in this miracle as a code.

[7] John uses the number seven throughout Revelation to represent the perfection of God's plan to do this.

Bad Bread (8:11–21)

"Be careful," Jesus warned them. "Watch out for the yeast of the Pharisees and that of Herod."

(Mark 8:15)

Every Roman knew a few things about the Jews. They circumcised their baby boys. They refused to eat the meat that was sold in the forum. They downed tools and rested on the Sabbath. And once a year they celebrated their nation's greatest feast: the Passover and the accompanying Feast of Unleavened Bread.

The disciples of Jesus were all Jews. They thought like Jews. They reacted against the word "yeast" like Jews. We tend to think of yeast very positively – it gives us our beer and our bread and, after all, Jesus likens the fast-growing Kingdom of Heaven to the rapid spread of yeast in Matthew 13:33 and Luke 13:21 – but Jews most definitely did not. The parable of Jesus is unusual because yeast is almost always used as a negative symbol throughout the Bible.[1] It is used as an outward picture of sin's inward power to corrupt and defile. The Jews saw it as a nasty little fungus and they used it as a metaphor for any kind of impurity that quickly spreads and defiles our entire lives.[2]

The early Christian leaders explained this to their Gentile converts. Although they did not expect them to abstain from leavened bread, they expected them to understand that "yeast" is an important biblical metaphor. Paul tells the Corinthians to get radical with sin, asking them incredulously,

[1] For example, see Genesis 19:3, Exodus 12:15–20, Exodus 23:18, Leviticus 2:4–11 and Judges 6:19.

[2] Jesus points out in Matthew 13:33 that a few grams of yeast can work their way through 42 litres of flour.

Don't you know that a little yeast leavens the whole batch of dough? Get rid of the old yeast, so that you may be a new unleavened batch – as you really are. For Christ, our Passover lamb, has been sacrificed. Therefore let us keep the Festival, not with the old bread leavened with malice and wickedness, but with the unleavened bread of sincerity and truth.

Paul also warns the Galatians to flee from false teaching, because *"A little yeast works through the whole batch of dough."*[3]

Mark expects his readers to understand this concept. When Jesus takes the disciples on a boat trip back from the Decapolis to the Galilean town of Dalmanutha, he is doing more than simply sailing across the lake from east to west. He is re-entering Jewish territory in order to provoke a confrontation that will help Peter and his friends to grasp that the message of the Kingdom is truly the entire world's story.

In verses 11–13, the Galilean Pharisees attack Jesus on sight. They demand he perform a miracle in order to prove his authority as a rabbi. That should strike you as odd. Jesus ministered almost exclusively in Galilee from chapter 1 to chapter 7, which means that these Pharisees had already seen Jesus' miracles for the best part of two years. They had seen him cast out demons and heal the sick in their synagogues. They had seen him heal the lepers, the paralysed and the diseased. If they had been humble enough to take a break from their own self-centred story and join the crowds who followed Jesus, they would also have witnessed the feeding of the five thousand. Their demand that Jesus perform a miracle to gain credibility is laughable, except Jesus isn't laughing. Mark tells us that Jesus *groaned deeply in his spirit* at the way in which their hearts were contaminated by sin.[4]

---

[3] 1 Corinthians 5:6–8; Galatians 5:9.

[4] The Greek verb *anastenazō* is an intensified form of the verb *stenazō*, which Mark used in 7:34. Jesus treats the Pharisees' deafness to his message more

The Greek word *genea* in verse 12 means either a *generation* or a *race* of people. Jesus used the same word in Matthew 12:38–45 to warn the Jewish leaders that their nation was more corrupt than the people of ancient Nineveh. Peter uses the same word in Acts 2:40 to urge his Jewish hearers to save themselves from their corrupt nation.[5] Jesus therefore tells the Pharisees in verse 12 that he will not perform any more miracles for the Galilean Jews. They have had their proof and now they must decide. He gets back in the boat with his disciples and returns to the mixed-race lands on the eastern shore.

In verses 14–21, Jesus uses this confrontation to warn his disciples that the Jewish leaders are selling bad bread to their nation. He tells them to *"Be careful. Watch out for the yeast of the Pharisees and that of Herod."* The disciples misunderstand. They assume that he must be rebuking them for only bringing one loaf of bread on their journey when they could have brought one of the seven basketfuls of leftovers. But Jesus isn't talking about their little catering problem. He is talking about the massive Jewish problem. The Pharisees might pretend to be strict enforcers of the Law of Moses, quoting Exodus 12:19 to demand that anyone who bakes with yeast during the Feast of Unleavened Bread must be cut off from Israel, but they are actually peddlers of the worst kind of yeast – the contaminating sin of self-righteousness and hypocrisy.[6] Herod and his supporters may pretend that their compromises with Rome are motivated by love for God and for his People, but they are peddlers of yeast too. Their cynical political pragmatism is the fruit of their unbelief in God and in his power.[7]

---

seriously than a man's physical deafness in the Decapolis.

[5] The word *genea* must refer to the Jewish *race* in Mark 13:30, Luke 17:25, Luke 21:32 and Acts 2:40. It is even clearer in the parallel Matthew 16:4 that Jesus uses the word here to refer to the Jewish *race*.

[6] Luke 12:1 clarifies that the yeast of the Pharisees is the sin of hypocrisy.

[7] The parallel passage in Matthew 16:5–12 equates the yeast of the *Herodians* with the yeast of the *Sadducees*. The Sadducees were the priestly class who cosied up to Herod in return for control of the Temple.

This day trip back across Lake Galilee is therefore not a departure from the message of part two of Mark's gospel. It is a demonstration of it. Jesus brings the disciples back to Jewish lands in order to show them that the Messiah's story is more than a continuation of the Jewish story. It is the world's story and it means rewriting the Jewish story wherever the Jewish leaders have got it wrong. Israel needs to eat up the message of God's Kingdom (*twelve* basketfuls in chapter 6) every bit as much as the Gentile nations (*seven* basketfuls in chapter 8). In verse 18, Jesus quotes from Jeremiah 5:21 in order to warn his disciples that the bad bread of the Pharisees has made them blind to what is obvious to the foreign crowds.

If you are Jewish, this is important. Jesus is first and foremost your Messiah. Don't allow the Gentiles to step into his story while you refuse. Get radical with the external rule-keeping and politicking which can still characterise much of Judaism today. Don't let the bad bread of the rabbis stop you eating your fill of the true Bread of Heaven.

If you are not a Jew, this is important for you too. Yeast is microscopically small. Each cell is a hundredth of the size of a grain of sand. Jesus therefore warns each one of us that sin and error are very easy to ignore. If the Jewish bread could go bad in the hands of the passionate preachers of purity, we must be on our guard too. Hypocrisy, religious formalism, unbelief and compromise can corrupt astonishingly quickly. Don't do a dirty deal with smooth-talking scholars, puffed-up politicians or pragmatic preachers. Live for Jesus and for his story alone.

Jesus still warns his followers in every nation: *"Be careful. Watch out for the yeast of the Pharisees and that of Herod."*

Yeast Extraction (8:22–26)

He took the blind man by the hand and led him
outside the village.

(Mark 8:23)

Jesus did not sail back to the Decapolis. He had only preached in two of the four mixed-race regions on the borders of Israel, so he was eager to move on to Trachonitis. It was time to demonstrate in the far northeast of Israel that the message of his Kingdom was a message for the whole world.

Bethsaida means *House of Fishing*. It was a fishing village close to where the River Jordan flows into Lake Galilee on its northeast shore. Although part of Trachonitis, it was on the border with Galilee and its population was so Jewish that John 12:21 refers to it as *"Bethsaida of Galilee."*[1] It was the last Jewish stop-off on the journey north and the town where Peter and some of the other disciples had been raised as children, so Jesus used it to show his disciples how subtle the yeast of the Pharisees and of Herod can be.[2]

A group of locals spot Jesus and plead with him to heal their blind friend.[3] The people of Bethsaida were more influenced by the culture of Galilee than the culture of Trachonitis, so

---

[1] It was so close to the border with Galilee that, when Luke 9:10 refers to the uninhabited fields east of Capernaum, it describes them as being near to Bethsaida.

[2] Even though they lived and worked at Capernaum in Galilee, John 1:44 tells us that Peter and Andrew were originally from Bethsaida in Trachonitis. It also tells us that so was Philip.

[3] Mark's choice of Greek words in 8:25 tells us that this man's sight was *restored*. He had not been born blind, but had become blind through an illness or an accident.

they instantly recognise Jesus as the miracle-worker from Capernaum. However, Jesus does two unusual things, which demonstrate to the disciples that the people of Bethsaida have become infected with the sinful attitudes of Galilee.

First, Jesus refuses to heal the blind man until he has left the Bethsaida city limits. He leads him by the hand and heals him in the countryside instead. Mark leaves us guessing why.[4] Some readers link it to 7:33 and suppose that Jesus is ensuring that he has his disciples' rapt attention, far away from the maddening blur of the crowds. Other readers link it to 8:12 and suppose that Jesus is making good on his promise to the Galilean Pharisees that he will not perform any further miracles in any of their towns. Still other readers link it to 5:40 and argue that Jesus is shutting out the cynical Bethsaidans, just as he shut out the cynical mourners at the house of Jairus. We know that Peter's home town had been compromised by the yeast of hypocrisy and cynicism because Jesus tells its people forcefully elsewhere: *"Woe to you, Bethsaida! For if the miracles that were performed in you had been performed in Tyre and Sidon, they would have repented long ago in sackcloth and ashes. But I tell you, it will be more bearable for Tyre and Sidon on the day of judgment than for you."*[5]

The second unusual thing Jesus does is even stranger. He fails to heal the blind man the first time around. He spits on the man's eyes and lays his hands on him, identifying with him in his physical disability, but as a result the man only sees blurred shapes instead of clear images. Jesus says to two blind men in Matthew 9:29, *"According to your faith will it be done to you."* That can be a curse and not a blessing if our hearts are contaminated with the yeast of unbelief. Jesus models what we should do when we fail to see complete healing in response to our prayers. He simply prays again, adding his own greater

---

[4] Mark is the only gospel writer to record this miracle, so there are no parallel accounts to clarify.

[5] Matthew 11:21–22; Luke 10:13–14.

faith to the flawed faith of the blind Bethsaidan. This time the man's sight is completely restored. Jesus tells him not to go back into the unbelieving fishing village. He needs to reflect on this miracle and extract the yeast of cynicism from his heart.[6]

This event is crucial if we are to play our part in carrying on Jesus' story. It is easy for us to look down on the Pharisees in much the same way as they looked down on others, but they are not the villains in the story: they are us but for the grace of God. John Calvin longed to bring revival to sixteenth-century Europe, but he proved that even Christian heroes are not immune to the yeast of the Pharisees and of Herod. Neither are we.

John Calvin spotted the yeast of the Pharisees in sixteenth-century Roman Catholicism. He exposed the hypocrisy and empty religious formalism of the age, declaring emphatically *"that the Pope hath but a devilish Synagogue, and that all his Clergy is but filth and stench."*[7] He devoted his life to defining the true Christian faith and to modelling it through the church he led in Geneva, Switzerland. But yeast is subtle. It is difficult to extract from our hearts. John Calvin fell for it and, as a result, he failed in his dreams.

Calvin was repulsed by the religious shrines across Europe. He hated the way the priests took money from the sick and needy who came to pray to dead saints for healing. He felt so strongly about it that he urged Christians to demolish shrines and to reject the notion of miraculous healing altogether. He told them that *"The gift of healing has vanished away, like the other miracles which the Lord willed to be brought forth for a time, in order to make the new preaching of the gospel marvellous*

---

[6] In Galilee and the Decapolis, Jesus tells people to keep quiet about their miracles so that he can continue preaching in the region without being mobbed. Here, he is about to leave Bethsaida and travel to the far north of Trachonitis anyway. The command is for the man's benefit and not for Jesus' benefit.

[7] Calvin said this while preaching on 1 Timothy 3:1–4 in his *Sermons on Timothy and Titus*.

forever... It has nothing to do with us, to whom no such powers have been committed."[8]

John Calvin resisted the yeast of the Pharisees, but in doing so he swallowed the yeast of Herod. He tried to protect the Gospel from hypocrisy by denying that healing was part of it. Robbed of a belief that they might be able to perform miracles like those in Mark's gospel, his followers were forced to resort to spreading the Gospel across northern Europe by striking dirty deals with sinful rulers. In doing so, they robbed the Gospel of its power.[9] In southern Europe they failed entirely because, in this most visible of areas, the corrupt medieval Church appeared more faithful than the Protestant Reformation to the teaching of Mark's gospel. John Calvin discovered what it costs when we ignore Paul's teaching in Romans 15:18–19: *"I will not venture to speak of anything except what Christ has accomplished through me in leading the Gentiles to obey God by what I have said and done – by the power of signs and wonders, through the power of the Spirit of God."*

So let's take these verses very seriously. Jesus could easily have healed the blind man in Bethsaida. After all, he cursed the town because it had refused to respond to the many miracles he performed there! He healed this blind man outside the village in order to show his disciples that Bethsaida was not the last outpost of orthodoxy before the wild borderlands of paganism. It had fallen for the yeast of the Pharisees and of Herod.

The Devil doesn't care whether we fall for the religious hypocrisy of the Pharisees or for the pragmatic rationalism of Herod. Both pollute the Christian faith as thoroughly and as fatally. Let's cry out for God to help us in the difficult work of spiritual yeast extraction.

---

[8] John Calvin wrote this in 1536 in his *Institutes of the Christian Religion* (4.19.18).

[9] John 11:23–24 warns us that treating the Bible's healing promises as beautiful metaphors for the distant future is as serious a sin as outright unbelief. We need to have faith for the here-and-now.

Mystery Story (8:27–30)

*"But what about you?" he asked. "Who do you say I
am?" Peter answered, "You are the Messiah."*

(Mark 8:29)

Everybody loves a good mystery story. Who enjoys a thriller
where all the facts are made obvious from the start? It therefore
shouldn't surprise us that Mark's record of Peter's three-year
journey with Jesus reads very much like a mystery story.

Demons keep attempting to spoil the mystery story.
Several times in the first half of Mark's gospel, Jesus has to order
demonised people to be quiet and to stop blurting out that he is
the Son of God (1:24–25, 34; 3:11–12). People who experience
Jesus' healing power also keep on trying unwittingly to spoil the
mystery story. Again and again in the first half of Mark's gospel,
Jesus forbids people from spreading the news too widely that
God has granted him use of heaven's power (1:44; 5:43; 7:36;
8:26). Instead of advertising his deity, Jesus frequently hides
away from the crowds in the first nine chapters of Mark's gospel
(1:35, 45; 7:24; 9:30). If we want to understand the conversation
that took place at Caesarea Philippi in the late summer of 29
AD, we need to understand that it isn't just the halfway point in
Mark's gospel. It is also the turning point where the mystery of
Mark's gospel begins to be revealed.

Caesarea Philippi was the capital city of the mixed-race
region of Trachonitis. It was in the far north of Israel in the
modern-day Golan Heights, at the foot of Mount Hermon, and

its prevailing culture was as Gentile as a pork pie.[1] The tetrarch Herod Philip II had renamed it in honour of himself and of the Roman emperors.[2] Even as Jesus walked among the villages which surrounded the capital city, Herod Philip was busy minting coins that bore his image and proclaimed that he was ruler of the area on behalf of mighty Rome. Jesus had brought his disciples right into the Gentile heartland in order to reveal the big mystery of Mark's gospel to them. It was in this pagan city which worshipped human rulers that Jesus would reveal himself to be the Messiah.

Even now, Jesus does not blurt out his identity to his disciples. He asks them questions, drawing out from them what they have discovered so far in the story. If you struggle to share the Gospel with unbelievers, this may be the coaching in evangelism that you need. Instead of blurting out your own discoveries, try following Jesus' example. Ask them, *"Can you help me? Why would you say most people aren't interested in following Jesus or going to church?"* Most people are willing to talk about what other people think. We only feel threatened when we are asked to justify our own thoughts. But talking about what other people think gradually makes us feel more comfortable about sharing our own thoughts too. Follow up by asking them, *"Which of those reasons is why you don't go to church?"* I can't guarantee that you will have a fruitful conversation about Jesus, but I can guarantee that it will be more fruitful than simply blurting out what you believe. Proverbs 20:5 reminds us that the thoughts of a person's heart are like the deep waters of a well, and that wise people use questions as a bucket with which to gently draw out a person's deepest thoughts.

Jesus does this with the disciples. He asks them, *"Who do*

---

[1] This northern part of Trachonitis was known as *Gaulanitis*, a name still preserved in *Golan Heights*.

[2] Do not confuse Caesarea Philippi with the city of Caesarea on the Mediterranean coastline of Judea. Do not confuse Herod Philip II with the former husband of Herodias. That was Herod Philip I.

people say I am?" The disciples are only too happy to reply. Some say he is John the Baptist, raised from the dead.[3] Others say he is Elijah, the great Old Testament prophet who ascended to heaven without dying and who the Old Testament prophesied would return to herald the arrival of the Messiah.[4] Others say he is one of the Old Testament prophets – perhaps the mysterious Enoch who also ascended miraculously to heaven, or the great Elisha who also healed the sick, raised the dead and multiplied loaves for a crowd of people to eat.

So much for the chattering of the Jewish crowds in Galilee and Judea. Jesus has brought the disciples to Caesar's city in order to reveal to them that he is far more than the latest player in Israel's long-running story. He is the Son of God. He is the Jewish Messiah. He is the Saviour of the entire world.

Jesus therefore moves from a general third-person question to a specific second-person question: *"But what about you? Who do you say I am?"* Quick as a flash, Peter gets in his answer before the other disciples: *"You are the Messiah."* Mark keeps his account typically brief and punchy, but Matthew expands on the significance of Peter's words. He tells us that Peter actually said, *"You are the Messiah, the Son of the living God,"* and that Jesus replied, *"Blessed are you, Simon son of Jonah, for this was not revealed to you by flesh and blood, but by my Father in heaven. And I tell you that you are Peter, and on this rock I will build my church, and the gates of Hades will not overcome it."*[5] Here in Caesar's city, Jesus has drawn out of Peter what

---

[3] Herod made this assumption in 6:14 due to Jesus' amazing miracles, even though John had not actually performed any miracles during his lifetime (John 10:41).

[4] 2 Kings 2:11; Malachi 4:5. The prophecy actually meant that John the Baptist would be like Elijah (9:11–13).

[5] Matthew 16:13–20. Matthew's account emphasises that Jesus affirmed Peter as the leading disciple and the principal bearer of heaven's keys of authority. Peter's humility may have prevented him from emphasising these same things as he recounted the story of Jesus to people across the Roman Empire.

God has revealed to him so far in the story. Peter has confessed that Jesus is a King far greater than any tetrarch or any Caesar. He is the divine ruler of heaven whose arrival on earth means salvation for the world.

This is a turning point in Mark's gospel. The first eight chapters are full of miracles and short on teaching. The next eight chapters are full of teaching and short on miracles. The first half of Mark's gospel is full of mystery and of commands to say nothing about who Jesus is. The second half of Mark's gospel is full of commands for the disciples to go out and preach the good news about Jesus to the world.[6] The first half of Mark's gospel tells us Jesus was very popular in Galilee but, as a result of this turning point, the second half tells us that he was hated and murdered in Judea.

The secret is out. This conversation at Caesarea Philippi is like the moment when the detective stands up at the end of a mystery story and begins to reveal all the answers. A new phase has begun in Jesus' ministry. He is about to reveal his identity to the world.

---

[6] Mark 8:31–33 and 9:9 explain the reason for this transition. They were not to proclaim the Gospel to the world until they understood the true significance of Jesus' death and resurrection. See Luke 24:44–48.

Speaking for Satan
(8:31–38)

*He spoke plainly about this, and Peter took him aside
and began to rebuke him.*

(Mark 8:32)

The name Richard Nixon is synonymous with failure. His role in
the Watergate scandal made him the only American president
in history to be forced to resign office. Polls rank him among
the worst ever occupants of the White House. Nevertheless, he
continued to protest his innocence long after his resignation.
He argued in a TV interview three years later that his only error
had been to show excessive loyalty to his bungling staff: *"Maybe
I defended them too long. Maybe I tried to help them too much.
But I was concerned about them, I was concerned about their
families."* When challenged to face up to his own illegal actions,
he insisted: *"When the president does it, that means it is not
illegal."*[1]

Watching a person look back on their life and attempt to
disguise and justify their sins is pretty ugly. Nixon's refusal to
admit his imperfections made his one-time colleague Barry
Goldwater conclude that *"He was the most dishonest individual
I ever met in my life. President Nixon lied to his wife, his family,
his friends, longtime colleagues in the U.S. Congress, lifetime*

---

[1] David Frost conducted these famous TV interviews with Richard Nixon in
March and April 1977.

members of his own political party, the American people, and the world."[2]

Whatever else we might say about Peter, he was definitely no Richard Nixon. Since the unanimous testimony of the Early Church is that Mark wrote down Peter's account of his three-year journey with Jesus, it is remarkable just how frank and honest Peter was with his listeners about his own failures. Matthew tells us that Peter walked on water, but Mark doesn't. Matthew tells us that Jesus gave Peter the keys to the Kingdom of Heaven, but Mark doesn't. Luke tells us that Jesus prayed that Peter would strengthen the other disciples after his crucifixion, but Mark doesn't. John tells us that Jesus reinstated Peter as the leading disciple after his denials, but Mark doesn't.[3] Peter refused to boast when he preached about Jesus because he didn't want us to be wowed by his successes. He was brutally honest about his own failures because he wanted to encourage us that we are just as able to step into Jesus' story as he was.

In verses 31–33, we read that Peter resisted the message of the cross of Jesus. He plunged from the heady heights of recognition that Jesus is the Messiah and tried to advise Jesus on what kind of Messiah he really ought to be. Killing the Romans would be fine. Winning independence for the Jewish nation from the Roman Empire would be fine too. But allowing Jewish priests and Roman soldiers to crucify him was definitely

---

[2] Barry Goldwater writes this in his memoirs, simply entitled *Goldwater* (1988).

[3] Matthew 14:22–33; 16:17–19; Luke 22:31–32; John 21:15–19. Jesus uses the Greek word for *you (singular)* rather than *you (plural)* in Matthew 16:19, only clarifying in 18:18 that this same authority belongs to all of Jesus' other followers too.

not fine.[4] Peter told Jesus firmly that this was not the kind of Messiah he was looking for.[5]

Jesus was just as willing to reject acceptance as he was to accept rejection. He was living for an audience of one, and it wasn't Peter. He was entirely submitted to his Father's will. Jesus rebukes Peter strongly, insisting that crossless Christianity is not Christianity at all, and informing him that anyone who preaches otherwise is speaking for Satan: *"You do not have in mind the concerns of God, but merely human concerns."* Jesus is telling Peter that his thinking is contaminated with the yeast of Herod.[6] He is well-meaning, but he has become Satan's tool to tempt Jesus to disobey his Father. Jesus only has to take one look at the faces of his needy disciples in verse 33 in order to reject Peter's advice entirely. Several times in the second half of Mark's gospel he repeats this message: The Messiah has to die, and anyone who wants to follow him has to walk the same path of death and resurrection too.

In verses 34–38, Jesus calls the largely pagan crowds to gather round him as he teaches the disciples that, just as there can never be a crossless Christ, nor can there ever be a crossless Christian. There are only two groups of people in the world: rebels against God who hang onto their own lives, and servants of God who lay down their lives for their new Master. Perhaps he invited the crowd to listen to this teaching in order to emphasise

---

[4] The other gospels tell us that Jesus talked about his death and resurrection before this point (Matthew 12:39–41; 16:4; John 3:14–18), but Matthew and Luke agree that from this point on Jesus began to speak about it far more openly. Mark mentions it now because the implications only dawned on Peter now.

[5] The Greek word *epitimaō* in 8:32 is a strong word. Mark uses it in 1:25, 3:12 and 9:25 to describe Jesus rebuking demons. He also uses it in 4:39 to describe Jesus rebuking the wind and the waves.

[6] It is good to be reminded that Satan thinks like a human and not like God. He is a fallen angel, a mere creature, and his thinking can never be any match for that of the Creator God.

that he is not describing an elite group of radical firebrands in these verses. He is simply describing normal Christianity.[7]

> **Whoever** *wants to be my disciple must deny themselves and take up their cross and follow me. For* **whoever** *wants to save their life will lose it, but* **whoever** *loses their life for me and for the gospel will save it... If* **anyone** *is ashamed of me and my words in this adulterous and sinful generation, the Son of Man will be ashamed of them when he comes in his Father's glory with the holy angels.*[8]

These are sobering verses and they force us to make a choice. Hold on to your life and you will die. Throw away your life for Jesus and you will live. Confess your faith in Jesus, regardless of the cost, and he will confess that you are his. Deny him for the sake of this world and he will deny you a share in the world to come. These are the terms that Jesus has set for all who follow him. Do we still want to step into his story?

Peter gulped hard and he struggled with Jesus' teaching. Nevertheless, he repented of his having spoken for Satan.[9] We know from John 21:18–19 that he was eventually martyred for his faith in Jesus. The early Christian writer Tertullian tells us that *"Peter endured the same suffering as his Lord... since he was bound to the cross."* Eusebius adds that *"Peter was crucified at Rome with head downwards, as he himself had desired to*

---

[7] Church leaders must not succumb to the yeast of Herod by demanding anything less than this from the people they lead. Jesus has set his terms of discipleship. It isn't kindness for us to alter them. It's deception.

[8] Jesus teaches very clearly here that he is God. Verse 38 is ludicrous in the mouth of anyone but God.

[9] Peter would continue to struggle with the message of Jesus' crucifixion (John 13:6–9; 18:10–11), but he would eventually come through to full faith in the Gospel (Acts 2:23; 1 Peter 1:10–11; 2:21–25).

suffer."[10] Peter did not treat these verses simply as a clever metaphor. Nor must we.

Jesus tells us that his death on the cross for our sake is the only way in which we can be saved. He tells us that dying to our old lives for his sake is the only way in which we can lay hold of this salvation. We may not need to end our days as an executed Christian martyr, like Peter, but we do need to live our days as cross-carriers for Jesus. Wherever God's will and your own will collide, that is where your cross is found. So let's put away the empty chatter of yeast-infected churches and let's commit to radical obedience to Jesus every day.[11] Let's tell him that, no matter what it may cost us, we still want to step ever deeper into his story.

---

[10] These quotations come from Tertullian in his *Prescription Against Heretics* (chapter 36) and *Antidote to the Scorpion's Sting* (chapter 15), and from Eusebius in his *Church History* (3.1.2).

[11] Mark 8:38 deliberately echoes 8:12. Jesus is telling his disciples and the largely pagan crowd at Caesarea Philippi that salvation is not found in living by corrupted Jewish rules, but in dying with the Jewish Messiah.

The Holy Mountain (9:1–13)

Jesus took Peter, James and John with him and led them up a high mountain, where they were all alone. There he was transfigured before them.

(Mark 9:2)

The Jews had a place that they called the holy mountain. It was so famous that even Mark's Roman readers knew about it.

The city of Jerusalem had been built on Mount Zion. Its Jewish citizens sang psalms that pleaded, *"Let them bring me to your holy mountain, to the place where you dwell."* They sang psalms that expressed their longing to *"Exalt the Lord our God and worship at his holy mountain."*[1] In the same way, their prophets proclaimed God's purposes for *"Jerusalem, your city, your holy hill,"* and they encouraged Israel with God's promise that *"You will know that I, the Lord your God, dwell in Zion, my holy hill."*[2] So when a Jew referred to "the holy mountain", nobody was in any doubt what he meant. Jews did not look to the seven hills of Rome. They looked to Jerusalem and its holy mountain.

Except for Peter, that is. Something happened to him at the beginning of Mark 9 that turned his Jewish thinking on its head. It affected him so profoundly that, even when he wrote a letter thirty-five years later, he still talked in awe of his experience

---

[1] Psalms 2:6; 3:4; 15:1; 43:3; 48:1; 87:1; 99:9. The name Zion is used 154 times in the Old Testament.

[2] Daniel 9:16, 20; Joel 2:1; 3:17. See also Jeremiah 31:23; Ezekiel 20:40; Daniel 11:45; Obadiah 16; Zechariah 8:3; Zephaniah 3:11; Isaiah 11:9; 14:13; 27:13; 56:7; 57:13; 65:11, 25; 66:20.

of God on a pagan mountain on the borderlands of Israel. He recalls excitedly in 2 Peter 1:16–18 that

> We did not follow cleverly devised stories when we told you about the coming of our Lord Jesus Christ in power, but we were eye-witnesses of his majesty. He received honour and glory from God the Father when the voice came to him from the Majestic Glory, saying, "This is my Son, whom I love; with him I am well pleased." We ourselves heard this voice that came from heaven when we were with him on the sacred mountain.[3]

We can tell that something dramatic happened to Peter at the beginning of Mark 9, because the holy mountain to which he refers is not Mount Zion. Incredibly, it is the pagan heights of Mount Hermon.[4]

In verses 1–2, Mark prepares us for the transfiguration of Jesus. He tells us that Jesus finished his teaching in Caesarea Philippi by promising that some of those listening to his invitation to die would not taste physical death until they had seen the Kingdom of God come in power. Six days later he took Peter, James and John – the inner circle of three within his inner circle of twelve – and he led them up a high mountain so that they could be alone together.[5] Mount Hermon lay to the north of Caesarea Philippi in the tetrarchy of Abilene, the fourth and final mixed-race region on the borderlands of Israel. It was so far north that it is not even in the modern state of Israel,

---

[3] Peter uses the same two words as the Greek Old Testament when it refers to Zion as the *holy mountain*.

[4] None of the gospel writers name the Mount of the Transfiguration, so some people assume it must have been Mount Tabor, to the southwest of Lake Galilee. However, it took place during Jesus' tour of the four mixed-race regions of Israel, while he was at Caesarea Philippi in the shadow of Mount Hermon.

[5] See 5:37 and 14:33. Luke 9:28 tells us that they climbed the mountain *"about eight days after Jesus said this"* – presumably including the day on which Jesus taught and the day on which he began the climb.

straddling the Lebanese border with Syria. There on the slopes of a faraway pagan mountain, Peter and his friends saw Jesus in his heavenly glory. It wasn't on Mount Zion, but the location could not have been more perfect. It was a strong reminder that Jesus came from heaven to earth in order to save people from every single nation of the world.

In verses 2–3, Jesus gives Peter and his friends a vivid reminder that he is far more than a Jewish carpenter.[6] He is transfigured before their eyes, revealing the glory which he now bears in heaven.[7] In 8:33, he rebuked the human thinking which attempts to confine his glory to the Jewish race within the borders of Israel, and this small glimpse convinces the disciples that his glory must fill the entire earth by saving people from every nation.[8]

In verses 4–6, Jesus gives Peter and his friends another vivid reminder that his mission cannot be boxed in by the borders of Israel. Moses and Elijah suddenly appear on the mountain with Jesus in order to strengthen him for the mission that lies ahead. Luke 9:31 tells us that Moses prepared Jesus to perform a better exodus than his own, so we can assume that Elijah also prepared him to call Israel to a more thorough repentance. The Pharisees revered both men as heroes, yet Moses had never entered the Promised Land and Elijah spent much of his public ministry among the pagans. Suddenly this pagan mountain becomes holy

---

[6] The Greek word Mark uses in 9:2 is *metamorphoō*, which has at its root the noun *morphē*, or *essential nature*. This is the word Paul uses in Philippians 2 to refer to Jesus being *in essential nature* God but taking *the essential nature* of a servant.

[7] John was on the mountain with Peter, so note the similarities between the description of the transfigured Jesus in 9:3 and John's description of the glorified Jesus in Revelation 1:12–16. John is the only gospel writer not to mention the transfiguration. Instead he records Jesus' prayer that the Father restore him to *"the glory I had with you before the world began"* (John 17:5).

[8] Isaiah 11:9 encouraged the Jews to expect this by calling Mount Zion the *"holy mountain"* at the same time as it promised a new day when *"the earth will be full of the knowledge of the Lord, as the waters cover the sea."*

in Peter's sight. He begins to grasp that Jesus is the Saviour, not just of Israel, but of people from every nation.

In verse 7, God the Father gives Peter and his friends a third reminder that they must not put Jesus' ministry in a box and exclude the Gentiles from the compass of his plan. Peter is alarmed when he sees two men who have been dead for several hundred years and, in his panic, he gives Jesus yet more unwanted advice about what he thinks he ought to do. God the Father booms out a rebuke from heaven, repeating the words that he spoke at Jesus' baptism, with one important modification: *"This is my Son, whom I love. Listen to him!"* God tells Peter to stop talking and to start listening.[9] He needs to understand that the Messiah's story is far bigger than Jewish hills and tabernacles.[10] Jesus has come to raise up an army of Jewish followers who will become like little tabernacles, filled with his presence, as they proclaim the glories of his Gospel to the nations of the world.

In verses 8–13, the cloud lifts and Jesus looks like a simple Jewish carpenter again. Peter and his friends are very confused. Was this the fulfilment of the prophecy in Malachi 4:5 that Elijah would return? No, Jesus tells them, that was fulfilled by the coming of John the Baptist. John has been killed, and the Messiah must also be killed and raised back to life before the Gospel can be proclaimed to the world. What are they to do with their confusion in the meantime? They are to listen to Jesus. They are to go wherever he leads them and to believe whatever he tells them. They are to reflect on what they have witnessed of his heavenly glory and they are to recognise that he is able to turn the entire earth into his holy mountain. They

---

[9] *"Listen to him!"* is more than a rebuke. It also draws Peter's attention to the prophecy in Deuteronomy 18:15.

[10] The Greek word *skēnē* was used throughout the Greek Old Testament to refer to the *tabernacle*. This is not the time to keep God's presence in a building. It is time to proclaim his presence to the world.

are to embrace the message of part two of Mark's gospel: The Messiah's story is a story for all the world.

We are to meditate on these amazing verses too. We are to grasp what Peter and his friends went on to grasp. Pagan mountains can become holy. Pagan cities can be saved. Unbelieving foreigners can become precious worshippers on God's holy mountain.[11]

---

[11] See John 4:19–24 and Hebrews 12:22–24. Peter was slow to understand this message, only fully grasping it in Acts 10–11, yet he then went on to preach it across the Roman Empire and in his letters.

Why Doesn't God Heal?
(9:14–29)

After Jesus had gone indoors, his disciples asked him privately, "Why couldn't we drive it out?"

(Mark 9:28)

Jesus heals a lot. That's pretty obvious when you read the pages of Mark's gospel. Chapters like these ones force N.T. Wright to conclude that

> *Jesus was not primarily a "teacher" in the sense that we usually give that word. Jesus **did** things and then commented on them, explained them, challenged people to figure out what they meant. He acted practically and symbolically, not least through his remarkable works of healing – works that today all but the most extreme sceptics are forced to regard as in principle historical... Jesus soon became better known for healing than baptizing. And it was his remarkable healings, almost certainly, that won him a hearing. He was not a teacher who also healed; he was a prophet of the kingdom, first enacting and then explaining that kingdom.*[1]

But if we read the pages of Mark's gospel slowly, we notice that there are also many occasions when Jesus doesn't heal. Despite the cries of the crowds in Capernaum, he goes elsewhere (1:35–38). When the Pharisees ask him to perform a miracle, he refuses and sails to the opposite shore (8:11–13). When he arrives in the

---

[1] N.T. Wright in *The Challenge of Jesus* (2000).

city of Tyre, Mark tells us that *"he entered a house and did not want anyone to know it"* (7:24). When he arrives in Bethsaida, a blind man receives only partial healing the first time that Jesus prays for him (8:22–26). We should find this very encouraging, because there are also many times in our own lives when we fail to experience Jesus' healing power. Are we therefore doing something wrong? That's the question Mark tries to answer for us at the end of part two of his gospel.

When Peter, James and John come down from Mount Hermon, they discover that their friends are in trouble. The remaining nine disciples are attempting to heal the crowds while Jesus is away on the mountain. They have gathered around a mute and deaf boy who is also suffering from the symptoms that we would normally associate with epilepsy.[2] No quantity of praying or shouting or binding or loosing or commanding has resulted in the boy's healing. They are frustrated and confused, the boy's father is distraught, and the boy himself is as mute and deaf and epileptic as before.[3] It's a bit of a mess. It's rather like our own experience when we try to heal people in Jesus' name.

Mark does not tell us what the teachers of the law are arguing about in verse 14, but we can guess. They are probably berating the nine disciples for raising the boy's hopes by praying for his healing. Do they not realise that the Old Testament promises about healing are simply metaphors for God's work of spiritual salvation? Are they not embarrassed that events have proved that they are presumptuous and pastorally insensitive? It is hard to fault their logic. Nine apostles, each with a successful track record of driving out demons and healing the sick, have

---

[2] Matthew 17:15 describes this in first-century language, telling us that the boy was *moonstruck*. Jesus addresses the demon in 9:25 as a *"deaf and mute spirit,"* not meaning that the demon was deaf (or else there would be no point in talking to it!), but that a demon was behind this particular boy's deafness, muteness and epilepsy.

[3] Many Greek manuscripts add two extra words in 9:24, telling us that the boy's father spoke to Jesus *with tears*. Luke 9:38 tells us that this boy was his father's only child.

prayed long and hard for this boy to be healed.[4] Surely this is an open-and-shut case of God simply not being willing to heal?

If Jesus had not appeared at that moment with Peter, James and John, we might be tempted to come to that conclusion. It is certainly tempting to come to that conclusion today whenever we pray for people and see nothing. Yet Jesus heals the boy instantly with a simple command. He tells the disciples that their problem is not presumption but unbelief, not believing too much of God but too little. *"You unbelieving race,"* he chides the Jewish teachers in front of the largely pagan crowd. *"How long shall I stay with you? How long shall I put up with you?"*[5] He rebukes the boy's father for his ambivalent faith: *"'If you can'? Everything is possible for one who believes."*[6] Mark therefore assures us that God wants to heal people even when we fail to see healing. He highlights three key factors that will help us to see more healings when we pray.

First, Mark draws our attention to *the presence of God*. In Exodus 34:29–30, the face of Moses shone brightly when he descended from God's presence on Mount Sinai. In the same way, Mark tells us literally that the crowds were *"struck with terror"* when they saw Jesus after his transfiguration. Something of his heavenly glory evidently still lingered, convincing the demon that there was no way it could resist him. After a last-ditch attempt to harm the boy, it flees in fear. The more we grasp of Jesus' glory and the more we receive his presence through the Holy Spirit, the more we will see healing.

Second, Mark draws our attention to *the promises of God*.

---

[4] They had been given power and authority to drive out demons and heal the sick (6:7). However, their successes in the past (6:13) were no substitute for fresh faith in the present.

[5] The Greek word *genea* means either *generation* or *race*. We saw in 8:12 and 8:38 that Jesus uses it during his travels through the mixed-race borderlands of Israel to refer to the Jews as God's People. See 13:30.

[6] Jesus' words in Greek are deliberately ambiguous. They can either mean *"'If you can'? Everything is possible for [me], the one who believes,"* or else they can mean *"If you can believe, then anything is possible for the believer."*

Jesus does not rebuke his disciples for being too weak for the demon. He was never under any illusions about their strength. He rebukes them for their failure to grasp the strength which we have over demons and sicknesses through God's promises. There is no beatitude which tells us that blessed are those who expect little from God for they shall not be disappointed. On the contrary, Jesus says,

> *Your faith has healed you... Don't be afraid; just believe... Have faith in God... Truly I tell you, if anyone says to this mountain, "Go, throw yourself into the sea," and does not doubt in their heart but believes that what they say will happen, it will be done for them. Therefore I tell you, whatever you ask for in prayer, believe that you have received it, and it will be yours.*[7]

The scope of Jesus' promises is too wide and God's desire to heal is too great for you ever to believe too much of him. We can only ever believe too little.

Third, Mark draws our attention to *the power of God*. When the disciples press him to explain further why they were unable to heal the boy themselves, he teaches them that some types of demons and sicknesses are harder to dislodge than others. We need to be strengthened through private prayer if we want to move in greater public power. Our expectations must not be shaped by our past discouragements. They must be shaped by our daily experience of the Holy Spirit clothing us with God's power.

In the next chapter we will get very practical. But before we look at how to pray for healing, let's settle in our hearts that God wants to heal far more than we see at present. Let's pray with this boy's father in verse 24: *"I do believe; help me overcome my unbelief!"*

---

[7] Mark 5:34, 36; 10:52; 11:22–24.

How to Pray for Healing
(9:28–29)

After Jesus had gone indoors, his disciples asked him privately, "Why couldn't we drive it out?" He replied, "This kind can come out only by prayer and fasting."

(Mark 9:28–29)

If we are looking for someone who can teach us how to drive out demons and heal the sick, Peter is our man. He healed people in the villages of Galilee. He healed a lame man outside the Temple in Jerusalem. He healed a paralysed man in Lydda and raised a dead woman to life in Joppa. He gained such a reputation as a miracle-worker that the people of Jerusalem *"brought those who were ill into the streets and laid them on beds and mats so that at least Peter's shadow might fall on some of them as he passed by."*[1] Peter told the astonished crowds that every Christian has authority to heal people through the Gospel. It is simply what God promises to do through us when we step into Jesus' story.[2]

Mark records Peter's description of how Jesus healed during his three months of public ministry. You will notice that he deliberately prevents us from relying on any special formula for healing. One time Jesus lays his hands on somebody. The next he declares that they are healed. The next time he rebukes a sickness. The next he tackles a demon lurking behind the

[1] Mark 6:13; Acts 3:1–10; 5:15–16; 9:32–43.

[2] Peter describes healing very simply as *"what I have"* (Acts 3:6). He goes on to explain that he is nothing special: it is also what everyone else who believes in Jesus' name has too (Acts 3:12–16).

physical symptoms. The next time he puts his spit on a person's tongue or rubs mud in their eyes. Peter didn't learn to heal by using a special formula.

We see this most clearly when we compare Mark's account with Matthew and Luke's own accounts of the same healings. If we only had Mark's account of Jesus healing Peter's mother-in-law, we would assume that helping her to her feet was the key factor; if we only had Matthew's, we would assume it was the laying on of hands; and if we only had Luke's, we would assume it was rebuking her fever. All of these things were factors but none of them was primary.[3] Again, if we only had Mark's account of Jesus healing the blind beggar Bartimaeus, we would assume that the key factor was proclaiming over him that *"Your faith has healed you."* If we only had Matthew's account, we would assume it was the laying on of hands; and if we only had Luke's, we would assume it was the authoritative command to *"Receive your sight!"*[4] These are important factors but they did not bring healing in and of themselves. If we want to see people healed in Jesus' name, we need to learn the same lessons as Peter.

Peter's healing ministry began in Mark 3:14–15 when Jesus *"appointed twelve **that they might be with him** and that he might send them out to preach and to have authority to drive out demons."* It matured when Jesus taught him here in verses 28–29 that consistent healing ministry only comes as a result of *"prayer and fasting."* Jesus does not mean that we need to pray more for people to be healed – the nine disciples must have done plenty of praying while Jesus was up Mount Hermon.[5] Nor does he mean that we have to fast while praying for people to be healed – the nine disciples had not run into problems because they were snacking while they ministered. The key to

---

[3] Matthew 8:14–15; Mark 1:29–31; Luke 4:38–39.

[4] Matthew 20:29–34; Mark 10:46–52; Luke 18:35–43.

[5] Jesus speaks 16 Greek words of command to the demon but not a single word of prayer. He is not telling us to pray in the moment, but to develop a close relationship with God through a lifestyle of prayer.

understanding verses 28–29 is found in John 11. Jesus pursued a lifestyle of deep friendship with his Father through long periods of prayer and fasting. As a result, he was able to confront death with a confident prayer: *"Father, I thank you that **you have heard me**... Lazarus, come out!"*[6]

Prayer and fasting is an expression of our deep friendship with God. We do not see people healed through healing formulae but through friendship with the Healer. Although some Greek manuscripts of verse 29 stress only the importance of *prayer*, many Greek manuscripts stress the importance of both *prayer and fasting.* Fasting is a statement that we care less about our physical needs than we do about our deep need to know God. Such prayer does not change God; it changes us. It helps us to experience God's heart towards the hurting. Too often we desire gifts of healing in order to draw attention to ourselves or to boost the numbers in our churches. Mark tells us that Jesus never performed miracles in order to attract a crowd, but only to express God's love and compassion.[7] Francis MacNutt reminds us that *"Jesus did not heal people to prove that he was God; he healed them because he was God."*[8] The more we spend time with God in prayer, the more we begin to share his compassion for the sick and hurting. The more we experience this, the more we begin to see breakthrough in healing.

Prayer and fasting also increases our faith in God. That's why Jesus tells us that it is the only remedy for an *"unbelieving generation."* Elijah saw great miracles because he knew that he had come from the presence of *"the God of Israel, before whom I stand."* The angel Gabriel found it hard to fathom Zechariah's unbelief because *"I am Gabriel, the one who stands in the presence*

---

[6] John 11:41–43. Jesus does not pray for Lazarus to be raised from the dead. He simply commands his corpse to come out of the tomb. His command is effective because of his prayer relationship with his Father.

[7] Mark 1:41; 5:19; 9:22. See also Matthew 9:35–36; 14:14; 20:34; Luke 7:13; John 11:33–36.

[8] Francis MacNutt in his helpful book *Healing* (1974).

of God."[9] The more time we spend in God's presence, the easier we will find it to believe in his power and his promises. The more we believe in his power and his promises, the easier we find it to minister his healing.

Prayer and fasting also helps us to pick a side in the spiritual battle. I pray for healing regularly but earlier this year, when my two-year-old's thumb was partially severed in a tragic accident, I discovered how lacklustre my prayers can be. Frankly, I often acquiesce to the presence of sickness in the world instead of treating it as Peter did in Acts 10:38 – as the work of the Devil in people's lives. I prayed for my son's injured thumb with a passion I had not known before and, with the help of doctors, he has now recovered perfectly. It makes me wonder what would happen if I picked a clearer side in the battle for healing by devoting more time to prayer and fasting. I intend to find out.

I intend to learn with Peter how to step more deeply into Jesus' story. I intend to pursue the same lifestyle of prayer and fasting which enabled him to see the crowds healed in Jerusalem. I intend to become like one of the ordinary Christians in the Early Church that the third-century writer Origen tells us cast out demons *"merely by prayer and by simple commands which the plainest person can use because, for the most part, it is uneducated people who perform this work... It does not require the power and wisdom of those who are good at arguing or who are most educated in matters of faith."*[10]

Will you join me? Will you listen to the words of Jesus and devote yourself to prayer and fasting? We have reached the end of part two of Mark's gospel so let's respond to its challenge. Let's throw off everything which stops us from stepping into Jesus' story.

---

[9] These are literal translations of 1 Kings 17:1 and Luke 1:19.

[10] Origen wrote this in *Against Celsus* (7.4). Anyone who steps into Jesus' story can heal people in his name.

Part Three:

The Costly Story

(Mark 9:30–10:52)

Road Trip (9:30–50)

They left that place and passed through Galilee.
Jesus did not want anyone to know where they were,
because he was teaching his disciples.

(Mark 9:30–31)

In part three of Mark's gospel, Jesus takes the disciples on a road trip. He waves goodbye to the mixed-race borderlands of Israel and takes the southern road through Galilee, from Mount Hermon to the main stretch of the River Jordan (9:30–50). He crosses over the river to avoid passing through the region of Samaria, and he continues south through the east-bank region of Perea (10:1–45).[1] He crosses back over the river just before the Dead Sea and he takes the mountain road through the region of Judea, from low-lying Jericho all the way up to Jerusalem (10:46–52). For this is no ordinary road trip. The Messiah is marching to Jerusalem, the mother city of the Jewish world. He uses the journey to prepare his disciples for his triumphal entry into Jerusalem.

Mark emphasises the importance of this march to Jerusalem by failing to mention any of Jesus' previous visits to the Jewish capital. The other gospel writers tell us that he frequently visited the Temple, but Mark omits this in order to increase the drama of this journey. Jesus takes the disciples on a road trip from his transfiguration to his crucifixion. He uses the

---

[1] Mark does not mention Perea by name, but it was the 60-mile-long and 13-mile-wide territory on the east bank of the River Jordan. Jews crossed over the river when travelling from Galilee to Jerusalem in order to avoid having to pass through Samaritan territory. Luke 9:51–56 shows us why Jesus had to do so.

journey to teach them that stepping into his story always costs us everything.

Note the shift in focus as we begin part three of Mark's gospel. Mark tells us that *"Jesus did not want anyone to know where they were, because he was teaching his disciples."* Parts one and two were about the crowds. Part three is about the disciples. Parts one and two were about preaching to the many. Part three is about preparing the few. Parts one and two were about the healing that comes through the message of the Gospel. Part three is about the suffering that comes to the messengers of the Gospel. Parts one and two invite sinners to step into Jesus' story for free. Part three invites those who have done so to surrender everything to the one who saved them.

In verses 31–32, Jesus models this by telling his disciples that he is about to die. He is travelling to Jerusalem in order to be betrayed and executed. For three days he will be a lifeless corpse on a cold slab of stone in the darkness of a tomb, until his Father grants him the reward of his suffering and raises him back to life again. The disciples do not understand what he is saying.[2] They are looking for a Messiah like the victorious Son of Man who is described in Daniel 7. They have forgotten the other Old Testament passages that chart the Messiah's path to that eventual victory. Psalm 22 and Isaiah 53 describe him as the Suffering Servant. The disciples struggle to grasp that their road trip will not end with a bed of roses, but with a crown of thorns.

In verses 33–37, the disciples show how much they still have left to learn. As they journey through Galilee, they argue about which one of them is the greatest. Perhaps Peter, James and John are boasting that they could have driven out the demon that resisted the other nine. After all, they alone had been permitted to catch a glimpse of Jesus' glory on the mountain.

[2] This is the third time that Jesus prophesies his death, after 8:31–32 and 9:9–10, but it is so far removed from what the disciples are expecting that their prejudices blind them to what he is saying.

Perhaps Peter is boasting that he has even greater authority than James and John, since Jesus has singled him out to lead the band of disciples after he has gone.[3] Whatever the reason, they are nothing like the Messiah they claim to follow. When they reach Peter's house at Capernaum, Jesus rebukes them.[4] He commends their desire to be of value to God's Kingdom but he warns them that such greatness does not come through self-promotion but through self-sacrifice. To reinforce this, he picks up a young child in Peter's house and commands them to imitate its willingness to assume the lowest position in the household.[5] Those who are great in the Kingdom of Heaven are those who are willing to be least. We can only be anything if we are willing to lay down everything.

In verses 38–40, Jesus addresses John's bad attitude in particular. John and his brother James had been nicknamed "the sons of thunder" for a reason in 3:17. They were quick-tempered and they had clashed with a man they met on the road who was driving out demons in Jesus' name.[6] John tells Jesus literally that *"we told him to stop because he was not following us."* He needs a reminder that the Kingdom of God is not about who follows us but about who follows Jesus. There is no place for the controlling spirit which afflicts church leaders and keeps their work small. There is no place for the denominational rivalry which afflicts church movements and prevents them from reaching the world as a united team. The path to fruitful ministry is paved with

---

[3] Jesus gave Peter the keys to the Kingdom of Heaven in Matthew 16:19, in between the events described in Mark 8:29 and Mark 8:30. The gift is only widened in Matthew 18:18, after the teaching in Mark 9:33–50.

[4] Mark refers to *"the house"* in Capernaum – in other words, the house mentioned in 1:29, 1:35 and 2:1.

[5] The parallel passage in Matthew 18:2–4 sheds light on what Jesus means here. Unless we are willing to take the humble position of a little child, we cannot enter God's Kingdom, let alone become great in it.

[6] Luke 9:49–56 describes another argument which James and John had on this road trip. Jesus rebukes John here in Mark using the plural Greek word for *you* because this bad attitude is common among his followers.

many little acts of humility. Church history has room for only one hero, and it isn't anyone of us.

In verses 41–50, Jesus warns the disciples not to look down on anyone who follows him.[7] We may write people off as insignificant, but Jesus is willing to die for each of *these little ones.*" He tells the disciples that any simple act of service towards a Christian will be rewarded in heaven. Conversely, any selfish act that causes a Christian to take offence and sin will be punished in hell. *"Be at peace with each other,"* Jesus warns his quarrelling disciples. If they want the Kingdom of God, they need to renounce the kingdom of self. If they want to experience the Messiah's victory, they need to join in with the Messiah's road trip to Calvary.

We live in a generation of Christians that treats John 3:16 as the entirety of the Gospel: *"God so loved the world that he gave his one and only Son."* But part three of Mark warns us that this only half the story. John 3:16 must be followed by 1 John 3:16: *"Jesus Christ laid down his life for us. And we ought to lay down our lives for our brothers and sisters."*

Jesus encourages us to trade in our semi-gospel for the real Gospel. He urges us to surrender to God's agenda. Jesus leads the way and he calls on us to follow him. So let's tell him that we are willing to lay down everything for him and for others. Let's tell him that we are happy to embrace his very costly story.

---

[7] Matthew 18:1–14 explains the meaning of Mark's shorter account of Jesus' teaching. Following Jesus means laying down our lives to serve other people instead of ourselves.

What Costs More (9:42–50)

*If your hand causes you to stumble, cut it off. It is
better for you to enter life maimed than with two
hands to go into hell, where the fire never goes out.*

(Mark 9:43)

Only one thing costs more than following Jesus: *not* following
Jesus. Many readers get upset with Jesus for talking so frankly
about hell at the end of Mark 9, but he does so out of love and
compassion. He has taken his disciples on a road trip in order
to convey to them that following him will cost them everything.
He therefore helps them to pay the price. He uses four vivid
pictures to show them that refusing to follow him will cost them
far, far more.

The first picture Jesus uses is that of being lynched by
an angry group of pagans. One of the cruellest ways in which
Roman and Greek rioters murdered their victims was to tie
a millstone around their neck and throw them into deep
water, rather like the Mafia godfather Carlo Gambino whose
trademark method of executing his enemies was to give them "a
pair of cement shoes and a short swim down". Jesus warns his
disciples that if we refuse to pay the price of following him now,
we will pay a far greater price later. If we play-act at following
him while compromising with sin, we will make those around
us think that self-centred church religion is genuine Christianity
and that Jesus wants them to copy us. We would be better off
pleading with a lynch mob to tie a large millstone around our

necks than to stand before Jesus as unfaithful ambassadors.[1] Refusal to follow Jesus on his road trip to Calvary means walking on the road to hell instead. An untimely death would be vastly preferable to a long walk along that road.

Instead of being offended by Jesus' teaching, let's note what he is trying to do here. Eleven of his disciples would choose to pay the price and travel on the Calvary road, but one of his disciples would not. Later on in 14:21, Jesus draws a link between these verses and the fate of Judas Iscariot when he tells us that *"The Son of Man will go just as it is written about him. But woe to that man who betrays the Son of Man! It would be better for him if he had not been born."* Jesus does not spare his listeners' feelings because he longs to spare their souls. Far from being cruel, Jesus could not be any kinder. Charles Spurgeon reminds us that *"He is the true lover of men who faithfully warns them concerning the eternal woe that awaits the impenitent; while he who paints the miseries of hell as though they were but trifling is seeking to murder men's souls under the pretext of friendship."*

The second picture Jesus uses is that of the rubbish tip outside Jerusalem. The Old Testament writers talked about the *fire*, the *pit*, the *grave* and the *place of the dead*, but Jesus brings the idea of hell far closer to home.[2] The word which is translated *hell* in these verses is *Gehenna*, the Greek form of the Hebrew name *Gey Hinnom* or the *Valley of Hinnom*, a deep and narrow gorge which ran along the southwestern wall of Jerusalem. This was where King Ahaz and King Manasseh built shrines to the Ammonite idol Molech and taught the Israelites to sacrifice their children as burnt offerings. It was such a place of torture that part of the valley became known as *Topheth*, or *Drums*,

---

[1] The Christian martyr Florian was executed by the Romans in this way in 304 AD. Jesus refers literally to a *donkey's* millstone – in other words, not just a small millstone taken from a hand mill but a full-sized one.

[2] Jesus uses the Greek word *Gehenna* in Matthew 5:22, 5:29, 5:30, 10:28, 18:9, 23:15 and 23:33, in Mark 9:43, 9:45 and 9:47, and in Luke 12:5. The only other place the word is used in the New Testament is in James 3:6.

because the priests of Molech had to play a loud and frenzied drum-beat to drown out the screams of dying children.[3] The Lord was so angered by what happened in the valley that he promised that the Babylonians would slaughter the wicked people of Jerusalem and pile up their corpses in Gehenna for the beasts and birds to feast upon their flesh. When this prophecy was fulfilled in 586 BC, Gehenna became a foul and terrible reminder that God always judges people's sin.[4]

Jesus is therefore warning us that there is something far costlier than laying down everything to follow him. Gehenna was a place of horror, a place of fire, a place of divine judgment and a place where maggots writhed continually on piles of waste and offal. Jesus quotes from the final verse of Isaiah's prophecy in order to remind us that, 600 years after the Babylonian massacre of Jerusalem, the valley was still ablaze. Hell is real and hell goes on forever. Hell is a place where *"the worms that eat them do not die, and the fire is not quenched."*[5]

The third picture Jesus uses in this passage is that of a person amputating parts of his body. He is not telling us to do this literally. He is simply telling us vividly that hell is so horrific that we can never be too radical with sin. The eighteenth-century theologian Jonathan Edwards points out that *"When metaphors are used in Scripture about spiritual things... they fall short of the literal truth."*[6] It would be better to limp through life with one foot and one hand and one eye than to be thrown into hell whole. Following Jesus may be costly, but rebelling against him is infinitely costlier.

---

[3] Joshua 15:8; 18:16; 2 Chronicles 28:3; 33:6; 2 Kings 23:10; Isaiah 30:33.

[4] Jeremiah 7:30–34; 19:1–15.

[5] In some Greek manuscripts Jesus quotes Isaiah 66:24 once in 9:48. In others he quotes it three times in 9:44, 9:46 and 9:48. How many times Jesus mentions the eternal fires of hell does not matter. What matters is that we avoid them! Jesus also says that hell's fires are *unquenchable* and *eternal* in Matthew 3:12, 18:8, 25:41 and 25:46.

[6] Taken from his sermon "The Torments of Hell Are Exceedingly Great" in *Sermons and Discourses 1723–29*.

That's why Jesus urges us in his fourth and final picture of hell to offer ourselves as living sacrifices to him. *"Everyone will be salted with fire,"* he warns. The Jewish priests mixed salt with many of the sacrifices they burned on the altar in the Temple, so he encourages us to escape the fires of hell by embracing Jesus' great act of sacrifice on our behalf and by making lots of little acts of sacrifice for him.[7] He echoes Matthew 5:13 when he calls us to be the salt of the earth, with a very sobering warning. If we pretend to be salt while not being salty at all, we will share in the terrible fate of Judas.

Jesus spoke more about hell than the whole of the Old Testament put together because he loves us. Even as he travelled to Jerusalem and to his own cross, he loved us enough to plead with us to take up our own crosses too. Hell was created for the Devil and for his demons because they chose to rebel against the Lord and, tragically, Judas chose to rebel with them too.[8] As we share in the road trip that took the disciples to Jerusalem, we therefore need to pause and pray. We need to tell Jesus that we will gladly accept the cost of stepping into his story. Better to endure the temporary costs of following Jesus in this life than to endure the horrific price tag of the only thing that costs more.

---

[7] Leviticus 2:13; Ezekiel 43:24. Jesus' teaching on saltiness here echoes his earlier teaching in Matthew 5:13–16, just as his teaching on being radical with sin echoes his earlier teaching in Matthew 5:29–30.

[8] Jesus tells us in Matthew 25:41 that he created hell as the place where rebellious demons will receive the just reward for their rebellion against God. Jesus experienced hell so that rebels like us can be spared it.

Invisible Gods (10:1–12)

"It was because your hearts were hard that Moses wrote you this law," Jesus replied.

(Mark 10:5)

The Jewish leaders detested images of foreign gods. They were willing to lay down their lives to resist them. When Pontius Pilate, the Roman governor of Judea, allowed his soldiers to enter Jerusalem with army standards bearing images of their gods, he almost provoked a revolution. The first-century Jewish historian Josephus tells us that

> *Pilate gave a signal to the soldiers that they should all coordinate their actions and suddenly surround the Jews with their weapons. So the band of soldiers surrounded the Jews in three ranks... Pilate told them that they would be cut to pieces unless they accepted Caesar's images, and he commanded the soldiers to draw their naked swords. At this the Jews, as if by a signal, knelt down together in vast numbers and exposed their bare necks, crying out that they would rather be slain than see their law transgressed. Pilate was greatly surprised at their prodigious superstition and he ordered that the army standards be carried out of Jerusalem straightaway.[1]*

The Jewish leaders hated idols, but idolatry is subtle. Ezekiel 14:3 reminds us that we can set up invisible idols in our hearts just as easily as golden images in our market squares and temples.

---

[1] Flavius Josephus records this in his *Wars of the Jews* (2.9.2–3).

Idols are more than statues. They are anything to which we turn for satisfaction and fulfilment instead of finding those things in God alone.[2] Jesus therefore uses his road trip to preach to the crowds that following him is very costly. It means renouncing every idol, even the invisible idols in our hearts.[3]

The first invisible idol Jesus exposes is the idol of *romantic love*. This is the idol that is worshipped today in love songs and romcoms and sexual encounters that seek ultimate joy and fulfilment through relationships with other people instead of with the Lord. The Pharisees detested the way in which Herod worshipped this idol by divorcing his wife in order to legitimise his affair with his brother's sister, and by asking his new stepdaughter to dance so that he could indulge his lust towards her body. They were appalled to hear what the Emperor Tiberius got up to at his private palace on the island of Capri: orgies, rape, homosexuality and paedophilia.[4] But Mark tells us that their purity is a pretence. They are not asking Jesus about divorce because they want to follow his teaching.[5] They are testing him to see if they can trick him into being executed like John the Baptist for condemning Herod's adulterous new marriage.[6] The Pharisees pretend to be pure but they are just as much idolaters as Herod.

Jesus asks the Pharisees what they think the Law of Moses

---

[2] Paul echoes the teaching of Ezekiel 14:3 in Ephesians 5:5, warning that sex and money can become idols just as easily as Zeus or Ganesh or the Buddha.

[3] Jesus crossed the River Jordan to Perea in January 30 AD. Mark does not record his early activity there (Luke 13:22–18:14; John 10:40–11:54), so we are now in early March, only a month before his crucifixion.

[4] The Roman historian Suetonius condemns all of these actions in his *Life of Tiberius* (chapters 43–45).

[5] Mark emphasises that Jesus *taught* the crowds in Perea, whereas the parallel verse in Matthew 19:2 emphasises that he *healed* them. Mark wants to focus part three of his gospel on the cost of following Jesus.

[6] Mark 6:17. Herod was tetrarch of Galilee and Perea, so the Pharisees are trying to trick Jesus before he leaves Herod's jurisdiction and crosses back over the River Jordan into Judea.

teaches them about divorce and remarriage. A debate was raging at the time between the liberal Rabbi Hillel, who tried to make divorce as easy for the Jews as it was for their Roman masters, and Rabbi Shammai who took a more conservative line.[7] When the Pharisees confess their conclusion that the Law of Moses permits divorce, Jesus tells them they have fallen for the same basic premise that motivated Herod and Tiberius: that romantic love is a path to true fulfilment and that, if a marriage isn't working, people should be free to trade it in and try again. Jesus resists the unaddressed idolatry in their hearts, explaining that *"It was because your hearts were hard that Moses wrote you this law."*

We worship an idol whenever we turn something that God has created into something primary instead of secondary. Jesus therefore reminds the Pharisees that marriage was not a human invention. God created it in order to whet our appetites for him. Jesus quotes from Genesis 1:27, which tells us, *"God created mankind in his own image, in the image of God he created them; male and female he created them."* The Lord created us male and female so that we would reflect something of his Triune nature – Father, Son and Holy Spirit – and so that the shortcomings of our two-in-one relationships would make us long for a relationship with the three-in-one God. Anyone who idolises marriage will end up disappointed and in the divorce courts. Tim Keller writes:

> *If we look to our spouses to fill up our tanks in a way that only God can do, we are demanding an impossibility... If I look to my marriage to fill the God-sized spiritual vacuum in my heart, I will not be in a position to serve my spouse. Only God can fill a God-sized hole. Until God has the proper place in my life, I will always be complaining that*

---

[7] Hillel died in about 10 AD and Shammai in about 30 AD. The debate continued long after their deaths.

my spouse is not loving me well enough, not respecting me enough, not supporting me enough.[8]

I live in the United Kingdom, a nation where 45 per cent of marriages end in divorce. Rather than being offended by Jesus' teaching, I need to be challenged by it.[9] He is saying that divorce is what happens whenever a culture worships romantic love instead of the Lord. He quotes from Genesis 2:24 to remind us that *"At the beginning of creation God 'made them male and female.' 'For this reason a man will leave his father and mother and be united to his wife, and the two will become one flesh.'"* The problem is not that a man marries the wrong woman, the wrong number of women, or even a woman instead of a man. The problem is that a man is looking to his romantic partner for fulfilment instead of to the Lord. However much we tinker with marriage as God made it, Jesus tells us that marriage partners remain one flesh: *"What God has joined together, let no one separate... Anyone who divorces his wife and marries another woman commits adultery against her. And if she divorces her husband and marries another man, she commits adultery."*[10]

If you are divorced, you already know that nothing devastates the human heart as cruelly as a broken marriage. Jesus is not trying to make you feel worse than you already do. God knows what it feels like to divorce, because Isaiah 50:1 and Jeremiah 3:8 tell us that he was forced to divorce unfaithful Israel. It is from personal experience that God tells us in Malachi 2:16 that *"I hate divorce."* Jesus tells us that, while human sin such as adultery, abuse or abandonment may make divorce necessary, we must not fall for the idolatry behind our nations'

---

[8] Timothy and Kathy Keller in *The Meaning of Marriage* (2011).

[9] British Office for National Statistics, March 2008. Second and third marriages are over twice as likely to fail as first-time marriages. The issue is not marrying the wrong person, but having a wrong view of marriage.

[10] Mark 6:17 reinforces this by telling us bluntly that, although Herod married Herodias under Roman law, she remained *"his brother Philip's wife."*

divorce laws.[11] Even the best marriage will disappoint us if we turn a good thing into a god thing. Even the worst marriage can glorify God if we make our two-in-one commitment to our wedding vows a reflection of the three-in-one God before whom we made them.

This message offended the Pharisees but it attracted those who had experienced the trauma of divorce and adultery and sexual immorality and all the other symptoms of a culture that worships romantic love as an idol. Don't cling to the mistakes of your culture like the Pharisees. Count the cost of following Jesus and throw away your idols.

---

[11] The Bible permits, but never promotes, divorce in cases of *sexual sin* (Deuteronomy 24:1), *abuse* (Exodus 21:10–11) or *abandonment* (1 Corinthians 7:12–16). Jesus refers to this in the parallel Matthew 19:9.

Respectable Idols
(10:13–27)

Jesus looked at him and loved him. "One thing you lack," he said. "Go, sell everything you have and give to the poor, and you will have treasure in heaven. Then come, follow me."

(Mark 10:21)

During the Reformation, John Calvin warned Protestants not to look down on Roman Catholics for praying to images of saints in their churches. *"The human mind is, so to speak, a perpetual idol factory,"* he warned them. *"The human mind, stuffed as it is with presumptuous rashness, dares to imagine a god suited to its own capacity... It substitutes vanity and an empty phantom in the place of God."*[1] Calvin warned Protestants that respectable idols in our hearts are just as toxic as any idol made with stone. He echoed the warnings which Jesus gave while continuing his journey south along the road through Perea.

161

The Roman Empire worshipped power. Quite literally. The Roman forum was dominated by a temple that called the city to worship the power of Jupiter by bringing offerings to the foot of a colossal statue of him flexing his muscles in a four-horse war chariot. The Jewish rabbis hated Roman images but they embraced the same foul idol. The city of Jerusalem was dominated by a temple to the Lord, but it was a temple which King Herod the Great rebuilt in order to bolster his political power and it was a temple run by the Sadducees who had cut a deal with Rome in return for being granted local powers. Having

---

[1] John Calvin issued this warning in 1536 in his *Institutes of the Christian Religion* (1.11.8).

confronted the worship of romantic love, Jesus now turns his attention to the worship of human power.

In verses 13–16, the disciples show that they have fallen for the rhetoric of Rome. They expect Jesus to want to spend time with priests and synagogue rulers, but they do not expect him to spend time with little children. Despite his teaching in 9:36–37, they rebuke the crowds for bringing their children to Jesus so that he will place his hands on them and bless them. Jesus is indignant. He rebukes them for pandering to the powerful and despising the weak.[2] He warns: *"The kingdom of God belongs to such as these. Truly I tell you, anyone who will not receive the kingdom of God like a little child will never enter it."*

Because the Jews relied on human power, their Temple would be destroyed in 70 AD. Because the Romans relied on human power, their city would be sacked in 410 AD. Followers of Jesus do not share in their fate. They recognise that God's weakness is stronger than human strength. They confess their weakness and find it is the doorway to all the blessings of God's Kingdom. Far from sending the little children away, Jesus tells the disciples that they ought to learn from them. Devoid of human strength, they help us understand the message of the Gospel: *"He was crucified in weakness, yet he lives by God's power. Likewise we are weak in him, yet by God's power we will live with him."*[3]

Wealth and power go together, so Jesus addresses the respectable idol of money in verses 17–31.[4] A rich man runs up to him and falls to his knees, asking *"Good teacher, what must I do to inherit eternal life?"* The disciples are over the moon. They take the man's wealth as proof that God is pleased with him.

[2] Mark uses the Greek word *aganakteō*, the same strong word he uses to describe the disciples being *indignant* in 10:41 and 14:4. It expresses a strong clash between two different ways of thinking.

[3] Paul writes this in 2 Corinthians 13:4. David also reminds us in Psalm 8:2 that God has chosen to use the weakness of children to shame the strong.

[4] The three gospel accounts of this encounter reinforce this link. Mark 10:22 and Matthew 19:22 say that the man is *rich*. Luke 18:18 says that the man is a *ruler*.

They believe his boast that he has kept the Ten Commandments since he was a boy. They are impressed by his body language as he runs to Jesus and kneels before him in the dust. They expect Jesus to answer him with a promise that eternal life will be his if he simply carries on doing what he is doing.[5] But they are in for a surprise. Jesus tackles the respectable idol in the man's heart by commanding him to sell everything he has. The rich man is sad but not sad enough to obey. He wants to step into Jesus' story, but only if the cost can be negotiated.

The first telltale sign is that he only wants to honour Jesus as a *"good teacher."* He is like many respectable churchgoers today. He doesn't want to follow Jesus as God and Lord and King. He simply wants to follow him as a spiritual adviser. Jesus asks him, *"Why do you call me good? No one is good – except God alone."* We cannot follow Jesus unless we throw away our respectable idols and confess that he alone is the real God.

Another telltale sign is the way that Jesus lists the Ten Commandments. He skips over the first four commandments, which deal with our love for God, in order to highlight the man's lack of love for other people. He changes the Tenth Commandment, *"do not covet,"* into a stronger command, *"do not defraud,"* because the man's problem is not lusting for what isn't his but thinking that what is his belongs to him alone. He thinks that helping the poor would be an act of mercy, whereas Jesus tells him that it would simply be an act of justice.[6] Treating money as a god always makes people defraud those around them because idols are grasped and carried, never given away. Mark tells us that *"Jesus looked at him and loved him."* He disciplines him in the same way that a loving father disciplines his child. He

[5] This is the first occurrence of the phrase "eternal life" in Mark's gospel. Whereas John uses the phrase to mean "the kingdom of heaven," Mark uses the phrase here and in 10:30 to mean "life beyond the grave".

[6] God's Word convicts of sin (Romans 3:20) but it needs to be explained for it to do so. That's why people need more than to be given a Bible. They also need to study it with friends who can help them understand it.

tells him to give away his respectable idol. Only then will his heart be humble enough to receive the eternal life he claims to crave.[7]

The disciples are astonished.[8] If this rich man has not earned his own salvation, then nobody can! Jesus adds to their astonishment by telling them that they have more chance of threading a camel through the eye of a needle than they have of seeing anybody saved who worships money as an idol.[9] If our earthly riches make us spiritually complacent, we will perish along with our money. If we admit that we are spiritual beggars and entirely unable to save ourselves, we will discover that *"With man this is impossible, but not with God; all things are possible with God."*

God loves the rich and powerful. In 15:43, he will save a rich member of the Jewish ruling council. Wealth and power are good things, but Jesus warns us that they can all too easily become god things and great impediments to our salvation.[10] They can become respectable idols which fool us that we are rich when we are poor, that we are strong when we are weak and that we are saved when we are hopelessly lost.

Jesus looks at you and loves you. He warns you that respectable idols are like a ball and chain around your ankles. He commands you to throw off everything that stops you from relying on him alone. He urges you to pay whatever price is needed to step into his very costly story.

---

[7] Softening the challenge of the Gospel to spare people's feelings is not loving. It is cruel. Jesus shows us that true love for people is to spell out the Gospel so clearly that we take a risk they will choose to walk away.

[8] Failure to challenge respectable idols results in churches full of false converts who ask, *"How can God send anyone to hell?"* Challenging them results in true converts who ask, *"How can anyone be saved?"*

[9] In 10:23 and 24 Jesus says that it is *duskolos*, or *difficult*, for the rich to enter the Kingdom of God. In 10:27 he explains why: it is *adunatos*, or *impossible*, for anyone who trusts in human strength to enter the Kingdom.

[10] Wealth makes us guiltier because it increases our ability to do good towards the poor. It also makes us more self-reliant and complacent about our need for God (Matthew 5:3; Luke 16:19–31; Hebrews 13:5–6).

Back to Front Story
(10:28–45)

Whoever wants to be first must be slave of all. For
even the Son of Man did not come to be served, but
to serve, and to give his life as a ransom for many.

(Mark 10:44–45)

If the road trip in part three of Mark's gospel had a soundtrack,
it would have to be this song by Jason Upton:

> *There's a power in poverty that breaks principalities*
> *And brings the authorities down to their knees.*
> *There's a brewing frustration and ageless temptation*
> *to fight for control by some manipulation.*
> *But the God of the kingdoms and God of the nations,*
> *The God of creation sends this revelation:*
> *Through the homeless and penniless, Jesus the Son,*
> *The poor will inherit the Kingdom to come.*
>
> *Where will we turn when our world falls apart*
> *And all of the treasures we've stored in our barns*
> *Can't buy the Kingdom of God?*
> *And who will we praise when we've praised all our lives*
> *Men who build kingdoms and men who build fame*
> *But heaven does not know their names?*[1]

The disciples are still struggling to sing this tune. Peter points
out that, unlike the rich man who went away sad, they have

---

[1] Jason Upton in his song "Poverty" on the album *Faith* (2001).

given up everything to follow Jesus – so where is their reward? Jesus has to show them that they have the story back to front. Following Jesus isn't about haggling with God for compensation. It is about giving up everything out of gratitude for the fact that he has saved us.[2]

Jesus tells Peter and his friends that they will get their reward. God will pay them back a hundred times more than anything they have given him.[3] These verses inspired Charles T. Studd, one of the greatest players in the England cricket team, to give up family and fame and fortune to become a humble missionary to China. C.T. Studd was a household name across the British Empire, but he gave it all up to become a nobody in God's Kingdom. He told his mystified fans that *"God has promised to give a hundredfold for everything we give to him. A hundredfold is a wonderful percentage; it is ten thousand per cent... What is it worth to possess the riches of the world, when a man comes to face eternity?"*[4]

It is indeed a wonderful promise, but in the longer account of this conversation in Matthew 19:27 to 20:16 Jesus makes it clear that Peter is very wrong to request a reward. He tells the Parable of the Workers in the Vineyard to point out that being saved from hell and admitted to heaven is reward enough.[5] We are still serving the idols of romance and money and power if we try to haggle with God for compensation. It means that we are relying on our acts of sacrifice to earn us merit with God every bit as much as the rich man relied upon his money. C.T. Studd

---

[2] Mark only uses the phrase *"eternal life"* twice in his gospel – in 10:17 and 10:30. This conversation is therefore a deliberate counterpart to the encounter between Jesus and the rich man.

[3] The rich man was therefore robbing himself by hanging onto his wealth, although Hebrews 10:34 and 11:37 remind us not to treat this promise as a mere financial formula.

[4] The quotes in this chapter come from Norman Grubb's biography *C.T. Studd: Cricketer and Pioneer* (1933).

[5] Mark's account is briefer, but verse 31 repeats the main theme of the parable in Matthew 19:30 and 20:16.

gave away a fortune and arrived in China with only five pounds in his pocket because he grasped this principle. He reflected that *"Either I had to be a thief and keep what wasn't mine, or else I had to give up everything to God. When I came to see that Jesus Christ had died for me, it didn't seem hard to give up all for him."*

The disciples are astonished, so Jesus tells them for a fourth time in verses 33–34 that he is going to Jerusalem to die.[6] He encourages them to sing along with him, but James and John are still singing a song of their own. At the very moment when Jesus is sharing that he will become nothing on the cross to save us, they sing about the glory they deserve on account of their own petty sacrifices.[7] The other disciples are indignant, but only because they think that their own sacrifices for Jesus are greater than those of James and John. Jesus has to tell them that they have the story back to front: *"Many who are first will be last, and the last first."* Greatness in the Kingdom of Heaven doesn't come to those who seek it through self-promotion. It comes to those who love God so much that they gladly sacrifice their own interests for his cause.[8]

Jesus therefore uses two of the most offensive words in the Roman Empire to convince the disciples that they don't need a reward, they need a ransom. The Greek word *lutron*, or *ransom price*, in verse 45 describes the payment that was made to free a slave or criminal or hostage or prisoner of war who had no hope of survival unless a powerful friend stepped in to save them. Jesus tells the disciples that he is about to take the punishment

---

[6] The first three times were in 8:31–32; 9:9–10 and 31–32. A fifth time comes in 10:45. The disciples are amazed and the crowds are afraid since everyone can see that Jesus is striding ahead because he means business.

[7] Matthew's longer account is even more pathetic. Matthew 20:20–23 tells us that James and John got their mum to make this request of Jesus for them!

[8] The disciples would grasp this later. They rejoiced when flogged for the name of Jesus (Acts 5:40–41). John was exiled (Revelation 1:9) and James was the first apostle to be martyred (Acts 12:2).

they deserve for their sin.[9] This is not the time to claim their just deserts. It is the time to be grateful that God doesn't give us what we deserve.

The other Greek word is *doulos*, or *slave*, in verse 44. Jesus tells the disciples that the sacrifices we make for the sake of God's Kingdom are simply part and parcel of stepping into the Messiah's story. We will be persecuted. We will be despised as common slaves. Some of us will die. In a world that worships romance and money and power, this is simply the normal price of following the one who died the death of the lonely and powerless and penniless to set us free.

Another missionary to Africa, David Livingstone, grasped this when he returned to Britain and was greeted by admiring crowds who spoke about the reward God would grant him in heaven for his many sacrifices. He told them:

> *For my own part, I have never ceased to rejoice that God has appointed me to such an office. People talk of the sacrifice I have made in spending so much of my life in Africa. Can that be called a sacrifice which is simply paid back as a small part of a great debt owing to our God, which we can never repay?... It is emphatically no sacrifice. Say rather it is a privilege. Anxiety, sickness, suffering or danger, now and then, with a foregoing of the common conveniences and charities of this life, may make us pause, and cause the spirit to waver, and the soul to sink; but let this only be for a moment. All these are nothing when compared with the glory which shall be revealed in and for us. I never made a sacrifice.[10]*

---

[9] Jesus did not pay a ransom price to Satan – he defeated Satan! He paid the ransom which satisfied God's justice towards the offence of our sin (Romans 3:26). Do not make too much of the fact that Jesus says he died for *the many*. 1 Timothy 2:6 clarifies that Jesus gave his life as a ransom for *everyone*.

[10] David Livingstone said this in an address to the students of Cambridge University on 4th December 1857.

Throw It All Away
(10:46–52)

Throwing his cloak aside, he jumped to his feet and came to Jesus.

(Mark 10:50)

Bartimaeus had virtually nothing. He didn't even have his eyesight. He was a blind beggar on the road that linked the old town to the new town of Jericho.[1] He had nothing except for the cloak that covered his skinny body by day and kept him warm on the cold streets at night.[2] Nothing, that is, except for his clear realisation that he was in desperate need of a saviour. That's why Mark uses him at the end of Jesus' road trip to challenge us to pay the price of stepping into his story,

169

Jesus has crossed over the River Jordan and has finally entered the Jewish heartland of Judea. Mark expects us to know enough about the geography of Israel to grasp this and to get excited. The Jewish Messiah has reached Jericho and is about to complete his march upon the capital. A large crowd of Jews are intrigued enough to follow him, but the one who sees his identity most clearly is blind Bartimaeus. He becomes a picture of what it means for us to reject the idols of our culture and to throw it all away for Jesus.

---

[1] Jericho consisted of an old town and a new town, which is why Mark 10:46 and Matthew 20:29 tell us that Jesus healed the man while *leaving* the city, whereas Luke 18:35 says he healed him while *approaching* it.

[2] As usual, Mark translates for his Roman readers. Bartimaeus was simply Aramaic for *the Son of Timaeus*. Even the man's name had been borrowed from his father.

Bartimaeus is weak but he has *faith in God's power*. The crowds talk about "Jesus of Nazareth" but the blind man recognises that he is far more than this. He cries out, *"Jesus, Son of David, have mercy on me!"* The Jewish leaders and the Romans may rely on human power, but this blind man looks to 2 Samuel 7 and 1 Chronicles 17 instead, where God promised to save Israel through a Messiah born to the fallen dynasty of David.[3] Bartimaeus sees what the power-blinded Jews and Romans cannot. Our hope is not in our money or in our politics or in our sacrifices. Our hope lies in throwing away those respectable idols and in laying hold of God's unmerited mercy.[4]

Bartimaeus is alone but he has *faith in God's love for him*.[5] The crowd despise him as much as the disciples despised the little children in Perea, telling him to be quiet and not to trouble the Galilean preacher.[6] A man with family or friends to comfort him might have been persuaded, but Bartimaeus persists because he knows his only comfort lies in the loving heart of God. He refuses to believe that the harsh response of those who follow Jesus is a true reflection of the heart of God towards him. He shouts all the more loudly, not caring if people hate him, just so long as Jesus shows him that he loves him. His faith is rewarded. The crowd suddenly tell him, *"Cheer up! On your feet! He's calling you."*

Bartimaeus is poor but he has *faith in God's resources*. Beggars hold onto their cloak tightly because they know it is

---

[3] This is why the Jews often referred to the Messiah as the *Son of David*. Matthew particularly emphasises this in Matthew 1:1, 20; 9:27; 12:23; 15:22; 20:30, 31; 21:9, 15; and 22:42.

[4] Jesus is about to be rejected by the powerful Jewish rabbis because he is not one of them, but in 10:51 Bartimaeus recognises their reject as Israel's true Rabbi.

[5] The parallel Matthew 20:29–34 tells us that Jesus healed two blind men, but Mark emphasises the aloneness of Bartimaeus in order to form a contrast with those who worship the idol of romantic love.

[6] Churches can be just as guilty of silencing rejects and outcasts. Mark wants us to grasp that the despised and unlovely are high up on God's loving agenda.

their sole protection from the scorching sun and the shivering cold. Blind beggars hold onto it even more tightly because they know if they misplace it, then they will struggle to relocate it. Nevertheless, when Bartimaeus hears that Jesus wants to see him, he throws his cloak away. He sees things too clearly to hang onto his possessions like the rich man or to complain about making sacrifices like Peter and his friends. Bartimaeus doesn't need his cloak any more because he can find everything he needs in Jesus.[7]

Asking Jesus to bless us is popular. Throwing things away to let him do so is painful. Few people are willing to do what Bartimaeus did. Even when we turn to Jesus as our Saviour, we tend to hang onto friends and money and human power as a backup plan in case our faith in Jesus fails us. But Mark is insistent. He will not finish part three of his gospel until he has pleaded with us to see things as clearly as this blind beggar. Stepping into Jesus' story always means throwing our respectable idols away.

A Chinese pastor sent his young son to America in 1920 so that he could receive a Western education. Seven and a half years later, when John Sung took the long journey back home across the Pacific Ocean to his father, his suitcase was full of diplomas and certificates which would open many doors for him across China. But he had recently been filled with the Holy Spirit and he had become convinced that he needed to throw those certificates away as an expression of his faith that Jesus alone could use him to revive China. *"Man's works do not even come close to the works of the Holy Spirit,"* he concluded. *"If the Holy Spirit does not work, all the efforts of man will come to naught."*[8] John Sung threw his diplomas and certificates overboard and landed in China with nothing but his faith in God, yet he went on

---

[7] Although Mark's more concise account omits it, the parallel Luke 19:1–10 tells us that Jesus also saved Zacchaeus on this visit to Jericho. He was a rich man who gave away his possessions to follow Jesus.

[8] He said this to his team of workers on 2nd December 1929. For a simple introduction to his life, read Leslie Lyall's *Biography of John Sung* (1954).

to become the most successful evangelist in China in the 1930s. By the time he died, it was estimated that 10 per cent of China's Christian converts had been directly influenced by him.

Jesus is delighted with Bartimaeus and his willingness to throw away his only possession. He asked James and John in verse 36, *"What do you want me to do for you?"*, but refused their selfish prayer. Now he asks the blind man the same question and gives him what he is looking for: *"Go, your faith has healed you."* Suddenly Bartimaeus is not blind any more. He has become a picture of what happens to us when we accept the cost of stepping deeper into Jesus' story. Bartimaeus gladly follows Jesus along the road.

It's decision time. We are about to end part three of Mark's gospel and move into the climactic part four. Have you stepped into the story? Are you willing to accept the price of following Jesus and to throw off the respectable idols that stop us living out his very costly story? If you are, Mark promises you that you will never lose out by sacrificing everything for Jesus. John Sung's diplomas and certificates were destroyed in the Pacific Ocean, but hopes for fruitful ministry in China were saved. He reflected shortly before he died:

> *Generally, people love to be uplifted and praised by others... The Lord Jesus, on the other hand... found fishermen and enlisted those with no learning and social status as his disciples... The Lord would have no use for the knowledgeable Saul if he had not been changed to the humble Paul. If Moses were still the prince in his palace and did not become a shepherd, the Lord would have no place for him either. O Lord, may you rid us of our towering ambitions... May we follow You to do the things that the world hates and walk the paths where few people want to travel.*[9]

---

[9] John Sung in a letter to his co-worker Leona Wu on 28th April 1941.

Part Four:

The Surprising Story

(Mark 11:1–15:47)

A Different Type of King (11:1–11)

"Blessed is the coming kingdom of our father David!"
"Hosanna in the highest heaven!"

(Mark 11:10)

Almost 200 years before Jesus entered Jerusalem, another Jewish saviour did the same. Against all odds, Judas Maccabaeus managed to defeat the heirs of Alexander the Great and to free the Jews from the oppressive Seleucid Empire. He entered Jerusalem in 164 BC in great triumph and acclaim. Many people wondered if he might even be the long-awaited Messiah. 2 Maccabees 10:7 tells us that the people of Jerusalem received their great deliverer with a shout: *"The people, carrying green palm branches and sticks decorated with ivy, paraded around, singing grateful praises to him."*[1]

Jesus is about to do the same. He has finished his road trip and he is about to enter the Jewish capital in triumph. Mark begins part four of his gospel by slowing down the action and describing the preparations that took place before he did so. Jericho is the lowest-lying city in the world, over 800 feet below sea level, so Jesus has climbed 4,000 feet by the time he reaches the Mount of Olives and catches his first glimpse of Jerusalem across the valley. He sends two of his disciples into a village to

---

[1] 2 Maccabees is the book in the Old Testament Apocrypha that records the victory of Judas Maccabaeus.

find him an animal to ride.[2] The time has come for the King to ride into his capital.

The people of Jerusalem instantly recognise that Jesus is their King. They throw their cloaks on the road, forming the equivalent of a modern-day red carpet for him, just as the Israelites did for the new King Jehu in 2 Kings 9:13. When they run out of cloaks, they cut down branches from the trees and turn the red carpet green. They understand that they are fulfilling the words of the messianic prophecy in Psalm 118:19–29: *"Open for me the gates of the righteous; I will enter... Join in the festal procession with boughs in hand."*[3] They begin to shout its words to Jesus. They shout the Hebrew word *"Hosanna!"* from verse 25, which means *"Please save us!"* and which was used as a cry of worship to God as Saviour. They shout from verse 26, *"Blessed is he who comes in the name of the Lord!"* In case his Roman readers fail to grasp what this means, Mark explains more clearly: *"Blessed is the coming kingdom of our father David!"* The crowds are celebrating the fact that there is a new King in town.

Mark's Roman readers understood the concept of a triumphal entry better than anyone. Nobody knew how to celebrate the victorious homecoming of a ruler better than the citizens of Rome. When Julius Caesar returned in triumph after defeating the Gauls in 46 BC, his war chariot was followed by a long train of captives and by soldiers who distributed 2,000 tons of silver and gold to the cheering crowds.[4] Mark's Roman readers can therefore have been in no doubt that this was a climactic moment in Jesus' story. Now Mark surprises them by showing that Jesus is a very different type of King.

---

[2] It is likely that one of these two disciples was Peter, because Mark gives us a surprising amount of eyewitness detail in 11:4. Literally, the colt was *tied up outside by a doorway at a junction in the road*.

[3] John 12:13 tells us that these were mainly *palm branches*. They were used as a carpet rather than as flags.

[4] See Appian of Alexandria's *History of the Civil Wars* (2.15.101–102).

Jesus is the King who does things God's way. He embodies the lessons he taught his disciples on his road trip to Jerusalem. Unlike Judas Maccabaeus or Julius Caesar, he refuses to enter the city with a show of power. Judas derived his nickname from the Aramaic word *maqqaba*, meaning *hammer*, because he shattered the Seleucid armies in the Battles of Beth-Horon and Emmaus. Caesar became ruler of Rome by slaughtering his foes. But Jesus is different. He carries no weapon in his hand and he has no troops or captives following in his train. He does not ride into Jerusalem on a mighty warhorse. He rides on a colt so young that it has never been ridden before. He rides on a little donkey to express his reliance on the power of heaven and not on the strength of man.[5] The crowds shout the words of Psalm 118, but Jesus embodies them: *"The Lord is with me; he is my helper... It is better to take refuge in the Lord than to trust in humans."*

Jesus is the King who does things with God's resources. Unlike Julius Caesar, he refuses to enter the city with gold and silver in his hands. He does not even own the little donkey on which he rides. It is borrowed from strangers. Once again he embodies the lessons he taught the disciples as they marched upon the capital.[6] If anyone expects Jesus to bring about his Kingdom through the marshalling of human resources, they are in for a surprise. He was nursed in a borrowed manger, he preached from a borrowed boat and he rides into Jerusalem on a borrowed donkey. Before the week is out, he will be buried as a corpse in a borrowed tomb.

Jesus is the King who does things according to God's timing. Don't miss the anticlimax at the end of these verses, because it

---

[5] Unlike Matthew, Mark does not emphasise that Jesus rode into Jerusalem on a donkey. He uses the Greek word *pōlos*, which can just as easily refer to a horse's *foal* as to a donkey's *colt*. Great kings might ride on a donkey (1 Kings 1:33), but no king would ever ride on an untested colt or foal.

[6] If Jesus finds this colt through a supernatural word of knowledge, then the miracle is repeated a few days later when a similar word of knowledge also finds him a room in which to eat the Last Supper (Luke 22:10–11).

is intentional. When Judas Maccabaeus rode into Jerusalem, he tore down pagan altars and immediately purified the Temple. When Julius Caesar rode into Rome, he dealt with his political enemies and became emperor in all but name. Note the contrast when Jesus finishes his triumphal entry in verse 11: *"Jesus entered Jerusalem and went into the temple courts. He looked around at everything, but since it was already late, he went out to Bethany with the Twelve."* He returns the donkey. He goes back to the home of Mary and Martha outside the city walls. Unless we feel the terrible anticlimax of verse 11, we will not grasp what Mark wants to tell us in part four of his gospel. Jesus is the King of heaven and he plays by heaven's rules. These final chapters will underline the fact that his is a very surprising story.

That's why the Jewish crowds who cheer Jesus now reject him only four days later. They are horrified to discover that his Kingdom's currency is not strength but weakness, not wealth but poverty, not impatient human action but patient waiting for God, not an army of soldiers but a band of apostles. Their cries of *"Hosanna!"* quickly turn to *"Crucify!"* They fulfil the prophecy in Psalm 118:19–29 that the Messiah will be *"the stone the builders rejected."*[7] Jesus rode into Jerusalem with no reliance upon the respectable idols which its blinded citizens held so dear. The Messiah rode into his idolatrous capital city, and the city preferred its idols to its Messiah.

This was important for Mark's Roman readers. They needed to know that following Jesus did not mean siding with Jerusalem against Rome. It was not an act of treason against their Emperor. It was an act of revolution against the entire world. It meant rejecting the false gods of this entire age, the whole world over. Make no mistake as the Messiah rides into his capital. This is a very different type of King.

---

[7] Jesus quotes from Psalm 118:22–23 in Mark 12:10–11.

On God's Team (11:11–23)

Is it not written: "My house will be called a house of prayer for all nations"? But you have made it "a den of robbers".

(Mark 11:17)

When Judas Maccabaeus rode into Jerusalem, it meant that the God of Israel's team had won. The pagan King Antiochus IV had treated the Temple in Jerusalem no differently from any other sacred building in his Seleucid Empire. He had defiled the Temple by erecting an image of Zeus in its courtyards and by sacrificing a pig to the pagan god on its altar. He had provoked a Jewish revolt, and the triumphant arrival of Judas Maccabaeus meant that God's team had emerged victorious. The pagan statues would be pulled down. The Gentiles would be barred from the Temple courtyards. Judas Maccabaeus had saved the Jewish religion from the pagan nations.

That's why the actions of Jesus are so surprising in Mark 11. His first act as King in the capital is to purge the Temple, but he makes it clear that he is not purging it *from* the nations. He is purging it *for* the nations. The crowds are so surprised that, in four short days, they change their shouts of *"Hosanna!"* into cries of *"Crucify!"* They had expected the Messiah to be on their side and they react very badly when he tells them to repent and to join his side instead.

The Jewish leaders assume that the Temple is pleasing to God because it is free from pagan images, but when Jesus looks around he sees idols everywhere. He sees a nation so steeped in the worship of money that they have turned the Temple courtyards into a cattle market. They exploit worshippers by cornering the market for sacrificial lambs and bulls and doves.[1] They even allow merchants to use the courtyards as a shortcut for hauling merchandise across the city if they are given a backhander along the way. The same Jews who chased Pontius Pilate's pagan images out of their city have turned the Temple courtyards into a shrine to money as their invisible god.

The Temple courtyards are also full of money changers. The Jewish leaders refused to accept Greek or Roman coins because they were decorated with pictures of pagan gods. They therefore forced pilgrims to exchange their pagan money for Jewish coins if they wanted to purchase animals to sacrifice, often at exploitative rates of exchange. They act like the heirs of Judas Maccabaeus by demanding that no foreign images defile the Temple, but Jesus sees it as a power play which forces Gentiles to line Jewish pockets instead of making it as easy as possible for them to experience the saving power of Israel's God. He overturns the tables and benches of the traders.[2] He forbids the merchants from trampling its sacred stones. Then he surprises the Jewish crowds by warning them that they may not actually be on God's team at all.

The outermost courtyard of the Temple was known as the Court of the Gentiles. Since uncircumcised pagans were forbidden from entering the main Temple courtyards, King Herod had built an outer square where unbelieving visitors could come and catch a first glimpse of what it would mean for them to worship Israel's God. Jesus quotes from Isaiah 56:7, reminding the Jewish leaders and traders that God's desire is

---

[1] Mark particularly emphasises the sellers of *doves* because those were the sacrifices offered by the very poor (Leviticus 12:8). God hates us profiteering from the Gospel (2 Corinthians 2:17; 1 Timothy 6:5).

[2] Jesus made a whip to clear the Temple two years earlier in John 2:13–22. We know that he did not drive out these merchants in unbridled anger, because he slept on his reaction to their sin in Mark 11:11.

that *"My house will be called a house of prayer for all nations."*[3] It was to be a place where Jews prayed for the salvation of the nations and where they made it easy for any interested pagan to come. Instead, Jesus quotes from Jeremiah 7:11 to declare that *"You have made it 'a den of robbers'."* He is quoting from a part of Jeremiah known as the "Great Temple Sermon", which warned the Jews not to trust in the Temple to save them unless they repented of their sins. He is telling the people of Jerusalem that they are not on God's team unless they understand his mission: Judas Maccabaeus came to purify the Temple from the pagans, but Jesus came to purify the Temple for the pagans.

This is so surprising for the disciples that Jesus illustrates his message for them through an incident on the two-mile journey from Bethany to Jerusalem. He sees a fig-tree in full leaf, which was unusual for April, since fig-trees only grow leaves when they are in fruit.[4] He searches its branches for breakfast and, finding no figs on it, he remembers that Jeremiah 24 describes the Jewish nation as a basket of good figs and a basket of bad figs. He makes this fruitless fig-tree a picture of what Israel has become – a nation with all the external trappings of devotion to the Lord but with none of the inner fruit. He curses the fig-tree – *"May no one ever eat fruit from you again"* – and, sure enough, Peter notices the following morning that the fig-tree has withered and died.[5] The Jews think that their Messiah has arrived in Jerusalem to show the world that they are right and that the nations are wrong. Instead, Jesus explains that he

---

[3] Matthew and Luke's accounts of this event simply say that it must be *"a house of prayer."* Mark gives us the full quotation in order to emphasise to his Roman readers that God wants them on his team too.

[4] In Israel, fig-trees normally bear leaves and fruit in the month of June. Jesus also used the picture of Israel as a fig-tree to issue a stern warning to the Jewish nation in Luke 13:6–9.

[5] Matthew's condensed account of this miracle remembers the fig-tree withering immediately (Matthew 21:18–22). Mark's fuller account says Peter reacted the following morning when it had withered completely.

has come to give the Jews an ultimatum: they need to repent of their sins and to step into his surprising story.

The disciples do not know which to be more surprised about: that the Jewish nation is not on God's team or that a simple curse from Jesus can wither a fig-tree. Jesus tells them that they ought to be surprised by neither. Anyone who utters a blessing or a curse or a prayer in faith that God will hear them can expect to move any mountain that stands before them as they seek to advance the Messiah's story. But he means more than that. He does not simply talk about faith moving a mountain, but about faith moving *this* mountain. He is talking about the mountain on which he saw the fig-tree in the distance while he was crossing the Kidron Valley from Bethany to Jerusalem. He is talking about Mount Zion! He is talking about the Temple Mount, which made the Jewish leaders so confident that God was with them that they plot in verse 18 how to kill the Messiah rather than accept his challenge to their invisible idols.

God is not on our team. He never was, as the Messiah's arrival in Jerusalem clearly shows. He has his own team and it is the team of faith. It is the team of anyone, Jew or Gentile, who throws off their confidence in money and power and religious traditions, trading them all in for simple faith in God's Messiah.

This was Mark's challenge to his Roman readers and it is still his challenge to us today. External appearances mean nothing. What matters is whether we are truly on God's team.

More Than Words
(11:20–26)

I tell you, if anyone says to this mountain, "Go, throw yourself into the sea," and does not doubt in their heart but believes that what they say will happen, it will be done for them.

(Mark 11:23)

Peter and his friends were descended from a man who knew that blessings and curses were more than words. Jacob risked his life by assuming a disguise in order to receive some words of blessing from his father Isaac. When Isaac realised that he had blessed the wrong son, he did not shrug it off and bless the right one. Like Jacob, he understood that blessings and curses are more than words. He told Jacob's older brother Esau that *"I have made him lord over you and have made all his relatives his servants, and I have sustained him with grain and new wine. So what can I possibly do for you?"* Isaac understood this. Jacob understood this. Even Esau understood this. Now Peter and his friends needed to understand it too, so that they could learn to participate in Jesus' Kingdom.[1]

It is very important that we understand this. These are no throwaway words which Jesus speaks to his disciples by the withered fig-tree. They are the crucial counterpart to what he has been teaching us about the folly of trusting in money and power and friends as invisible gods. There is no inherent power in weakness. By definition, it means not having power! There

---

[1] The Lord never condemns Jacob for his flawed faith in the power of words of blessing in Genesis 27.

is no inherent power in poverty. By definition, it means being in need! When the Lord says to Paul in 2 Corinthians 12:9 that *"My power is made perfect in weakness,"* he is not telling us that weak people are automatically strong. If that were the case, the Jewish leaders would have been very strong indeed. The Lord is telling us that we are strong when we cast aside all trust in human strength and wealth and friendship, because only then are we able to gamble everything on God. Understanding that these things have no currency in heaven is only half the story. The other half is understanding that the currency of heaven is faith in God.

The New Testament writers commend Isaac and Jacob for grasping the power of speaking blessings and curses in God's name. Hebrews 11:20–21 tells us that *"By faith Isaac blessed Jacob and Esau in regard to their future. By faith Jacob, when he was dying, blessed each of Joseph's sons."* If these twelve apostles were to kick-start the story that began with Jacob's twelve sons and had stalled, they needed to possess the same faith as Isaac and Jacob that words spoken in God's name carry great power to change the world.

Jesus tells the disciples not to be surprised that a simple curse from his mouth has caused the fig-tree to wither. There are too many good things to be surprised about in part four of Mark's gospel for us to waste time being surprised at what is really quite straightforward. Jesus spoke the world into existence in Genesis 1. He healed the sick by proclaiming that they were healed.[2] It therefore should not surprise us that the fig-tree withered from its roots. The earth could no longer support it once the Lord of the universe spoke a decree of execution. When Jesus blesses and curses, all of creation lines up to what he says.

Jesus informs the disciples that this is how his Kingdom advances on the earth. When people stop relying on their own

---

[2] See John 1:1–3, 10; Colossians 1:15–17; Hebrews 1:1–3; Mark 5:34; 7:29; 10:52.

finite human resources, they put themselves in a position to tap into the infinite resources of heaven. Instead of comparing obstacles with their own strength and saying, "I cannot," they start comparing obstacles with God's strength and saying, "Through God I can." Jesus tells the disciples that they have as much power as he does whenever they speak words on his behalf. If they bless, people are surely blessed. If they curse, people are surely cursed. If they pray, their prayers are surely answered. The messianic promise in Zechariah 4:6–7 belongs also to them: "'Not by might nor by power, but by my Spirit,' says the Lord Almighty. 'What are you, mighty mountain? Before Zerubbabel you will become level ground.'"

When most of us read the promises Jesus makes to us in these verses, we immediately rush to qualify them. We argue that these promises are for the disciples, not for us. We point out that many times our prayers appear to go unanswered. We decide that these words are simply too good to be true. We are right to qualify them, but only if we qualify them in the right way. Jesus gives us three provisos that qualify these words, but only three provisos.

The first proviso is the context in which he speaks these words. He is challenging the people of Jerusalem not to rely on the invisible idols of romance and wealth and power. If we take these words to mean that we can name and claim our future husband or a financial windfall or a promotion, we are missing the whole thrust of the second half of Mark's gospel. Jesus does not give this promise to reinforce our reliance on little manmade gods. He gives it in order to help us to advance his countercultural cause.[3]

The second proviso is the warning he gives us. He speaks about the importance of forgiving others who sin against us so

---

[3] John 14:14 and Matthew 18:18 and 28:18–19 also tell us that our authority to let loose God's Kingdom on earth through our words depends on our speaking words in line with the nature of that Kingdom.

that we may be forgiven by God our Father.[4] If we refuse to forgive others, we cannot be forgiven, and if we are not forgiven, we have no authority to issue commands or petitions in Jesus' name. Our ability to wield God's authority is directly linked to our willingness to submit to it ourselves. Only if we truly make Jesus our Lord have we any authority to speak powerful words in his name.

The third proviso is the big one, and it is where so many of us fall down. Jesus warns us that our words only carry as much authority on earth as we believe they carry in heaven. *"Have faith in God,"* Jesus encourages us. This promise belongs to anyone who *"does not doubt in their heart but believes that what they say will happen."* The Greek word Jesus uses for doubting is *diakrinō*, and it means literally *to hold two opinions*.[5] If we think we have enough resources of our own to have a backup plan, we will struggle to have this faith, but if we put our trust in heaven's power alone, we will move mountains.

Later, I will share some of the baby steps I have been taking recently in faith that this promise is really true. But you don't need my testimony. You have Peter's. You have the testimony of the water-walking, shadow-healing, corpse-raising fisherman from Galilee who heard these words and believed them. He was just as surprised as we are when he started acting as if these words were true and found that, by God's strength, he was able to carry on Jesus' story.

---

[4] Mark 11:25 echoes Matthew 6:14–15 so strongly that some scribes later inserted an extra verse 11:26 (not in the most accurate Greek manuscripts) in order to echo it more completely.

[5] If you know about Hebrew parallelisms, you will also notice that Jesus uses one in 11:23 to emphasise that *doubt* and *faith* over God's promises simply cannot coexist within the same heart.

Eviction Notice
(11:27–12:12)

What then will the owner of the vineyard do? He will come and kill those tenants and give the vineyard to others.

(Mark 12:9)

The members of the Jewish Sanhedrin were furious that Jesus had dared to purge their Temple.[1] As soon as he returned from Bethany the following morning, they accosted him in the Temple courtyards. *"By what authority are you doing these things?"* they demanded. *"And who gave you authority to do this?"*

The question was a very first-century Jewish one.[2] Their leaders spoke a great deal about authority. The members of the Sanhedrin knew they had authority because they had negotiated it from the Roman governor. They had authority because they had been recognised as priests and rabbis. Even though the Sanhedrin was a relatively new body, they had used their position as interpreters of the Old Testament to argue that they had authority as heirs to the seventy elders appointed by Moses in Numbers 11. Furthermore, they had authority because they were largely drawn from the aristocracy of Israel. They were wealthy, well-connected and well-qualified. They were everything that this upstart Galilean carpenter was not. Who

[1] The *chief priests* were the leaders of the 24 priestly families. The *teachers of the law* were the leading rabbis. Together with the *elders*, they formed the 71-member council that administered Jewish affairs for Governor Pilate.
[2] See Mark 2:7–10; John 2:18; Acts 4:7.

did he think he was to quality-control the religious wares that they were peddling in their Temple?

If the Jewish leaders thought that their aggressive questioning would bully Jesus into beating a hasty retreat, they were in for a surprise. The King of heaven had not ridden into his capital to be intimidated by a bunch of usurpers and charlatans. He darts back a question of his own. He will gladly talk about the source of his authority if they can tell him their assessment of John the Baptist. Now that Herod has eliminated the rugged prophet who baptised the repentant crowds in the River Jordan, surely they can take an honest view. Did his authority come from heaven or from men?

Jesus' simple question exposes the hypocrisy of the Jewish leaders. They cannot admit that John came with authority from heaven, or Jesus will rightly ask them why they refused to confess their own sins and repent with the crowds down at the river. Nor can they confess what they really believe, that John was an uneducated upstart who refused to listen to his elders and his betters. If they do, the crowds will know that their religious leaders are so spiritually blind that they tried to silence a powerful revival. *"We don't know,"* they respond glumly to Jesus. *"Neither will I tell you by what authority I am doing these things,"* Jesus replies. If the Jewish leaders were offended when he cleared the Temple yesterday, things are going to be even worse today.

Now Jesus goes on the offensive by telling the Parable of the Tenants.[3] It is the week of the Passover, the greatest festival in the Jewish calendar, so Jesus knows the Temple courtyards are filled with pilgrims listening to his every word. Having likened Israel to a fig-tree based on Jeremiah 24, Jesus now likens Israel to a vineyard based on several passages in the

---

[3] Mark says that Jesus told them several parables, even though he only recounts one of them. Matthew 21:28–22:14 adds that he also told them the Parable of the Two Sons and the Parable of the Wedding Banquet.

Psalms and Prophets.[4] The Jewish nation belongs to God. He brought it out of Egypt and into the Promised Land, and he has tended it throughout its long and turbulent history. The Jewish leaders are merely tenant-farmers who have been entrusted with overseeing God's vineyard for him.[5] Jesus issues them an eviction notice.

God has been sending prophets such as John the Baptist to the Jewish leaders for centuries in order to remind them that they are tenants and not owners of the vineyard. They have treated these prophets in a manner that reveals the hardness of their hearts towards God. They are not questioning Jesus about his authority because they want to spot a true messenger of God. They are questioning him because they find it easier to attack God's messengers than to listen to the penetrating challenge of their message. Herod murdered John the Baptist and they owe their own authority to a dirty deal with Herod. They have John the Baptist's blood on their hands.

Now Jesus moves onto the question of his own authority. He is the Messiah, the beloved Son of God, the one about whom the Lord might legitimately say: *"They will respect my Son."* Jesus warns the Jewish leaders what will happen if they persist in their plan to act like the wicked tenant-farmers in the parable and say, *"This is the heir. Come, let's kill him, and the inheritance will be ours."* Jesus predicts his death for the sixth time in Mark's gospel, and for the first time to anybody but the disciples. He does so in order to warn the Jewish leaders not to crucify him outside the city walls, as they are planning. If they do, God will not give up on the story of Israel. He will

---

[4] Some of the clearest passages are Psalm 80:8–16, Isaiah 3:14, 5:1–7 and 27:2, Jeremiah 2:21 and 12:10, Ezekiel 17:6–8 and 19:10–14, Hosea 10:1 and 14:7 and Micah 7:1.

[5] In Matthew 21:43, Jesus tells the Jewish leaders plainly that these tenant-farmers represent them. This is a parable, so God has not built a literal wall, pit and tower, any more than he has *"moved to another place."*

simply destroy them and invite the pagans to step into the story instead.

The crowds were right two days earlier to fulfil the prophecy in Psalm 118 by cutting branches off the trees and shouting *"Hosanna!"* and *"Blessed is he who comes in the name of the Lord!"* Now they need to follow this up by taking heed of the Psalm's solemn prediction that the Messiah will be rejected by the Jewish leaders, discarded by the Jewish nation and vindicated by God in the eyes of all the world: *"The stone the builders rejected has become the cornerstone; the Lord has done this, and it is marvellous in our eyes."*[6]

Jesus has just served the Jewish leaders with an eviction notice. He has told them they are tenant-farmers who refuse to pay their rent. Their questions about authority are a smokescreen to hide their rebellious desire to wield complete control of the nation of Israel, a desire so all-consuming that they are not even willing to share it with God himself. Jesus warns them that it is rent-payment day and that, unless they are willing to surrender everything to God, they are about to lose it all.

Jesus asks learned teachers of the law, *"Haven't you read this passage of Scripture?"* He asks Jewish priests to watch out what they are sacrificing. He asks members of the supreme court of Jewish affairs to pass judgment on themselves: *"What then will the owner of the vineyard do? He will come and kill those tenants and give the vineyard to others."*[7]

The irony is lost on his enemies. Instead of repenting, they start plotting how to fulfil the words of this parable by killing him. Instead of confessing their rent arrears, they resolve to

---

[6] Psalm 118:22–23 is such an important prophecy that it is also quoted in Matthew 21:42, Luke 20:17, Acts 4:11 and 1 Peter 2:7. A cornerstone was the foundation stone that anchored and aligned an entire wall.

[7] Jesus teaches us an important evangelistic tactic by using questions to trap these unbelievers into passing judgment on themselves. Matthew 21:41 says he even forced them to reply. See also 2 Samuel 12:1–7.

defy this eviction notice. They hold back for fear of the crowd but they have already made up their minds: This is not the Messiah they are looking for. This man has to die.

Revolution (12:13–17)

*Is it right to pay the poll tax to Caesar or not? Should
we pay or shouldn't we?*

(Mark 12:14–15)

There was a word for subjects of the Roman Empire who dared
to defy the edicts of their rulers. The word was *dead*. Roman
emperors did not hesitate to murder their parents, their
brothers and their children to cling onto power. They would not
hesitate to kill a Galilean preacher who told the Jews to defy the
tax collectors of Rome.

Don't miss how cynical the Jewish leaders are in their first
attempt to murder Jesus after he serves them with their eviction
notice. The Pharisees were separatists who hated Roman
culture, Roman laws and any Jew who cosied up to Roman
rule. Their natural enemies were therefore the Herodians, but
Mark 3:6 tells us that the two groups formed an odd alliance
after clashing with Jesus, uniting around him as an even greater
enemy. The stench of hypocrisy is overwhelming as they
praise Jesus for being a rabbi of great integrity and willingness
to speak God's truth, no matter who it may offend. All this is
blarney. Mark tells us they are trying to trick him into inciting
a revolution. If he refuses to condemn the payment of taxes to
the Romans, the crowds will stop looking to him as their long-
awaited Saviour. If he opposes the payment of taxes, they can
hand him over to the Roman governor to be executed. It's heads
they win and tails he loses.[1]

---

[1] See Luke 23:2. The Greek word *agreuō* in 12:13 means literally *to hunt
an animal*. They are trying to snare Jesus but he makes them step into their

They want to force Jesus into making a *political statement*. The Roman *kēnsos* was a poll tax paid by the subject peoples of the empire as a tribute to their Roman masters. Roman citizens were exempt and so it came to represent the oppressive rule of Rome.

They want to force Jesus into making a *religious statement*. The denarius with which the poll tax was paid bore the head of the Emperor Tiberius. In case there was some room to doubt whether or not this counted as an image of a false god, the head was surrounded by an inscription that hailed him as *"Tiberius Caesar, Son of the Divine Augustus."* Many devout Jews refused even to touch such dirty Roman coinage.

They want to force Jesus into making a *messianic statement*. The war cry of the Maccabean revolt had been, *"Pay back to the Gentiles what they deserve, and always obey the Law and its commands."*[2] They therefore want to know if Jesus will follow up his triumphal entry into Jerusalem with a call to a new Maccabean revolution. Perhaps he is friendly with the tax collectors because he is as comfortable with Roman rule as they are.

Jesus sees straight through their hypocrisy. He tells them that he knows they are trying to trap him but, instead of sidestepping their question as they did his in 11:33, he turns the trap back on them. He uses it to expose their sinful rebellion against the Lord.

He asks them to bring him a denarius. Some people assume that this is evidence he was so poor that he did not have one himself, since the coin was equivalent to a day's wages. John 12:6 tells us this is not the case. Jesus asked to borrow one of their coins in order to highlight their hypocrisy to the crowds. As the ranks of money changers in the Temple courtyards testified, the

hunting trap themselves.

[2] 1 Maccabees 2:68. In contrast, Jesus taught in Matthew 5:41 that obeying the Law meant loving the Romans.

Jewish leaders were only too happy to handle Caesar's money. They had grown rich by profiteering from its pagan images.

When they bring him one of Caesar's coins, Jesus pushes his point further. Drawing attention to the image of the Emperor Tiberius and to the blasphemous inscription around his head, he rephrases the Maccabean war cry for a new generation: *"Give back to Caesar what is Caesar's."* Jesus is being deliberately ambiguous. Is he supporting the Roman regime? No. He is calling the Jews to send Roman images back to Rome. They have no place in the Temple courtyards. Is he inciting armed rebellion against the Roman regime? No. His is not a revolution of vengeance on the pagans, but a revolution of personal holiness.

The crowds are very surprised. They expected the Messiah to spearhead the Jewish fight against the Romans. Even the disciples expected this, still asking him hopefully after his resurrection in Acts 1:6, *"Lord, are you at this time going to restore the kingdom to Israel?"* Jesus' call to revolution was unexpected and surprising. He proclaimed that the biggest enemy of the Jews was not the Romans but themselves. Their greatest fight was not against foreigners on the outside but against sin on the inside.

Jesus has done what the Jewish leaders wanted. He has launched a massive revolution. But it is not the revolution they are expecting. It is not a revolution against the Roman Empire. It is God's Kingdom revolution, which calls the nations to reject the invisible idols of this sinful world. Caesar can keep his failed currency of human wealth and human power. *"Give back to Caesar what is Caesar's and to God what is God's."* Don't miss the second part. It is a call to revolution. Jesus urges us to throw away everything this world holds most dear in order to step into God's unfolding story.

We were made to bear the image of God in the same way that a denarius was made to bear the image of Caesar.[3] Far from

---

[3] Genesis 1:26–27; 9:6; 1 Corinthians 11:7; James 3:9.

dividing the world into sacred and secular spheres through his reply to the Jewish leaders, Jesus is telling us that our entire lives belong to God.[4] The Messiah did not come to free 7,000 square miles of Middle Eastern territory from the Romans. He did not come to purify a sacred building or to vindicate one people group against another. He did not come to defeat Rome, but Satan. He did not come to kill the Romans, but to save them. He did not come to destroy the pagans through an army of Jews. He came to recruit an army of sinful Jews and pagans who will march behind their common Saviour.

So away with the failed currency of this world. Jesus asks you to join his revolution. He asks you to believe that pierced hands will triumph over jewelled fingers, that a crown of thorns will triumph over a crown of gold, and that submission will triumph over swords and spears. Give back to Caesar what belongs to his fading world – he is welcome to have all of it – and give yourself entirely to following the King of heaven.

---

4 These verses have been used to promote a sacred–secular divide, as well as to sanction slavish obedience to earthly powers. Both of these interpretations miss the point. They minimise God's Kingdom revolution.

Dead Poets (12:18–37)

He is not the God of the dead, but of the living. You are badly mistaken!

(Mark 12:27)

In the classic movie *Dead Poets Society*, Robin Williams warns a class of students not to analyse great poetry in the same way that a scientist studies a machine. He tells them to read an essay by Mr J. Evans-Pritchard, which teaches them to assess the greatness of a poem by scoring it on various measures. Then he explodes:

> *Excrement. That's what I think of Mr J. Evans-Pritchard. We're not laying pipe. We're talking about poetry. How can you describe poetry like American Bandstand: "I like Byron, I give him a 42, but I can't dance to it"? Now I want you to rip out that page. Go on, rip out the entire page.... I want it gone. History. Leave nothing of it. Rip it out. Rip! Begone, J. Evans-Pritchard, PhD! Rip, shred, tear! Rip it out!... Make a clean tear. I want nothing left of it... Keep ripping, gentlemen! This is a battle, a war, and the casualties could be your hearts and souls. Armies of academics going forward, measuring poetry? No! We'll not have that here!"*[1]

The Jewish leaders treated the Old Testament Scriptures as the words of dead poets.[2] They continue to circle Jesus, vying

---

[1] *Dead Poets Society* (Touchstone Pictures, 1989).

[2] They say *"Moses wrote for us"* (12:19), whereas Jesus says *"David spoke by the Holy Spirit"* (12:36).

with one another to see which one of them can provoke him into saying something that will either lose the support of the crowds or provoke the ire of the Romans and therefore get him killed. He deals with them as they come at him, one by one, but his message remains the same. They need to grasp the true faith of the Old Testament. If they do not, they are about to lose the battle for their souls.

In verses 18–27, Jesus responds to a question from the Sadducees. These were members of the sect that ruled the Temple, having convinced their Roman governors that they were pragmatic politicians who could be trusted to administer Jewish affairs for Rome. They were so committed to the Law of Moses that they rejected the other thirty-four books of the Old Testament, as if Moses could teach them everything they needed. The Pentateuch says little about life beyond the grave, so they despised the common Jews for believing in heaven and hell.[3] They therefore pose a question to Jesus – if a woman marries seven brothers in accordance with the rules about levirate marriage in Deuteronomy 25:5–10, to which of them will she be married in heaven?[4]

Jesus tells the Sadducees that they know about as much about the Law of Moses as Mr J. Evans-Pritchard knows about poetry: *"Are you not in error because you do not know the Scriptures or the power of God?"*[5] They are so fixated on romantic love as an invisible idol that they cannot conceive of any paradise where marriage does not continue as today, but Jesus is a single thirty-something who has found complete fulfilment

---

[3] Acts 23:8 tells us that the Sadducees refused to believe in the resurrection of the dead or in angels.

[4] God commanded this in order to raise up an heir for a man who died without a child to carry on his name.

[5] Jesus accused the Jewish leaders of misreading the Old Testament in 2:25 and 12:10, but he goes one step further with the Sadducees in 12:24. At least the Pharisees believed in God's miraculous power.

in his relationship with his Father.[6] Since the Sadducees do not believe in angels, Jesus highlights their blindness by informing them that we will no more marry in heaven than do the angels. Then he takes a quotation from Exodus 3:6, one of five books of the Old Testament that they claim to honour, and uses it to prove that there is life beyond the grave. Faith in God is not about analysing dead poets. It is about living with him forever!

In verses 28–34, one of the teachers of the law has a turn.[7] He tries to draw Jesus into their practice of dissecting the Law of Moses and playing verses off one against another. He asks him to tell the crowds which Old Testament commandment he sees as the most important. Jesus chooses two, and both are extremely practical. Deuteronomy 6:4–5 tells us to love the Lord with all our being, and Leviticus 19:18 tells us to love other people as much as we love ourselves.[8] The teachers of the law were great at compiling lists of dead rules but they were very poor at remembering to live a life of love towards the Lord and one another.[9] Jesus exposes how much the lawmakers of Israel are lawbreakers in Israel.

The teacher of the law beats a hasty retreat, praising Jesus for his answer and claiming that this is what he and his Pharisee friends would also say. Jesus is not fooled. He warns him, *"You are not far from the kingdom of God"* – in other words,

---

[6] Jesus is not saying that we will fail to recognise our former spouses in heaven. He is simply saying that things will not be the same as on earth. This is good news for single, divorced or unhappily married people!

[7] Matthew 22:34–35 tells us that this teacher was a Pharisee and that he was also trying to trap Jesus.

[8] Deuteronomy 6:5 only tells us to love the Lord with all our *heart*, *soul* and *strength*. Jesus adds the command to love him with all our *mind* because the answer to dead theology is not anti-intellectualism. It is to use our minds as God intended them to be used, as an aid to genuine worship.

[9] See Matthew 9:13 and 12:7. Jesus also taught this "law of love" in Luke 10:25–28. It is repeated in James 2:8, Galatians 5:13–14, Romans 13:8–10, 1 John 3:23 and 1Timothy 1:5.

you are not saved yet but you will be saved if you turn your dead rhetoric into living faith.

Robin Williams addresses this theme again in the film *Good Will Hunting*. He challenges an arrogant student:

> *If I asked you about art, you'd probably give me the skinny on every art book ever written. Michelangelo. You know a lot about him. Life's work, political aspirations, him and the pope, sexual orientation, the whole works, right? But I bet you can't tell me what it smells like in the Sistine Chapel. You've never actually stood there and looked up at that beautiful ceiling... If I ask you about love, you'd probably quote me a sonnet. But you've never looked at a woman and been totally vulnerable, known someone that could level you with her eyes.*[10]

Analysing the words of Scripture cannot help us unless we learn to imitate the living faith of the dead.

In verses 35–37, Jesus goes on the offensive. He challenges the teachers of the law to tell the crowds how to interpret Psalm 110:1. How can David, inspired by the Holy Spirit, call the Messiah his *"Lord"*?[11] If the Messiah is nothing more than the son of David, he would not be worshipped by his ancestor. It usually works the other way around. But if the Messiah is more than just the son of David, if he is in fact the Son of God, why do they refuse to listen to what he says? Why do they cling to their muddled ideas about dead poets when they are standing in the presence of the living Word of God?

The crowds are surprised but delighted. They have never heard anybody stand up to the Pharisees and Sadducees like

---

[10] *Good Will Hunting* (Miramax Films, 1997).

[11] Jesus affirms in 12:36 that all Scripture is God-breathed (2 Timothy 3:16; 2 Peter 1:20–21). It is not the words of dead poets. It is the words of the living God.

this before.[12] They recognise the truth: that their teachers read the Old Testament in the same way that Mr J. Evans-Pritchard reads poetry. They begin to understand why the Messiah has not come to affirm first-century Judaism, but to undermine it through a clear restatement of the faith of Abraham. They begin to understand that they need to repent of treating Scripture as the work of dead poets and to start treating it as the God-inspired record of people's living faith in him. So do we.

---

[12] Ironically, preaching which compromises with the world attracts very few listeners. Radical preaching which confronts this world's idols in the name of God, however, never fails to find delighted hearers.

Cinderella at the Ball
(12:38–44)

Many rich people threw in large amounts. But a poor widow came and put in two very small copper coins, worth only a few pence.

(Mark 12:41–42)

The story of Cinderella strikes a chord with people of any culture. There is a universal ugliness in sinful people believing they are righteous and a universal pleasure in seeing virtue rewarded in the downtrodden. That's why I love the last few verses of this chapter. They are the Cinderella story of Mark's gospel.

Jesus turns to the Jewish crowds in the Temple courtyards and warns them that their leaders are like Cinderella's ugly sisters. They think they are beautiful to God, but their actions are grotesque and repulsive. They are consumed with externals: wearing fine robes, receiving fine greetings, sitting on fine seats in the synagogues and receiving fine honours at banquets. They are concerned to look like good believers, making lengthy prayers and throwing their money into the Temple treasury with a great fanfare, but they are not concerned with actually being good believers.[1] They assume that God is bound to show them favour, in the same way that the ugly sisters blindly assume that Prince Charming is bound to choose them to become his bride.

---

[1] The parallel passage in Matthew 23 emphasises that pretending to be spiritually better than we are is one of the primary things which turns us into ugly sisters. Jesus uses the word *hypocrite* seven times.

But Jesus replies with a terrible verdict: *"They devour widows' houses… These men will be punished most severely."*[2]

Offensive though this message was in Jerusalem, it was music to the ears of Mark's original readers in Rome. One of their biggest objections to Christianity was that they thought it was an invitation to become like the sinful Jews in their city. Mark records Jesus' teaching in the Temple courtyards to reassure them that the Christian Gospel is not a call to adopt the ugly-sister attitude of the Pharisees. It is a call to become like Cinderella. Paul constantly reaffirmed this as he preached to pagans across the Roman Empire: *"It is because of my hope in what God has promised our ancestors that I am on trial today. This is the promise our twelve tribes are hoping to see fulfilled."*[3] The Christian Gospel is a call to return to the faith of the ancient Hebrews before it became corrupted by the yeast of the Pharisees and Sadducees.

Now enter Cinderella. Jesus looks over towards the offering box in the Temple courtyards where worshippers are bringing their financial gifts to the Lord. He sees wealthy establishment Jews making much of their generosity as they throw large sums of money into the offering box, but his attention is captivated by a poor widow. She doesn't come in fine clothes, but in rags. She doesn't receive any welcome greeting. But in her poverty she refuses to offer God a tithe using the meticulous measuring stick of the Pharisees.[4] She throws two tiny copper coins into the offering box, despite the fact that they are all she has to

---

[2] Jesus tells us that there will be different levels of reward and punishment in heaven and in hell. Those who seek their reward on earth through ugly-sister religion will be punished all the more severely later.

[3] Acts 13:32–33; 24:14; 26:6–7; 28:20; Galatians 4:25–26; 6:16; Ephesians 3:6.

[4] Jesus is not condemning tithing. He affirms it in Matthew 23:23, but stresses that we ought to give away enough to force us to rely completely on the Lord. For the rich this is far more than 10% of what they have.

live on.[5] Jesus singles her out to his disciples as the kind of worshipper that God is looking for. God is never impressed with ugly-sister religion, but he always delights in Cinderellas.

If you are Jewish, don't be offended, or at least be offended in the right way. Mark is writing for Gentiles so he only gives us a brief summary of Jesus' teaching. Matthew writes for Jews so he expands Mark 12:38–40 into a whopping thirty-nine verses of detail in Matthew 23. Jesus spoke these words for Jews as much as for Gentiles. He exposes the ugly-sister weaknesses in Judaism in order to call you back to the faith of your fathers as it was experienced by Abraham, Jacob, Moses and David.

In the Disney movie of the Cinderella story, the ugly sisters resist this challenge right to the very end. When the servants of Prince Charming arrive at their house with a glass slipper and tell them what kind of bride he is looking for, they carry on pretending. One of them says, *"There. I knew it was my slipper. Exactly my size... Well, it may be a trifle snug today. You know how it is, dancing all night. I can't understand why. It's always fit perfectly before... It must have shrunk or something. A glass shoe isn't always reliable."*[6] Don't resist what Jesus says about the Jewish religion, as many people are experiencing it today. He offends us because he wants us to discover the faith of Abraham in all its original beauty.

Jesus encourages us that conversion to Christianity is not an invitation to put on the grotesque slipper of the Pharisees and Sadducees. It is not an invitation to analyse the Scriptures as the writings of dead poets or to measure out our minimum devotion to the Lord. What matters is not how much we give to God, but how much we hold back. We are to give so generously that we are forced to rely on him instead of on our money. We are to live so servant-heartedly that we are forced to rely on him

---

[5] The Greek text says she gave two tiny brass coins called a *lepton*. A denarius was worth 128 lepta, so her entire offering was worth less than 2% of the coin Jesus held up earlier.

[6] *Cinderella* (Walt Disney Productions, 1950).

to promote us instead of our own power. We are to obey him so radically in everything that it costs us the approval of our family and friends, leaving us with no comfort save our relationship with him. Jesus encourages us in the parallel passage in Matthew 23:12: *"Those who exalt themselves will be humbled, and those who humble themselves will be exalted."*

Mark encourages us not to view the demands of true religion as an attractive but essentially unrealistic fairy tale. We must not be like the King's cynical servant in the Disney film, who sneers: *"A pretty plot for fairy tales, Sire. But in real life, oh no. No, it was foredoomed to failure."* He is ashamed when the King points to the happy couple together and asks him triumphantly, *"Failure, eh? Ha ha! Take a look at that, you pompous windbag!"*

So let's take a good look at this widow, the Cinderella of Mark's gospel, and let's celebrate that Jesus is restoring the ancient religion of Israel to the world. He is sounding the death-knell for the pompous rule-keeping of the Pharisees and for the pragmatism of the Sadducees. He is restoring to us the faith that made the childless Abraham believe he would become a mighty nation, that made the nomad Jacob believe he would possess the Promised Land, that made the Hebrew slaves in Egypt believe God had chosen them to be his People, and that made the prophets believe God would save people from every nation through the Messiah dying at the hands of the Jewish leaders.

Let's be surprised and elated that the Gospel is much more than the news of a Jewish victory over the Romans. It is a call for Jew and Gentile to believe together that God's Prince Charming has come into the world to rescue many unworthy Cinderellas.

The Surprise of All History
(13:1–37)

Be on guard! Be alert! You do not know when that time will come.

(Mark 13:33)

To say that the thirteenth chapter of Mark's gospel is surprising would be a massive understatement. For a start, it sticks out from the rest of the gospel because it consists of one long sermon which was spoken by Jesus on a particular day. Nowhere else in this action-packed gospel does Mark slow down to give us such a detailed account of Jesus' teaching on a particular theme. These verses are therefore of crucial importance. Jesus uses the walk back to the Mount of Olives to teach his disciples what is going to happen throughout AD history. This chapter is full of surprises. Very little of what God had planned for the centuries to come was going to be as the disciples had expected.

In verses 1–2, Jesus talks about *the future for the Jewish nation*. As they are leaving the Temple, one of his disciples remarks on the size of some of its stones, which are eleven metres wide.[1] Jesus tells them sadly that his showdown with the Jewish leaders has not gone well, and that their stubbornness is about to prove fatal.[2] A time is shortly coming when the Temple will

---

[1] Josephus tells us in his *Antiquities of the Jews* (15.11.3) that some of the stones were 11 metres long, 5.5 metres wide and 3.5 metres high. The disciples were impressed for a reason!

[2] Since there is no record in the gospels of Jesus ever going back to the Temple after his resurrection, it appears that he says this as he leaves the Temple for the very last time.

be destroyed. Forty years after Jesus spoke these words, in 70 AD, the Romans would fulfil this prophecy by sacking Jerusalem. They would slaughter over a million Jews as they razed both the city and its Temple to the ground.[3] They would build a temple to Jupiter on the site of the old Jewish Temple. If the Sanhedrin thought they could reject God's Messiah and survive, they were in for a terrible surprise.

In verses 3–8, Jesus talks about *the future for the world.* When he arrives at his evening camp in the Garden of Gethsemane on the Mount of Olives, Peter and three other disciples ask him to explain this further.[4] He warns that, although his Kingdom has arrived on earth, it has not yet reached its completion. The period between his ascension to heaven and his return in glory will be marked by trials and conflict, like an expectant mother in the throes of labour. There will be false messiahs peddling false religion. There will be wars and natural disasters and famines.[5] News reports will make people think that the world is about to come to an end, but we should not be alarmed. These are simply the signs of a sinful world order taking its last stand before its rightful King returns to usher in the fullness of the age to come.

In verses 9–13, Jesus talks about *the future for the Church.* We really should not find it surprising that the world hates us as it hated Jesus but, because we often do, Jesus spells it out for us in detail. Church history will be a combination of fierce opposition and of glorious advance for the Gospel throughout the nations. Whenever believers tone down their message for the sake of a quiet life, the Church will go the same way as

---

[3] Josephus tells us this in his *Wars of the Jews* (6.9.3), adding that *"nothing was left there to make visitors believe it had ever been inhabited"* (7.1.1). Jesus was so distressed by this that he wept over Jerusalem in Luke 19:41–44.

[4] Although Jesus stayed at Mary and Martha's house in Bethany on previous nights, he now camped on the Mount of Olives (Luke 21:37; 22:39–40). This is how Judas knew where to find him the following evening.

[5] The parallel Luke 21:9–11 also adds to this list *revolutions* and *plagues.*

Jerusalem, but whenever they speak up for their Lord in spite of the terrible consequences, they will emerge victorious through the fire.

In verses 14–23, Jesus uses *the fate of Jerusalem as a picture of the fate of the whole world.* Some of the detail in these verses is clearly talking about what befell Jerusalem in 70 AD. Jesus quotes from the book of Daniel to describe the Temple being defiled by "the abomination which causes desolation",[6] and most of the Christian inhabitants of Jerusalem were saved from its destruction because they obeyed the command, *"Let those who are in Judea flee to the mountains."*[7] At the same time, some of the detail is also clearly talking about the end of world history. Mark says, *"let the reader understand,"* because Jesus did not speak these words for a single generation. Daniel 9:27 suggests that the defilement of the Temple was a picture of what the Devil and his false messiahs will try to do to the Church throughout the centuries of AD history. We must not be impressed or intimidated by the counterfeit miracles they perform to gain a hearing for their message. God will protect his chosen People, even as he protected his chosen remnant in Jerusalem in 70 AD.[8] Despite the enemy's attacks, God's Kingdom cannot fail.

In verses 24–27, Jesus tells us *how world history is going to end.* It will not be through a manmade catastrophe, although he refers back to Isaiah 13:10 and 34:4 to remind us that the whole of creation will reap the terrible consequences of human sin. History will end when God gives the word and when Jesus

---

[6] This referred to King Antiochus IV's statue of Zeus in Daniel 9:27, 11:31 and 12:11, so Jesus uses it to describe the way in which the Romans would respond to the Jewish Revolt in 66–73 AD.

[7] Eusebius of Caesarea tells us this in his *Church History* (3.5.3), written just after 300 AD.

[8] Jesus speaks three times in 13:20, 22 and 27 about God's sovereign decision to predestine those he has chosen to salvation. Although we may not understand this fully, we can be fully reassured.

returns to assert fully the fact that he is King of all the earth.[9] For now, he allows sin and rebellion to continue because he wants to save sinful rebels instead of destroying them. But a day is coming when our opportunity to step into his story will be taken away.[10]

In verses 28–37, Jesus therefore warns us to *get ready for the surprise of all history*. When a fig-tree sprouts leaves, we know that summer is almost here. When we experience the things Jesus predicts in this chapter, we know that his triumphant return is also just around the corner. Jesus promises in verse 30 that the Jewish race will not be extinguished, no matter how hard Satan tries, because the Jews have not been replaced in his heart by the Gentiles. He has simply invited the Gentiles to step into the Jewish story.[11] Since nobody knows when he will return – neither Jesus nor any of his angels, but only God the Father[12] – we must therefore live in readiness, watching for the return of Jesus at any time.[13] One day those who wait expectantly for his return will be proven right and will be rewarded for siding with the King before his great return in power.[14]

[9] What Jesus says about himself in 13:26 is ludicrous unless he is claiming to be God. He is in fact referring back to Daniel 7:13–14, assuring his disciples that he will completely fulfil those messianic promises.

[10] Jesus explains in Matthew 13:24–30 and 36–43 that this is why he delays his return.

[11] We have already seen that in Mark's gospel the Greek word *genea* often refers to the Jewish race rather than simply to a particular *generation*. The survival of the Jewish race against all odds is a powerful testimony that all of God's promises will come true. In 13:31, Jesus equates his own words to the words of God.

[12] Although he is fully God, Jesus submits to his Father as a perfect example of how we are to submit to him. Jesus limited his knowledge during his earthly ministry, modelling how to trust in the Father's wisdom.

[13] Jesus tells the disciples literally to *"Stay awake!"* in 13:33, 35 and 37. He says this knowing full well that Peter, James and John are likely to fall asleep at a vital moment in 14:32–42.

[14] Matthew 24 gives a longer account of Jesus' teaching in Mark 13. Matthew 25 follows it up with three parables that emphasise that how we wait for his return will affect our reward in the age to come.

The thirteenth chapter of Mark's gospel is therefore very surprising but, as a result, the events of AD history should come as no surprise to us at all. Jesus has warned us what will happen between his ascension to heaven and his return to earth in glory. The King has readied his subjects to be unsurprised as the surprise of all history unfolds.

Christians Die (13:9–13)

Everyone will hate you because of me, but the one
who stands firm to the end will be saved.

(Mark 13:13)

I have read many encouraging verses in Christian greeting cards over the years, but I have never read the verse Jesus used to encourage his disciples a couple of days before his crucifixion. He told them: *"Everyone will hate you because of me, but the one who stands firm to the end will be saved."*

Perhaps that's part of the problem. Most of us have been taught to expect the Christian life to be an easy ride, so we get offended when we discover that it isn't. We are somehow surprised to discover that following a person the world hated does not result in our being loved. We are somehow astonished that following a person who was murdered for what he said does not result in our own words being accepted and applauded. Unless we understand that being hated and rejected by the world is very normal for a Christian, we will never develop the resilient faith which Jesus' followers need in order to be able to carry on his story.

Peter and Andrew would be crucified. James would be beheaded. John would be exiled from his home. Jesus therefore warns them that they will be hauled before councils and synagogues and kings as part and parcel of what it means to be his witnesses.[1] They will be betrayed by family members

---

[1] Jesus refers to two sets of Jewish bodies (*sanhedrins* and *synagogues*) and to two sets of Gentile rulers (*governors* and *kings*) in order to emphasise that we will be hated by the whole world.

and friends. They will be executed by religious leaders who are so deluded that they actually think they are doing God a favour by ridding the earth of them.[2] Jesus prepares the disciples for persecution so they will be ready to face it when it comes. Unless they understand that following the one who wore a crown of thorns can never be a bed of roses, they will be surprised at persecution and will tone down their message, thinking that they must be doing something wrong.[3]

Jesus gives us three wonderful promises in these verses to help us if people persecute us for proclaiming the Gospel. No, scrub that. Jesus does not say if – that everyone *may* hate us because of him. He tells us that everyone *will* hate us. Jesus therefore gives us three wonderful promises in these verses to help us when the inevitable happens and people start to persecute us for following him. If we do not need these promises then it is probably an indication that we have misread what it means to step into his story.

Jesus promises in verse 10 that the Gospel will be preached in every nation. Don't miss how oversized this promise is when given to four fishermen from Galilee. Their world was so small that Matthew, Mark and John refer to a body of water only thirteen miles long and eight miles wide as the *Sea* of Galilee. Luke, an educated doctor from Antioch, knows the world well enough to call it what it really is: *Lake* Galilee.[4] After Jesus' resurrection, the disciples would lock themselves inside a house because they were afraid of the Jews, let alone the Gentiles. The idea that these men might take the Gospel "*to all nations*" was

PART FOUR: THE SURPRISING STORY

210

[2] See John 16:2. The parallel Matthew 24:10 warns us that some of our greatest opponents will be so-called Christians. Jesus teaches on this theme in greater detail in Matthew 10:16–39.

[3] Jesus tells us that successful evangelism draws hatred and opposition as well as converts.

[4] Compare Matthew 4:18 and 15:29, Mark 1:16, 3:7 and 7:31, John 6:1 and 21:1, with Luke 5:1 and 8:23. The exaggerated terminology which the disciples use to describe the hub of their little world is so embarrassing that some English translations even change their word *sea* to read *lake* in these verses.

laughable, but Jesus promised he would empower them through the Holy Spirit to do so.

Jesus promises in verse 11 that they do not need to worry about what they will say when persecuted. When the world hurls its greatest resources against them, God will ensure that they have all the resources they need from heaven. The Holy Spirit will inspire them, so they can relax: *"Just say whatever is given you at the time, for it is not you speaking, but the Holy Spirit."* The advance of the Gospel will not depend on the brilliance of their sermon preparation. It will depend on their willingness to suffer on behalf of Jesus' name.

Jesus promises in verse 13 that they and their Church will eventually prevail. Every believer who stands firm to the end will be saved. Every congregation that refuses to compromise with the culture around it will succeed in renewing that culture. Every group of Christians that determines to follow in the footsteps of its suffering Saviour will become the means of God's salvation to the nations. Travelling across the globe, they will eventually persuade people from every single nation to submit to Jesus' name.[5]

These three promises encouraged the early Christians to accept persecution as part and parcel of stepping into Jesus' story. When Polycarp was put on trial for his refusal to pray to Caesar as Lord in 156 AD, he asked the prosecutor, *"I have served Jesus for eighty-six years and he has never done me any wrong. How can I blaspheme my King who saved me?"* When the prosecutor pleaded with him not to go to death at the stake, he laughed at the sacrifice: *"You threaten me with fire which burns for a season and is quickly quenched, for you are ignorant of the judgment fire which is coming, and of the eternal punishment*

---

[5] Paul sees his own suffering for the Gospel as the continuation of the suffering Saviour's story in Colossians 1:22–24. John sees people from every ethnic group, not just nation, worshipping Jesus in Revelation 7:9–10.

which awaits the ungodly. Why are you taking so long? Bring it on. Do what you wish."[6]

These three promises encouraged Martin Luther to accept persecution as part and parcel of stepping into Jesus' story. When his friends pleaded with him not to go and defend the Gospel at his trial in the German city of Worms, he told them that *"Even if there were as many devils in Worms as tiles on the roofs I would still come."*[7] These promises encouraged Bishop Latimer to accept being burned at the stake for the sake of the Gospel in the English city of Oxford in 1555, telling one of his friends: *"Be of good comfort, Master Ridley, and play the man. We shall this day light such a candle, by God's grace, in England, as I trust shall never be put out."*[8] They encouraged John Knox to endure being made a galley slave, praying just before he died:

> *Lord, grant faithful pastors, men who will preach and teach, in season and out of season. Lord, give us men who would gladly preach their next sermon even if it meant going to the stake for it. Lord, give us men who will hate all falsehood and lies, whether in the Church or out of it. Lord, grant to Your struggling Church men who fear You above all.* [9]

In the movie *Oblivion*, Tom Cruise is faced with a choice. He has discovered a secret which will save the world but only if he is willing to sacrifice his own life in the process. When somebody tries to deter him, he instantly replies: *"Everybody dies, Sally. The thing is to die well."*[10] How will we respond to the Gospel message in a world that hates Jesus? Will we compromise in

---

[6] His words were recorded shortly after his death in *The Martyrdom of Polycarp* (chapters 8–11).

[7] Quoted by Hans Hillerbrand in *The Reformation in Its Own Words* (1964).

[8] Quoted in *Foxe's Book of Martyrs* (1563).

[9] Quoted by Douglas Wilson in *For Kirk and Covenant: The Stalwart Courage of John Knox* (2000).

[10] *Oblivion* (Universal Pictures, 2013).

fear or will we believe in the Gospel to triumph through our painful sacrifice? Will we draw faith from the promises of Jesus in these verses? Everybody dies, even Christians. The thing is to die well.

Riches to Rags (14:1–11)

*"Why this waste of perfume? It could have been sold
for more than a year's wages and the money given to
the poor." And they rebuked her harshly.*

(Mark 14:4–5)

Everybody knew what the Passover festival was – even Mark's
Roman readers. It was the yearly celebration of the day 1,500
years earlier when God had rescued his chosen People from
slavery in Egypt. One day they were slaves. The next they were
plundering their former masters and leaving town with their
carts full of the best of Egypt's treasures. The blood of the
Passover lamb had changed everything. It was the ultimate
rags-to-riches story.

But that was only half the story. The one-day Passover was
immediately followed by the week-long Festival of Unleavened
Bread. Jews across the Roman Empire would rid their homes of
yeast and go through the motions of humbling themselves before
the Lord. Their poor man's bread demonstrated that having our
rags turned to riches by God must always result in our being
willing to turn our riches into rags for God. Moses had been
brought up in Pharaoh's palace, served by slaves, but his faith
in the God of his Hebrew fathers had meant turning his back
on Egyptian wealth, Egyptian power and his Egyptian adoptive
family. He is commended for this in Hebrews 11:24–26:

> *By faith Moses, when he had grown up, refused to be
> known as the son of Pharaoh's daughter. He chose to be
> ill-treated along with the people of God rather than to*

*enjoy the fleeting pleasures of sin. He regarded disgrace
for the sake of Christ as of greater value than the treasures
of Egypt, because he was looking ahead to his reward.*

Mark expects us to know this background at the start of chapter 14. He reminds us in verse 1 that the Passover and the Festival of Unleavened Bread go hand-in-hand together. He uses the reactions of the people around Jesus to challenge us. Have we truly grasped that following Jesus is not just a rags-to-riches story? Have we grasped that it also calls us to turn our riches into rags?[1]

In verses 1–2, we are reminded that the Jewish leaders are unwilling to do so. Even though the chief priests are meant to be preparing for the slaughter of many lambs, they are instead consumed with plotting how to slaughter Jesus. They view the crowd of Passover pilgrims as an irritant, an impediment to killing Jesus quickly because they may riot if their leaders arrest their Messiah. It has taken these priests and rabbis many years to turn their rags into riches through collaborating with the Romans. They are not about to let Jesus upset everything by turning their riches into rags.

In verse 3, we are reminded that Jesus is willing to do what they are not. He left the glory of heaven to become a tiny baby and a humble carpenter and a hated street preacher. Mark emphasises this by telling us that he ate dinner in the home of a man named Simon the Leper – a leper who had presumably been healed by Jesus, if he were able to host a dinner party, but a man whose nickname still spoke about his former shame. Mark wants to remind us that Jesus stooped very low so that he could save and set us free. While the Jewish leaders fretted about losing their favour with Rome, Jesus was extending a hand of friendship to former lepers and nobodies.

In verse 3, we have a challenging example of somebody

---

[1] John 12:2–8 tells us that Mark 14:3–11 actually took place the night before Jesus' triumphal entry into Jerusalem. Mark recounts the event out of order so that he can use it to bring us to a point of decision.

who was willing to turn her riches into rags for the sake of Jesus. Mark does not name her as Mary of Bethany (we only discover this in John 12:3) because she could be anyone of us. We may not have seen somebody we know healed of leprosy or our brother raised from the dead, but we have our own reasons to be grateful towards Jesus.[2] She brings an alabaster jar of nard, a perfume which had to be imported from India and which was therefore so expensive that it was normally reserved for kings.[3] It is worth 300 denarii – over a year's salary – but she gladly smashes open the jar and anoints Jesus' head and body with her perfume.[4] Her gift is 20,000 times more valuable than the two copper coins the widow threw into the offering box in the Temple, but it means the same.[5] It means that Jesus is worth far more to her than her money. It means that she is willing to throw away all she holds dear in order to step into his story.

In verses 4–9, the dinner guests are offended by the price Jesus expects his followers to pay. Mark does not tell us that those most offended were the disciples, and principally Judas (we are only told this by Matthew and John), because again he wants to stress that they could be anyone of us. They are so affected by the respectable idols of this world that they are appalled someone might throw away their riches as an act of worship. Doesn't this woman know that money makes the world go round?[6] This expensive perfume could have been

---

[2] See John 11:1–12:11. Since John tells us that Martha served as hostess at this dinner, it appears that Simon the Leper was a close relative – possibly Martha's husband.

[3] Perhaps Mary is deliberately re-enacting Song of Songs 1:12, where King Solomon's royal bride expresses her love for him by telling us literally that *"While the king was at his table, my nard spread its fragrance."*

[4] Mark says she anointed his head, but John 12:3 says she anointed his feet. Jesus clarifies in Mark 14:8 that she anointed his whole body.

[5] Mark 14:5 tells us that the perfume was worth over 300 denarii, deliberately linking back to 12:15 and 42.

[6] The unbelieving world always approves of the Church when it helps the poor, because it believes that money solves all ills. What it never understands is such devotion to Jesus that we throw away our money.

sold and used to promote Jesus' ministry, especially his desire to help the poor. Jesus knows that their concern for the poor is just a sham. Their true concern is rooted in their worship of money as an idol.[7] Jesus commends the woman for grasping that the Gospel is not just an offer to exchange our earthly rags for heaven's riches. It is also a command to exchange our earthly riches for earthly rags.[8]

In verses 8–11, Judas Iscariot acts as a picture of anyone who refuses to pay this price. Jesus predicts his death again, telling his disciples that Mary has anointed his body with perfume now because he is about to die the type of death that does not permit the normal practice of anointing a corpse before burial. Her act of worship is a prophecy about the kind of death he has to die and about the kind of death we need to die in turn. Jesus tells his disciples that wherever the Gospel is preached throughout the world, people will be called to remember her action and to follow her example.

Judas refuses to listen. He is too offended by this dishonouring of his cherished idol, money.[9] He sides with the chief priests and rabbis, telling them that if they give him enough money he will lead them to Jesus' night-time camp in the Garden of Gethsemane so that they can arrest him away from the crowds. Judas refuses to turn his riches into rags, like Mary. Instead he sells out Jesus. In doing so, he sells his own soul.

---

[7] John 12:6 tells us that Judas led the attack on the woman because he was in charge of the disciples' purse, and because he was in the habit of helping himself to its contents.

[8] Jesus is not excusing our ignoring poverty in 14:7. Far from it. He tells us that one of the signs a church has grasped the Gospel is that it attracts poor people. This poses a difficult question: Does yours?

[9] Luke 22:3 tells us that, as a result of this sinful reaction, *"Satan entered Judas."* Mark recounts this event out of order to emphasise that this reaction was the decisive turning point in his defection from Jesus.

There Will Be Blood
(14:12–31)

> *"This is my blood of the covenant, which is poured out for many," he said to them.*
>
> (Mark 14:24)

Part one of Mark's gospel devotes six and a half chapters to recounting the first two years of Jesus' public ministry. Part two of Mark's gospel devotes two chapters to his next six months of ministry. Part three of Mark's gospel devotes one and a half chapters to his six-month road trip from the north of Galilee to Jerusalem. So we must not miss the significance of the fact that Mark slows down dramatically in part four of his gospel. He devotes five long chapters to just five days leading up to the crucifixion. He leaves us in no doubt that we have come to the dramatic moment in the story. There will be blood.

In verse 12, Mark spells this out for us by telling us that it is Passover, the first day of the week-long Festival of Unleavened Bread, the day *"when it was customary to sacrifice the Passover lamb."* Mark expects us to grasp the symbolic significance of this, as the early Christians did: *"Look! The Lamb of God, who takes away the sin of the world!" "Christ, our Passover lamb, has been sacrificed."*[1]

First-century rabbis could not agree on the exact day when worshippers should eat the Passover feast, in much the same way that modern imams disagree over the exact dates of Ramadan. This works to Jesus' advantage, because it means that

[1] John 1:29, 36; 1 Corinthians 5:7. Note also the quotation from Exodus 12:46 in John 19:36.

he can eat the Passover meal with his disciples now and yet still die at the exact moment that the priests have chosen to sacrifice lambs in the Temple courtyards. Having made his triumphal entry into Jerusalem on the same day that flocks of Passover lambs were driven into the city, he now prepares to die with them as the great Passover Lamb.

In verses 13–16, Mark spells this out further by emphasising that Jesus is Lord of the Passover. First-century Jewish men did not carry water jars. They considered it to be a woman's task. Even if one of them broke convention, he was extremely unlikely to live in the one house in Jerusalem with a fully furnished upper room which could seat thirteen people for dinner and which had not already been booked by the crowds of pilgrims who more than trebled the normal population of Jerusalem at festival time. Nevertheless, Jesus receives a prophetic revelation which echoes the earlier way in which he knew the exact location of a suitable donkey on which to enter the city. His disciples find things precisely as Jesus predicted they would be. This will be no ordinary Passover meal. The fingerprints of God are all over their dinner preparations.

In verses 17–21, Jesus warns that his is not the only blood which will be shed. A fatal battle is raging in the heart of one of the disciples. Jesus warns the Twelve that one of their number is a traitor. One of them is about to fulfil David's prophecy in Psalm 41:9 about the Messiah's death: *"He who shared my bread has turned against me."*[2] He dips his bread into the Passover dish which contains a bitter sauce of raisins and vinegar, representing the bitterness of slavery in Egypt. He hands the bread to Judas. Will he surrender and be forgiven or will he choose to die as a slave to Satan?[3] Jesus warns him, *"Woe to that*

---

[2] Mark only hints at this because many of his Roman readers did not know the Psalms. John 13:18 states it explicitly.

[3] Mark does not tell us that Judas accepted the bread. We are told this in John 13:26–27. Mark leaves the decision hanging in the air because he wants us to treat it as a challenge to make a decision of our own.

man who betrays the Son of Man! It would be better for him if he had not been born."[4]

In verses 22–26, Jesus uses the Passover meal to teach the disciples that he has to die. He takes the unleavened bread – part of the same loaf which he has just offered to Judas – and he breaks it as a symbol of his body broken on the cross to free us from slavery to Satan and to sin. He hands them the bread to eat as a practical symbol that they are putting all their faith in him: *"Take it; this is my body."*[5]

Next, he takes the cup of wine which was drunk at the Passover meal to give thanks for the blood which was smeared on the vertical and horizontal wooden doorframes of the Israelite houses in Egypt and which saved them from the judgment of God.[6] He uses it as a picture of his own blood, which is about to be smeared on the vertical and horizontal wooden frame of a Roman cross: *"This is my blood of the covenant which is poured out for many."*[7] Jesus tells them they will drink this cup forever in the age to come. There will be blood, and that blood will be the most important object in the Christian story.

Jewish families would sing Psalm 115–118 together at the end of the Passover meal. This is what Mark is referring to when he tells us that Jesus and the disciples sang a hymn together before they left the upper room and returned to the Garden

---

[4] Mark 14:21, John 17:12 and Acts 1:25 all imply that Judas went to hell. He opened a door to Satan when he rejected Mary's act of worship (Luke 22:3) and he opened it further by taking this bread (John 13:27). What is frightening is the disciples' failure to guess instantly that the traitor is Judas. He looked just like one of them.

[5] Jesus is not claiming that the bread and wine are physically turned into his body and blood when we take the Lord's Supper. He is speaking symbolically, just as he does when he says he *is* the Gate in John 10:9.

[6] He uses the third of the four cups of wine drunk at the Passover meal, which was known as "the cup of blessing". Paul refers to the wine at the Lord's Supper as "the cup of blessing" in 1 Corinthians 10:16.

[7] Like all the covenants in the Old Testament, this one would be made with blood. Although Jesus says that his blood was shed for *many*, we read elsewhere that it was shed for *all* (1 John 2:2; 1 Timothy 2:6).

of Gethsemane on the Mount of Olives.[8] These four psalms celebrated the freedom which the Lord won for the Israelites through the Passover lamb. As they finished drinking the wine, they could now sing the words of Psalm 116:13 in a far better key: *"I will lift up the cup of salvation and call on the name of the Lord."*

In verses 27–28, Jesus prophesies one final time that there will be blood. As they cross the Kidron Valley and begin to climb the Mount of Olives, he quotes from Zechariah 13:7 and tells them that the Scriptures will be fulfilled this very evening: *"I will strike the shepherd, and the sheep will be scattered."* He is about to be killed and buried in a tomb. All of them will run away. But he will rise from the dead and will go back to Galilee to meet them there. Their failure will not disqualify them. He will take them back to where it all began and he will invite them afresh to step into his story.[9]

In verses 29–31, Peter struggles to accept this. Jesus is preparing to go the way of the cross, but Peter still feels very much alive. He insists on his own abilities. He assures Jesus that he is more reliable than his friends. He would rather die than disown Jesus. No, Jesus warns him. There will indeed be blood and, with it, Peter's pride will also die.

These verses are full of death – the death of Jesus as our Passover Lamb; the death of Judas for his invisible idols; the death of Peter and his friends to their self-confidence.[10] Mark leaves us in no doubt: there will be blood. Jesus and anyone who claims to follow him must die.

---

[8] These four psalms are known by Jews as the "Egyptian Hallel". They end with the same messianic promises in Psalm 118:19–29 which inspired the crowds in Mark 11.

[9] Jesus rose from the dead in Jerusalem and ascended to heaven from the Mount of Olives (Acts 1:9–12). There was therefore no reason for him to take them back to Galilee except to restart them on their journey.

[10] Typically, Mark focuses on Peter's mistakes, but 14:31 says they all made this proud boast.

The Cup (14:32–42)

"Abba, Father," he said, "everything is possible for you. Take this cup from me. Yet not what I will, but what you will."

(Mark 14:36)

On one level, the Roman Empire was an extremely tolerant place. A person could worship almost anyone or anything they pleased. The streets of the empire were lined with a myriad of shrines to gods and goddesses of every shape and size. A person could experiment and choose whichever one worked best for them. When it came to religion, there was only one thing the Romans really hated. They were fiercely intolerant of any belief system that talked about only one God and only one way of reaching him.

This was one of the major reasons why the Romans hated the Jews. Even the great Julius Caesar had been forced to accept their stubborn insistence that the God of Israel was unlike the Roman gods. He had purchased peace by granting the Jews a concession that declared their faith to be a "permitted religion", a legalised exception to the rule. If the Jews were willing to keep their faith to themselves and not foist it on their pagan neighbours, their claim to worship the only true God would be indulged and tolerated.[1]

This peace had been shattered by the time that Mark wrote his gospel. Peter and his friends had refused to keep their heads down. They broke the ultimate Roman taboo when they preached about Jesus, proclaiming that *"Salvation is found*

---

[1] Josephus records this concession in *Antiquities of the Jews* (14.10.17–26).

in no one else, for there is no other name under heaven given to mankind by which we must be saved."[2] It was fine to say that Jesus was a new saviour alongside the Roman gods. It was even fine to claim that he was the preferred option. But to claim that Jesus was the only way to God was definitely not permitted. It seemed so arrogant and intolerant that Roman pride refused to tolerate it. It helps to understand all of this background when we read what Jesus prayed in the Garden of Gethsemane.[3] Mark is answering this great Roman objection.

Mark demonstrates in verses 32–34 that, unless Jesus is the only Saviour, *God is very cruel*. He tells us that Jesus was in agony in the Garden of Gethsemane as he faced up to the need for his blood to be shed in order to pay the penalty for the sins of the whole world. Mark tells us that he was deeply distressed and troubled, asking his closest three friends to stay close by and telling them that *"My soul is overwhelmed with sorrow to the point of death."*[4] If there were no such thing as sin, or if there were any other way that devout and godly people could be saved, then the loving Father would have intervened to spare his Son. To claim that there are many ways for our sins to be forgiven is not humble. It is a grave insult to the character of the God to whom Jesus prayed in Gethsemane.[5]

Mark demonstrates in verses 35–36 that, unless Jesus is the only Saviour, *God is a liar*. The agony Jesus feels revolves

---

[2] Acts 4:12. See also Acts 14:15, 17:29–30 and 19:26, and 1 Thessalonians 1:9. Before the coming of Jesus, people were saved through faith in blood sacrifices which anticipated his final blood sacrifice (Hebrews 9:22).

[3] The Aramaic word Gethsemane means *Oil-Press*. John 18:1 tells us that it was the name of a garden. It was therefore one of the many olive gardens which gave the Mount of Olives its name.

[4] The word *ekthambeō* in 14:33 can be translated *deeply astonished*. No amount of preparation could ready Jesus for feeling the weight of the human race's sin. Luke 22:44 tells us that he sweated drops of blood.

[5] Mark emphasises the deep love between God the Father and the Son by telling us in 14:36 that Jesus called God *Abba*, the Aramaic word for *Dad* or *Daddy*. See also Romans 8:15 and Galatians 4:6.

around his conviction that he must drink "the cup" – a recurring Old Testament metaphor for the righteous anger God pours out on human sin.[6] Christians do not claim that every other religion is wrong. They claim that every religion is right about at least one thing. They may use many different words to describe wrongdoing and the penalty it incurs, but the major religions all agree that sin and its consequences are very real. Even the Romans did not deny this – our own culture is uniquely arrogant in the way that it shrugs off this uniform idea – so Jesus is not grappling with a uniquely Christian question in Gethsemane. He is accepting the teaching of the Jewish Old Testament and of all the great world religions, and he is asking the Father if he needs to drink the cup as the only true solution to them all.

Mark also demonstrates in verses 35–36 that, unless Jesus is the only Saviour, *God is ignorant*. Jesus pleads with the Father three times that he be spared this ordeal if there is any other way to save people from the cup of judgment.[7] Is God therefore not aware of Judaism or Hinduism or Buddhism or paganism – all of them well established by the early first century? Is he really that ignorant? Or is it our culture which is ignorant, typified by Homer Simpson when he blurts out a panicked prayer: *"I'm gonna die! Jesus, Allah, Buddha – I love you all!"*?[8] The more we study different religions, the more we realise that they are not the same at all. A crossless religion is a religion which is powerless to save. God's justice must be satisfied through the blood of his Son.

Mark demonstrates in verses 37–42 that, unless Jesus is the only Saviour, *God is making a mistake*. If there are many

---

[6] God refers to *"the cup"* of his righteous judgment upon sin in Psalm 75:8, Isaiah 51:17, Jeremiah 25:15–17, Lamentations 4:21, Ezekiel 23:31–34 and Habakkuk 2:16. Jesus also refers to it in Mark 10:38–39.

[7] Matthew 6:7–8 doesn't tell us not to repeat ourselves in prayer. It tells us not to babble lots of empty words.

[8] *The Simpsons*, Season 10, Episode 15 – "Marge Simpson in: 'Screaming Yellow Honkers'" (1999).

saviours, it means that the disciples are right to sleep instead of praying since this is not a crisis moment for the human race at all. It means that Jesus is wrong to challenge them for being too weak to pray, because there are other options for salvation if this one fails.[9] It means that the Father is wrong to send his Son to die, and that Jesus is wrong to tell his disciples in verse 49 that his crucifixion is necessary because *"the Scriptures must be fulfilled."*

We live in a culture that is very similar to first-century Rome. Oprah Winfrey summed it up when she shared her view that *"One of the biggest mistakes humans make is to believe there is only one way... There are many paths leading to what you call God."*[10] What we discover in the Garden of Gethsemane is that, while there may be many paths to what we call God, there is only one path to the real God. Jesus demonstrates that he is the only Saviour, the only blood sacrifice for sin and the only one whose resurrection proves he knows the way beyond the grave. This is what believing in Jesus means. It means accepting what he discovered and what he taught in the Garden of Gethsemane.

There is no offence in claiming that Jesus is one among many saviours – but nor will such a statement of faith bring us any salvation. It will not spare anyone from having to drink the cup of God's righteous judgment against their sin. Salvation comes through recognising that Jesus alone has made a way for us to step into God's story. Don't sleep through this Gethsemane prayer, like the disciples, and miss out on what Jesus is saying. Accept the truth of his statement: *"I am the way and the truth and the life. No one comes to the Father except through me."*[11]

---

[9] Mark emphasises in 14:37 that Peter failed to pray since he was the one who needed to pray most. He was about to deny Jesus (14:66–72), and he would take the lead in rallying the scattered disciples (Luke 22:31–32).

[10] Oprah Winfrey made this claim on her talk show in 1998.

[11] John 14:6. This is not an isolated statement. See also Mark 16:16 and John 3:36 and 10:8.

Show Trial (14:43–65)

"You have heard the blasphemy. What do you think?"
They all condemned him as worthy of death.

(Mark 14:64)

There have been some very famous show trials throughout history: the Salem witch trials, the Dreyfus Affair in France, the Moscow trials under Joseph Stalin, the trial of the Gang of Four in China, the trial of Nicolae Ceausescu in Romania. But none of these notorious show trials was as unjust as the show trial of Jesus at the Passover of 30 AD.

The Jewish leaders have finally succeeded. They have Jesus exactly where they want him. Judas has helped them to find him at his evening camp outside the city and far away from the support of the crowds. They will not wait until after the Passover to try and execute him. It must happen straightaway, before the crowds wake up to what is happening. The outcome of this show trial has already been decided: Jesus has to die.

But even as the Jewish leaders put Jesus on trial and concoct evidence to legitimise his execution, Mark recounts events in a manner which emphasises that it is in fact the Jewish nation which is on trial. These verses are full of detail that highlights the unrighteousness of Jesus' enemies. They may think they have Jesus in their clutches, but he has them exactly where he wants them too. The prisoner in the dock is the true judge of Israel, and he is about to pass his verdict over their nation.

In verses 43–46, they arrest Jesus through a foul act of treachery. It is worse than Iago and Othello. It is worse than Benedict Arnold and the American revolutionaries. It is worse than Quisling and the Norwegians. When Judas Iscariot identifies Jesus to the Sanhedrin's soldiers by greeting him as his *"Rabbi"* and kissing him like a friend, he performs the most notorious act of duplicity in history.[1] This traitor and this legalised lynch mob clothe the Jewish leaders in shame. They may be dragging Jesus away to a show trial, but the way in which they do so proves that they themselves are guilty.[2]

In verses 47–52, their cowardice is exposed for all to see. They need Judas to identify Jesus for them because it is dark. They could easily have arrested him in broad daylight as he taught in their own Temple courtyards, but they were too afraid. They are several hundred in number but, when one of the disciples draws his sword, they need Jesus to defend them.[3] Jesus is no rebel. He promises to come peacefully because *"the Scriptures must be fulfilled."* Even as his followers abandon him, Jesus remains surrounded with integrity. In contrast, the Sanhedrin's soldiers are so cowardly and ill at ease with what they are doing that they cannot prevent all of his followers from running away.

In verses 53–54, the Sanhedrin's contempt for the Jewish Law becomes evident. The fact that they need Judas to identify Jesus and the fact that Peter needs to warm himself by a fire in the month of April tells us that this trial took place at night. The Jewish Law explicitly forbade criminal courts from holding session at night in order to outlaw shady kangaroo courts like this one.[4] Their contempt for the Law of Moses is proven by

---

[1] Mark emphasises this by telling us for the third time in this chapter that Judas was *"one of the Twelve."* The Greek word **kata**phileō means that Judas didn't just *kiss* Jesus. He *kissed repeatedly and lovingly*.

[2] *"The chief priests, the teachers of the law, and the elders"* means the entire Sanhedrin. These were not simply the actions of a few rogue leaders. They were the united actions of the entire Jewish ruling council.

[3] John 18:10–11 tells us that this disciple was Peter and that Jesus rebuked him. John 18:12 tells us that there was a *cohort* of soldiers (roughly 500 men). John 18:4–9 tells us that Jesus was entirely in control of the situation, and Luke 22:51 even tells us that he healed the servant's severed ear.

[4] Sanhedrin 4:1, which is part of the Mishnah in the Jewish Talmud.

their failure to question Jesus over his statement that his death is somehow predicted by the Scriptures. They are not interested in God's Word. They are interested in getting a dangerous threat to their authority silenced and put out of the way.

In verses 55–59, their contempt for basic justice is revealed. They are not seeking the truth about Jesus. Mark says that they are simply *"looking for evidence against Jesus so that they could put him to death."* When they find none, they make some up instead.[5] When their false testimony contradicts itself, they ignore it and carry on. Think of how many weeks a high-profile court case normally features in the news. Compare that with the way in which this trial is concluded in less than an hour.[6] They think they are convicting Jesus of wrongdoing but all they are doing is exposing their own. This show trial shows the profound sinfulness of first-century Israel.

In verses 60–62, Jesus shows his own love for the Law. Although he must feel angered by their lies, he exercises such self-restraint that he fulfils the prophecy in Isaiah 53:7 that the Messiah will be silent before his killers. When he is directly challenged to state clearly whether or not he is the Messiah, the Son of God, he refers back to the prophecy in Daniel 7:13–14 and tells them that he is indeed the *"one like a son of man, coming with the clouds of heaven."* His evident love of Scripture contrasts strongly with the pragmatic disdain of his judges towards any Scripture that might hinder their wicked plans. He is an innocent law-keeper, but they are lawbreakers who are happy to twist and abuse God's Word in order to sanction murder.

---

[5] They know they are misquoting his words from John 2:19–21. Having watched Jesus like a hawk for over two years, their failure to list any sin he has committed actually testifies to his perfect deity!

[6] Between his late-night arrest and his execution early the following morning, Jesus actually had six hurried trials: one before the high priest (John 18:12–24), two before the Sanhedrin (Mark 14:53–65 and 15:1), two before Pilate (Mark 15:2–15 and Luke 23:1–25) and one before Herod (Luke 23:7–12). None was a fair trial.

In verses 63–65, the Sanhedrin reveal their hatred towards God. Although they go through the motions of honouring God by calling him *"the Blessed One"* in order to avoid using his name, like any good Jew, they think nothing of murdering his Son. They know full well that Jesus is claiming in verse 62 to be the Son of God whose coming is predicted throughout the Old Testament, yet they take no time to examine seriously whether or not this claim is true.[7] With unseemly haste, the high priest tears his clothes in a false show of piety. He declares that no more witnesses are needed (despite the fact that he has not allowed Jesus to call any defence witnesses at all), and he brings the Sanhedrin to a suspiciously speedy consensus. They break the Law again by blindfolding Jesus, spitting on him and asking him to prophesy who hit him, mocking his claim to have divine insight through the Holy Spirit.[8] These men are God-haters who finally have God in their clutches. They will not squander their moment of power.

The Jewish show trial of Jesus is over. A unanimous guilty verdict has been recorded. Yet Mark wants us to grasp that, in truth, the Sanhedrin has been put on trial before Jesus. The seventy-one priests and elders and rabbis who form the senior ruling council of the Jews have issued their formal response to God's story. As Jesus predicted in the Parable of the Tenants, they have rejected God's purposes for Israel. It is a poignant picture of Israel's sin when the Jewish leaders tie up their Messiah and hand him over to the Gentiles.

---

[7] Even Jesus' fiercest enemies could not deny that he was claiming to be God in 14:62. It takes 2,000 years and a great deal more ignorance about the Old Testament to enable a person to do that.

[8] See Deuteronomy 25:1–2, which is probably the passage referred to in Acts 23:3 and John 7:51.

God Accepts Rejects
(14:51–52, 66–72)

Peter remembered the word Jesus had spoken to him: "Before the cock crows twice you will disown me three times." And he broke down and wept.

(Mark 14:72)

I used to be responsible for what came out of a large soft-drinks factory. I didn't perform the quality-control testing myself, but I made decisions about what needed to be done with any faulty products that were found. Sometimes I would have to destroy several pallets at a time. My customers were paying top-notch prices for top-notch products. Any rejects needed to be thrown away.

Judas Iscariot believed that God has the same attitude towards sinners. When he betrayed Jesus, he assumed there was no turning back for him. Mark does not tell us what happened to Judas (he keeps the focus on what happened to Peter), but the other gospel writers fill in the blanks. He felt convicted about his terrible sin but, instead of repenting, he fell into despair. How could God ever forgive him for conspiring in the crucifixion of his Son? Judas decided to do to himself what I told the workers to do at the soft-drinks factory. He believed there was no hope for rejects, so he threw his life away.[1]

It is tragic when people misunderstand the Gospel like Judas. As a church leader, I see it all the time. Non-Christians come close to faith in Jesus but then shrink back at the last

---

[1] Matthew 27:1–10. There is a big difference between faith-filled repentance and mere remorse.

minute, believing that their sins have placed them beyond all hope of redemption. Christians are so appalled by their post-conversion sins that they begin to doubt their own salvation, drift away from church and return to the folly of their former lives. That's why it is important that we grasp what happened to Peter and his friends. God is not like the manager of a soft-drinks factory. He accepts rejects through Jesus' blood.

This was very good news for Peter. His boasting earlier in the evening had not prevented him from falling asleep when he should have been praying, and his prayerlessness had left him unprepared. Like the other disciples, he abandoned Jesus in the Garden of Gethsemane and ran away but, unlike most of the other disciples, he changed his mind and followed the soldiers as far as the high priest's inner courtyard. He had promised Jesus, *"Even if all fall away, I will not... Even if I have to die with you, I will never disown you."* He was determined to fulfil this pledge to his Master on the night when his Master needed him most.

It did not take very long for Peter's resolve to crumble. The man who drew his sword against a cohort of soldiers beat a hasty retreat before a lowly servant-girl. When she recognised him as one of Jesus' disciples, he denied it. When she insisted, he denied it a second time. When another man recognised his Galilean accent, he called down strong curses on himself and swore an oath to convince them that he did not know Jesus at all.[2] Suddenly the cockerel crowed to announce the break of dawn. He remembered Jesus' prediction on the way to the Garden of Gethsemane and broke down in guilty tears.[3]

Unlike Judas, however, Peter believed that God accepts

---

[2] The Greek word *anathematizō* does not merely mean *to curse*. It means *to curse so as to be cut off from God's People and go to hell*. This was the most serious of Jewish oaths (Acts 23:14).

[3] Luke 22:31–34 and John 13:36–38 tell us that Jesus also warned Peter that he would betray him while they were still in the upper room. He received a double warning but still he failed.

rejects. Even though he had cursed himself with the same fate as Judas, he refused to believe it was the end of the story. If God would accept lepers and prostitutes and tax collectors, there must be hope for a failure like him. He had not deserved his salvation, so how could he have undeserved it? If he was not beyond the need of God's forgiveness on his best days, how could he be beyond the reach of God's forgiveness on this, his worst day? If Jesus had chosen him and had believed that an impetuous fisherman named Simon could become a rock-steady apostle named Peter, then Jesus must be right.[4]

Because Peter believed that God accepts rejects, he went on to become the leader of the band of apostles. He would see 3,000 people saved through a single sermon. He would see sick people healed when his shadow fell upon them. He would see a dead woman raised at his command. He would preach the Gospel across the Roman Empire and would eventually be crucified as a witness to his Lord. I don't know what is happening in your life right now, but God does. I don't know what setbacks and failures and disappointments you are facing, but I do know this: rejects are always accepted by God if they fix their eyes on the perfection of Jesus instead of on their own imperfections. The blood of Jesus is enough to restore anyone, including you and me.

To reinforce this point, Mark makes a cameo appearance in the story. Like Alfred Hitchcock or Peter Jackson, he appears briefly in his gospel as a reminder that he has experienced this grace of God first hand. Since it adds nothing to the story when he mentions the young man who was grabbed by his clothes by one of the soldiers in the Garden of Gethsemane and who struggled free to flee home naked, most scholars assume that the young man must have been Mark himself. It would not be the last time that he ran away when the going got tough. We

---

[4] Jesus encouraged us in 13:20, 22 and 27 that faith in his sovereign election will give us strength to persevere under discouragements, setbacks, failures and trials.

are told in Acts 13 that he also deserted Paul's team at a crucial point in his first missionary journey.

Before he wrote his gospel, Mark had therefore faced a choice. He could assume that he had blotted his copybook forever. He could drift away to the edges of church life, like many old and jaded Christians today, and act as if his best days were behind him. Or he could choose to believe that God accepts rejects. If Paul would not have him on his team, he would join Peter's team instead. If Peter would not let him preach, he would take such thorough notes from Peter's preaching that he could turn them into the first of the New Testament gospels. Because he chose wisely, Peter learned to call him, *"my son Mark."* Paul recruited him back into his team, telling his friends that *"he is helpful to me in my ministry."* Paul may even be commending Mark's new book when he tells believers to welcome *"the brother who is praised by all the churches for his service to the gospel."*[5]

Mark's gospel is too action-focused to include Matthew's teaching about practical Christian lifestyle. Nevertheless, this simple message that God accepts rejects changes everything about the way in which we live. It revolutionises how we treat other people, how much we forgive them, how much we believe in their potential, how we reach out to unbelievers, how we engage with the culture around us, how we relate to people from other ethnic groups and how we treat people whenever they fail us.

Knowing that God accepts rejects changed everything for Peter and Mark. It will change everything for us too, if we truly grasp it. No matter who you are and where you have come from and what you have done, God is ready to accept you through Jesus' blood.

---

[5] 1 Peter 5:13; Colossians 4:10; Philemon 24; 2 Timothy 4:11. Since Luke wrote his gospel in c.60 AD and used Mark as one of his sources, we know that Mark wrote his gospel before then. If 2 Corinthians 8:18 is indeed a commendation of Mark's newly published gospel then he had already written it by 55 AD.

Rome on Trial (15:1–20)

*Knowing it was out of self-interest that the chief
priests had handed Jesus over to him... he had Jesus
flogged, and handed him over to be crucified.*

(Mark 15:10, 15)

Mark was not anti-Semitic. He was a Jew. He had been raised by
a devout Jewish mother in one of the most expensive houses in
Jerusalem.[1] He does not expose the ugliness of first-century
Judaism in his gospel because he dislikes those who practise it.
He loves his Jewish countrymen enough to hold up a mirror to
their culture so that they will rediscover the true faith of their
ancestors. Now, at the start of chapter 15, he suddenly changes
tack. He holds a mirror up to the culture of his Roman readers
and urges them to turn their back on the ugliness of first-century
Roman culture too.[2]

Perhaps Mark is concerned that his Roman readers will
feel that stepping into Jesus' story is somehow a betrayal of
their culture. Perhaps he wants to address their assumption
that Rome should be exporting its culture to the barbarians, not
learning from a Galilean carpenter. Whatever the reason, as the
Jewish leaders tie up Jesus and hand him over to Pontius Pilate,
Mark puts Rome on trial. He wants to persuade his readers that
Roman culture really isn't worth dying for.

In verse 1, the very mention of Pontius Pilate is

[1] Acts 12:12. Mark's family owned a house large enough to accommodate
a large prayer meeting and they were wealthy enough to employ a servant to
wait on them.

[2] Matthew writes mainly for Jews and stresses Jewish guilt in the crucifixion.
Mark writes mainly for Romans and stresses Roman guilt.

embarrassing for Mark's Roman readers. He was well known in Rome – a harsh man with a reputation for blasphemy and brutality. The first-century writer Philo says he was *"very merciless as well as very obstinate,"* famous for *"his cruelty and his continual murders of people untried and uncondemned."*[3] He was such a bad ruler that the Emperor Tiberius removed him from office in 36 AD and the Emperor Caligula exiled him to Gaul, where he committed suicide in shame.[4] As governor of Judea, therefore, Pontius Pilate exemplified the sinfulness of Roman culture. Mark's readers should be glad to throw much of it away.

In verses 2–5, Pontius Pilate exhibits the lazy arrogance of Rome. The late hour of Jesus' arrest and the early hour of his arrival at the governor's palace make it obvious that he has only been given a hurried and illegal night-time trial by the Sanhedrin. Nevertheless, Pilate legitimises their judgment and does not intervene to stop the Jewish lynch mob. The Sanhedrin only has authority to execute those who trespass on restricted areas of the Temple, so Pilate alone can decide to have this prisoner crucified.[5] He can see that Jesus has already been beaten, but still he does not intervene. When Jesus confirms to him that he is the Messiah, Pilate is amazed but again he does nothing.[6]

In verses 6–8, Pontius Pilate displays the hypocrisy of Rome. One of the reasons why they adorned their public squares with statues of the Virtues was as a substitute for having virtue

---

[3] See Luke 13:1, Josephus in his *Wars of the Jews* (2.9.2–4) and *Antiquities of the Jews* (18.3.2), and Philo in his *Embassy to Gaius* (38.1–7).

[4] See Josephus in *Antiquities of the Jews* (18.4.1–2) and Eusebius in *Church History* (2.7.1).

[5] The Sanhedrin's lack of authority to execute Jesus ensured that he was crucified in Roman fashion and not stoned to death in Jewish fashion. This fulfilled Old Testament prophecies about how the Messiah would die.

[6] Jesus confirms this by answering *"You said it!"* to Pilate's repetition of the Jewish charge. They drop the blasphemy charge because it is more effective in a Roman court to accuse him of claiming to be a rival king.

on the inside. Rather than stand up to his murderous subjects, the governor concocts a coward's plan to play the Jewish crowds off against their Jewish leaders.[7] He agrees to free one of his guilty prisoners as an act of Passover clemency: do the crowd want him to release Jesus or the insurrectionist Barabbas?[8] The gamble fails spectacularly. The crowd request Barabbas and the governor is forced to free a genuine enemy of Caesar while condemning an innocent man.

In verses 9–15, Pontius Pilate exposes the corrupted nature of Roman justice. He knows full well that the Jewish leaders have only put Jesus on trial out of jealousy and self-interest. Nevertheless, he takes a pragmatic view and decides not to antagonise his subjects while such large crowds are in Jerusalem. *"What crime has he committed?"* Pilate asks the crowd, knowing full well that Jesus is not claiming to be a rival Caesar. His silent integrity in the face of death proclaims loudly that his Kingdom is unlike those of this world. Basic justice demands that Pilate postpone judgment at least until after the Passover so that tempers have had a chance to cool down. But the Jewish leaders are too smart for him. They stir up the same crowds that shouted *"Hosanna!"* a few days earlier to shout *"Crucify!"* now. In the end, Pilate's commitment to justice is less than his commitment to a quiet life and to avoiding a riot which will make trouble for him in Rome.[9] He takes the easy option. *"Wanting to satisfy the crowd,"* he sends out an innocent man to die.

In verses 15–20, Mark uses the actions of Roman soldiers to make his readers feel ashamed of the culture they hold so

[7] Luke 23:7–12 tells us that Pilate also failed in a cowardly attempt to use the fact that Jesus was a Galilean to foist the responsibility for making a decision onto Herod the tetrarch.

[8] Barabbas was Aramaic for *Son-of-the-Father*. The Jewish crowd chose to embrace a parody of their Messiah instead of the real thing. They chose a sinful man instead of the sinless Son of God.

[9] Our pragmatic workplace decisions really matter to God. He refuses to compartmentalise our lives. Sin is sin, wherever we commit it.

dear. They flog Jesus using a special whip which was designed to tear chunks of flesh out of the victim's back. It was such a cruel weapon that many prisoners died before they could be crucified.[10] When the soldiers finish, they mock his claim to be Messiah by clothing him in one of their purple army cloaks and by twisting together a crown of thorns for him to wear. They beat it deep into his brow by hitting him over the head with a staff, and they fall down on their knees in mock worship of heaven's King. When I read accounts of some of the cruel acts committed under the British Empire, I feel ashamed to be British. When Mark's original readers finished these verses, they must have felt ashamed to be Roman.[11]

Following Jesus is always costly. It always means celebrating what is good about our culture, while submitting all that is bad about it to Jesus Christ as Lord. If you are from a Muslim or Hindu or atheist background, you can probably feel this cost acutely, but if you are from a churchgoing background then you need to pay the same cost too. We all have things we treasure in our culture that hold us back from stepping into Jesus' story. Mark tells us to throw such baggage away. The values of any earthly culture are not worth dying for.

---

[10] The Greek word which Mark uses for *flogging* in 15:15 is *phragelloō*, which comes from the Latin word for a whip known as a *flagellum*, tipped with many sharp little pieces of bone and metal.

[11] Mark tells us in 15:16 that the whole *cohort* of soldiers took part in this. They outnumbered Jesus 500 to 1.

The End of the Road
(15:21–37)

With a loud cry, Jesus breathed his last.

(Mark 15:37)

When Jesus finally reaches the end of his road trip to Calvary, we come face to face with the most surprising moment of them all. The Son of God dies. The Messiah becomes a corpse. The one who is the Resurrection and the Life becomes a lifeless cadaver in a tomb. What Jesus predicted during his road trip would happen has happened. He has finally reached the end of the road.

We must not lose our sense of surprise at this. I was reading a children's Bible to my young daughter recently, when she pointed to a picture of Jesus being taken down from the cross and asked me, *"Daddy, what's happening here?"* I replied without thinking: *"That's a picture of Jesus when he was dead."* Then it suddenly hit me afresh and I felt like crying. The author of life died. It's not an event we should ever get over. Let's not grow familiar with the detail in these verses. It should overwhelm us.

Jesus has been brutally flogged. When the blood starts to clot on his back, the wounds are reopened by the soldiers tearing off the robe they used to mock him. They put a cross on his bleeding shoulders and, when he buckles under the pain and loss of blood, they make him go on ahead as the cross is carried behind him by a passer-by. They offer Jesus a primitive analgesic to dull the pain, but he refuses. He is determined to drink to the very last dregs the cup of his Father's judgment upon sin. Then he is nailed to a wooden cross through his wrists and feet. While the blood that will save the world flows out of his dying body, he sees the soldiers gambling for his clothes, the crowds jeering at him, the Sanhedrin gloating over him, and even the criminals who are crucified alongside him insulting him.[1]

Crucifixion was not just one of the most painful ways to die. It was also one of the most shameful. It was so hideous that it was usually reserved only for slaves and pirates and revolutionaries. The Roman orator Cicero declared that it was

a most cruel and disgusting punishment... To bind a Roman citizen is a crime, to flog him is an abomination, to kill him is almost an act of murder. What shall I say of crucifying him? There is no fitting word that can possibly describe so horrible a deed... The very word "cross" should be far removed not only from the body of a Roman citizen, but also from his thoughts, his eyes and his ears... The mere mention of them is unworthy of a Roman citizen and a free man.[2]

Mark tells his Roman readers that Jesus endured the worst kind of death their city meted out. The only greater voluntary act of self-abasement in history was his original decision to descend from sinless heaven to sinful earth. Creation itself reacts with horror to the scene, plunging Jerusalem into darkness between noon and three in the afternoon. When Jesus cries out in pain, the crowds react by taunting him with a vinegar drink, which will only make him thirstier. He takes one final look at the bloodstained battleground where he has fought for the souls of the human race. Then, with a loud cry, the Son of God dies.

---

[1] Mark emphasises that the two criminals crucified on either side of Jesus insulted him. Luke 23:39–43 adds that one of them was so impressed with Jesus' reaction that he repented and was saved before he died.

[2] Cicero said this in his legal speeches against Gaius Verres in 70 BC (2.5.165–170) and in defence of Gaius Rabirius in 63 BC (5.16).

The final few steps in Jesus' road trip to Calvary should therefore surprise and shock us.[3] We must never grow accustomed to reading about the Son of God's date with death. Yet at the same time, this ending is precisely what we should have been expecting all along. Mark litters these verses with clues about what Jesus meant in 14:49 when he told his disciples that *"the Scriptures must be fulfilled."*

In verse 20, Mark hints that Jesus is the true blood sacrifice for sin. The Law of Moses commanded that priests take the bodies of their sacrificial victims outside the camp to be burned. Later New Testament writers would link this to the fact that Jesus was led outside to be crucified beyond the walls of Jerusalem: *"The high priest carries the blood of animals into the Most Holy Place as a sin offering, but the bodies are burned outside the camp. And so Jesus also suffered outside the city gate to make the people holy through his own blood."*[4]

In verses 33–37, Mark hints that Jesus is the true Passover Lamb. Since Jesus ate the meal a day early in the upper room, he is crucified as the city starts to celebrate the Passover. Mark emphasises that Jesus was crucified at nine in the morning (the *third hour* of the Jewish daytime clock, which ran from six in the morning to six in the afternoon) and that he therefore hung on the cross while the flocks of lambs were being driven into the Temple courtyards in order to be slaughtered. Mark emphasises that Jesus died at three in the afternoon (the *ninth hour* of the Jewish daytime clock), at the very moment when the priests oversaw the ritual slaughter of the lambs.[5] The chief priests are therefore not merely murdering Jesus. They are sacrificing

---

[3] Our word Calvary comes from *Calvaria*, the Latin word for *skull*. Mark translates the Aramaic word *Golgotha* in 15:22, telling us that the location where Jesus died was called *the Place of the Skull*.

[4] Leviticus 4:21; Numbers 19:3; Hebrews 13:11–13.

[5] The Hebrew phrase *"between the two evenings"* in Exodus 12:6 means any time between 3 p.m. and 6 p.m. Paul picks up on this in 1 Corinthians 5:7.

him at the exact hour stipulated by Moses. Unwittingly, they are fulfilling the very Scriptures they despise.

Mark also hints that Jesus is the fulfilment of the Old Testament prophecies about the Messiah. By gambling to see which one of them will get his clothes in verse 24, the Roman soldiers fulfil the prophecy in Psalm 22:18.[6] Jesus confirms this in verse 34 by shouting out the words of Psalm 22:1 as an anguished prayer.[7] Verse 28 is only in certain Greek manuscripts but, if it is part of Mark's original text, it tells us that Jesus is fulfilling the words of Isaiah 53:12. When the crowds mock Jesus in verse 29 for claiming that he would destroy and rebuild the Temple in just three days (John 2:19–21), they remind us that all of the Old Testament passages about the Tabernacle and Temple are prophetic images of what is happening here. Even as they taunt Jesus with a vinegar drink in verse 36, the crowds unwittingly fulfil the messianic prophecy in Psalm 69:21.[8] So don't rush over this detail. If we know these messianic prophecies, then Mark is telling us that the surprising end to Jesus' road trip shouldn't really be all that surprising after all.

Jesus is the true Passover Lamb. He is the true blood sacrifice for sin. He is the Messiah who drinks the cup of God's judgment against sin down to its very last dregs so that we can be forgiven. But there is something very different between the way that Jesus dies and the way that the lambs are being slaughtered at this very moment in the Temple courtyards. He dies this death by choice. He is the willing sacrifice. He chose to do this for you and for me.[9]

---

[6] Mark hints at this. John 19:24 tells us explicitly. By beating Jesus with a staff, they also fulfil Micah 5:1.

[7] Matthew 27:43 also tells us that the Sanhedrin's taunts fulfilled the messianic prophecy in Psalm 22:8.

[8] John 19:28 says that Jesus told the crowds he was thirsty *"so that Scripture would be fulfilled."*

[9] The Greek word *ekpneō* in 15:37 means *to breathe your last*. It is only ever used in the New Testament to describe the death of Jesus on the cross. This was not just murder. It was willing self-sacrifice.

Surprising Cry (15:34)

Jesus cried out in a loud voice, "Eloi, Eloi, lema sabachthani?" (which means "My God, my God, why have you forsaken me?").

(Mark 15:34)

The movie *Gandhi* is a bit of a classic. It's pretty hard not to enjoy it. But I'm sure that this has something to do with the way in which the scriptwriter focuses much more on Gandhi's inspiring life than on his sudden death. It is a three-hour movie, but less than two minutes at the end of the film portrays Gandhi's surprise assassination.[1]

Frankly, that's pretty normal. You would not expect a biography of Abraham Lincoln to focus as much on his death at the hands of John Wilkes Booth as it does on his early life or on his leadership during the American Civil War. You would not expect a book about John Lennon to talk as much about his shooting in Manhattan as it does about the 600 million albums that The Beatles sold worldwide.

That's why we need to slow down to the same pace as Mark as we reach the end of part four of his gospel. He devotes almost half of his entire gospel to the death of Jesus – one and a half chapters of road trip towards Calvary, four chapters of action and teaching leading up to Calvary, and one chapter describing Calvary in detail. Mark's gospel is a story that revolves around the death of Jesus, so before we move on let's ensure that we have fully grasped the depth of what Mark is telling us in these

---

[1] *Gandhi* (Columbia Pictures, 1982).

verses. Let's ensure that we grasp the message behind Jesus' very surprising cry.

Mark tells us that, just before Jesus died, he shouted out a phrase that proclaimed to the world what had been achieved through his very costly sacrifice. It is so important that Mark tells us his exact words in Aramaic: *"Eloi, Eloi, lema sabachthani?"* The crowds misunderstand, because the Aramaic word for God sounds a bit like the Aramaic word for Elijah. They think that Jesus must be calling to the prophet who ascended to heaven without dying and who was supposed to return to prepare Israel to receive its Messiah. Mark translates the words for his Roman readers, because Jesus is not calling to Elijah at all. He is calling to his Father as he prepares to die: *"My God, my God, why have you forsaken me?"*[2]

First, Jesus is proclaiming that *he is saving us*. He is quoting the first verse of Psalm 22, one of the greatest Old Testament prophecies about the Messiah. It predicted that the Messiah would be despised (22:6), mocked (22:7–8), surrounded by his enemies (22:12–13) and terribly thirsty (22:15) while his enemies gambled over his clothes (22:18). It predicted that he would be pierced through his hands and feet (22:16) and hung so cruelly that his limbs were dislocated (22:14). Jesus drew great comfort from this psalm in his hour of need but, more than that, he proclaimed that he had achieved all of the salvation promises the Lord gives to us through David's song.

Jesus proclaimed that he would be raised to life (22:22).[3] Although his Aramaic words speak of abandonment, Jesus knew that the Father would not despise his suffering or hide his face from him for long (22:24). He celebrated the fact that the lifeblood flowing from his body was purchasing people from *"all*

---

[2] Mark clearly sees this cry as very significant because it is the only one of Jesus' seven sayings from the cross that he records. The other six can be found in Luke 23:34, 43 and 46, and in John 19:27, 28 and 30.

[3] Hebrews 2:12 quotes from Psalm 22:22 and tells us that this is the triumphant cry of the risen Messiah.

the families of the nations" and even from *"a people yet unborn"* (22:27–31). Mark tells us in verse 37 that Jesus shouted before he breathed his last, and John 19:30 tells us what he shouted. He quoted from the final line of Psalm 22 and cried out that he had drunk the cup of God's judgment to its very last dregs: *"It is finished!"*, or *"He has done it!"*[4]

Second, Jesus is proclaiming that *he is replacing us.* He wants us to grasp that he is being punished in our place and that he is experiencing the punishment we deserve. If you want to catch a glimpse of the despair that reigns in hell, just listen to the anguish in his voice as he shouts, *"My God, my God, why have you forsaken me?"* Jesus speaks twenty-one recorded prayers in the gospels, and in all but this one he addresses God intimately as *"Abba"* or *"Father"*. As he becomes the sponge that soaks up all the sin and filth of the human race, Jesus feels the horror that pervades hell, the place of *"outer darkness"* and, for the first time in his life, he feels the Father withdraw his presence from him.[5] Jesus has not lost hope – he still calls his Father *"my God"* – but he reveals to us how we will feel one day in hell if we

refuse to step into his story.[6]

Mark reinforces this by using Barabbas as a picture of what Jesus is achieving as he dies on the cross. Barabbas was a murderer and a rebel against Rome. It should have been him hanging on the cross between these two brigands. Jesus remained silent before Pilate because he knew he could easily argue his way to freedom. He made a willing choice to step into the sandals of Barabbas and drink the cup of judgment

---

[4] The Hebrew word *tsedāqāh* in Psalm 22:31 means *righteousness*, *vindication* or *being declared innocent before God*. Jesus took our sin so that we might take his perfect standing before God.

[5] 2 Corinthians 5:21: Galatians 3:13; Matthew 8:12; 22:13; 25:30.

[6] The Greek word *enkatelipes* is an aorist rather than a perfect tense. It therefore speaks of a sudden sense of separation from the Father – *"why did you forsake me?"* rather than *"why have you forsaken me?"*

he deserved. Even as Jesus dies, Barabbas is celebrating his freedom. Jesus died instead of you and me.

Third, Jesus is proclaiming *his victory for us*. The Greek word Mark uses for his crown of thorns in verse 17 is *stephanos*, which means a *victory crown* like the ones winning athletes were awarded after the gruelling ordeal of the Olympic Games. Mark tells us in verse 26 that above Jesus' head is a proclamation that he is *"The King of the Jews."*[7] His separation from the Father means that he has achieved the final goal of his road trip. It is a victory cry. It signifies the completion of his mission, stated in 10:45: *"The Son of Man did not come to be served, but to serve, and to give his life as a ransom for many."* We were slaves, criminals, hostages, prisoners of war. But now that has all changed. We are on the winning team.

Fourth, Jesus is *calling us to step into his story*. That's why Mark tells us about Simon of Cyrene in verse 21. The Roman soldiers pick Simon out of the crowd and tell him to follow Jesus, carrying his cross and walking behind him in his blood-soaked footsteps. As Jesus shouts in pain that he has taken our place, Mark wants us to understand that Jesus invites us to step into his blood-soaked footsteps too: *"Whoever wants to be my disciple must deny themselves and take up their cross and follow me. For whoever wants to save their life will lose it, but whoever loses their life for me and for the gospel will save it."*[8]

Don't miss what is going on behind the scenes as Jesus shouts his surprising cry. Jesus has not simply endured the cross. He has embraced it. He has won a resounding victory for you and for me. He is calling us to step into his story.

---

[7] John 19:19–22 tells us that this proclamation was written in Aramaic, Latin and Greek. This victory belongs to people from every nation of the world.

[8] Mark 8:34–35; Luke 9:23–24. It is to illustrate these verses that Luke 23:26 makes so much of the fact that Simon of Cyrene carried the cross *behind* Jesus, following him.

Surprising Response (15:38–47)

When the centurion, who stood there in front of Jesus, saw how he died, he said, "Surely this man was the Son of God!"

(Mark 15:39)

I will never forget the first time I watched *The Return of the Jedi* with my oldest two children. They knew all about Darth Vader. He is one of the most famous cinema villains of all time. So when I told them before the movie started that Darth Vader would become a goody at the end, they looked at me and laughed. They simply couldn't believe that an arch-villain like Darth Vader would ever be able to change.

Part four of Mark's gospel doesn't end with the death of Jesus and his surprising cry. It ends with a collection of Darth Vaders and their surprising response to the sacrifice they have just seen. Mark uses their example to challenge us and to build our faith. He uses them to help us step into Jesus' story.

First, Mark draws our attention to *the sinful*. He mentions Simon of Cyrene in verse 21. Most modern readers are not sure where Cyrene was, and even those who can pinpoint it on the map of modern-day Libya are generally unaware of what it meant to anyone in the first century. Cyrene meant one thing: it was the city that monopolised the world's supply of silphium, the medicinal herb that was used to procure abortions. It was so essential to the city's economy that a picture of the silphium herb appeared on all its coins. If a woman was pregnant and didn't want to be, she knew what to do. She would buy some

Cyrenian silphium. Simon's city was the abortionist capital of the world.

Mark uses a Greek word in verse 21 that tells us that Simon was compelled by force to take up the cross and follow Jesus. But he also gives us a massive clue that what started out as a reluctant chore soon became a willing choice. Mark tells us that Simon was *"the father of Alexander and Rufus."* That's an irrelevant piece of information unless those two men were known to the Christians in Rome. Add to this the fact that Paul writes to the church at Rome and addresses a believer named Rufus and his mother, and we begin to see the full story. Mark is telling us that even people from the most sinful of places can still step into Jesus' story.[1]

Second, Mark draws our attention to *the Jews*. God has not finished with them after today's events. Mark tells us in verse 38 what happened to their beloved Temple. As Jesus died, the crowded courtyard of worshippers looked up over their Passover lambs at the thick curtain that barred the way into the inner sanctuary, and they saw it completely torn in two. It wasn't just torn slightly to be repaired. It was split from top to bottom, signifying the dawn of a new initiative from heaven to earth. God did not give the Jewish nation the silent treatment for rejecting his Messiah. He performed a miracle which proclaimed that the presence of God, once reserved for high priests, was now something that their entire nation could enjoy. The writer to the Hebrews celebrates this:

> Brothers and sisters, since we have confidence to enter the Most Holy Place by the blood of Jesus, by a new and living way opened for us through the curtain, that is, his body... let us draw near to God with a sincere heart

---

[1] Romans 16:13. Luke 23:39–43 also emphasises this by telling us that one of the two robbers was converted.

*and with the full assurance that faith brings, having our
hearts sprinkled to cleanse us from a guilty conscience.*[2]

Third, Mark draws our attention to *the Romans*. This was
important because his readers must have been appalled to read
that the Son of God had not been killed by Jewish hands, but
by Roman ones.[3] It is important to us too because, as Martin
Luther pointed out, we all carry around his nails in our pockets.
Jesus was crucified at the behest of the Jews and at the hands of
the Gentiles in order to emphasise that the entire human race
caused him to die, including you and me. What happens next
is therefore far more surprising than what happens to Darth
Vader in *The Return of the Jedi*.

Mark tells us in verse 39 that the centurion in charge of
the Roman soldiers who beat and mocked and crucified Jesus
repented and decided to step into his story. While his men
were gambling for Jesus' clothing, he had taken note of the way
in which his prisoner died. Crush a fruit and you will quickly
discover from its juice whether it is an orange or a lemon. Crush
a man and you will quickly discover from his reaction what kind
of man he is on the inside. The centurion looks at Jesus and is
convicted of the terrible sin he has committed. *"Surely this man
was the Son of God!"* he exclaims with a mixture of horror and
faith. Even as Jesus died, the centurion was made alive.[4]

Fourth, Mark draws our attention to *outcasts*. Women
were often disregarded by first-century men. We can see that in
verses 40–41 because, unlike the male disciples, Jesus' female
followers felt no need to run and hide. First-century rulers were

---

[2] Hebrews 10:19–22. The tearing of the curtain declared a new and better
day for the people of Israel.

[3] Mark reminds us in 15:42 that his primary readership is Roman, not Jewish,
by explaining Jewish customs.

[4] This was such a surprising response that Matthew and Luke mention it too.
Matthew 27:54 tells us that some of his soldiers were saved with him, and John
19:32–35 says they were among the early Christians.

not overly concerned about the beliefs of women, which is one of the reasons why Mark focuses his Roman readers mainly on the men who followed Jesus. At this point, however, he mentions the large number of women who followed Jesus on his journeys. He commends their continued faithfulness and reminds a world that values men and devalues women and children that outcasts have a crucial role to play in Jesus' story.

Fifth, Mark draws our attention to *the in-crowd*. The danger of grasping God's love for the poor is that we can assume this means he somehow cares less for the rich. The danger of realising that God loves outcasts is that we can assume he therefore rejects members of the in-crowd. That's why Mark tells us in verses 42–47 that, while the disciples remained in hiding, a member of the Sanhedrin nailed his faith in Jesus to the mast for all to see. Unlike his colleagues, he was genuinely waiting for the coming of the Kingdom of God, and he recognised in Jesus that the King had come. In spite of all his questions and confusion (who can imagine how the disciples must have felt between the crucifixion and the resurrection?), Joseph of Arimathea goes to Pontius Pilate and requests the corpse of Jesus. He lovingly buries his dead Saviour in his own new tomb cut into the rocky hillside.[5] Better late than never to step into Jesus' story.[6]

These are five very surprising responses. The dead Jesus finds new followers in a man from a sinful city, among the Jews, among the Romans, among outcasts and among the members of the in-crowd. As we finish part four of Mark's gospel, make a surprising response of your own. Tell Jesus unreservedly that you are stepping into his story.

---

[5] The fact that the tomb was carved into a rock face made it easy for the soldiers appointed by the Jewish leaders to guard the corpse of Jesus. A large stone blocked the only entrance to the tomb.

[6] Joseph disagreed with the supreme Jewish council's decision (Luke 23:50–51) but he kept his faith to himself out of fear (John 19:38). John says a second member of the Sanhedrin was also saved with him.

Part Five:

The Unfinished Story

(Mark 16:1–20)

It's Your Move (16:1–8)

"Don't be alarmed," he said. "You are looking for Jesus the Nazarene, who was crucified. He has risen!"

(Mark 16:6)

The death of Jesus was not the end of the story. We discover in the fifth and final part of Mark's gospel that it was only just getting started. The sixteenth chapter of Mark ends the story in three possible ways. We will look at the first ending in this chapter and the other two endings in the next, but all three possible endings have one thing in common: They tell us that the story of Jesus is an unfinished story.

The first possible ending of Mark's gospel is 16:1–8. Whatever else we might need to say about the second half of this chapter, we can know for sure that Mark definitely wrote these eight verses. These are included in every Greek manuscript and they were among the verses that were given full endorsement by the Early Church: *"Mark, having become the interpreter of Peter... committed no error while he wrote down things as he remembered them. For he was careful not to omit anything which he had heard, and not to state anything which was false."*[1]

In these eight verses, Mark proclaims the amazing news that Jesus' story has not finished. The female followers of Jesus watched where he was buried and returned at first light after the Sabbath day of rest in order to anoint his decaying corpse with perfume. They never had the chance. When they arrived

---

[1] Papias said this just after 100 AD, quoted by Eusebius in *Church History* (3.39.14–15).

at the tomb, the heavy stone was rolled away from the door and an angel was sitting near to where the corpse of Jesus had been laid. Sensing their panic and fear, the angel proclaimed to them the message which Peter subsequently preached across the Roman Empire: *"You are looking for Jesus the Nazarene, who was crucified. He has risen! He is not here."*

At this point, the patronising attitude of the first-century world towards women actually corroborates Mark's story. The testimony of women was considered suspect in the law courts, so anybody setting out to invent a tale of resurrection would not have chosen women to be its star witnesses. Mark knows that an honest statement of the facts will therefore make his story less convincing to his Roman readers, but he refuses to pretend otherwise for the simple reason that the first witnesses were women and not men. This is a powerful proof that he is telling us the facts as they really happened.

Mark was in Jerusalem that morning, so he also confirms the accuracy of Peter's teaching. A sealed and guarded tomb in Mark's hometown burst open. Hardened soldiers cowered and fainted like dead men because they saw angels.[2] The stone was not rolled away from the entrance of the tomb to let Jesus out (John tells us that he could appear to people inside locked rooms after his resurrection). It was rolled away to let in the women and Peter and Mark and everybody else in Jerusalem so that they could see that the corpse of Jesus was no longer there. Their crucified Messiah was alive!

Now Mark turns the spotlight onto Peter. After all, this gospel has largely been the record of Peter's journey with Jesus. When the angel tells the women to go and tell the disciples that Jesus is risen, he singles out Peter in particular. The apostle must not think that his three denials have disqualified him

---

[2] Mark keeps his account brief. We can read more about what happened in Matthew 27:65–28:4. Luke and John tell us that there were at least two angels but, since the gospel accounts differ as to whether the angels were inside or outside the tomb, there may well have been several more.

from continuing to play a leading role in this unfinished story. He must lead the other apostles as they preach to the world about the miracle that took place inside the tomb of Joseph of Arimathea.

We can only imagine how the eleven surviving disciples were feeling. Their friend Judas was dead. The rest of them had abandoned their Master when he needed them most. Their hopes had died with him on the cross and had been buried with him in the tomb. We are told in Luke 24:17 that their faces were gloomy. They felt as though the story to which they had given their lives had come to an abrupt end. The angel therefore reminds the women that Jesus has arranged a practical way to convince them that his story has only just started. In 14:28, Jesus set up a post-resurrection rendezvous with them in Galilee. They needed to go back and meet him at the lake where he called many of them to follow him at the beginning. There he would re-enact their initial call and launch them back into his unfinished story.[3]

This is where Mark's original ending becomes unsatisfactory for many readers. He does not tell us about Peter running to the tomb and confirming that it was empty. He does not tell us about Peter's encounter with the angels. He does not tell us about Peter meeting the risen Jesus with the disciples in Jerusalem or back on the shores of Lake Galilee. We only read this in the other gospels.[4] Mark leaves his gospel unfinished, not even finishing his sentence properly at the end of verse 8. A literal translation reads:

> *Trembling and bewildered, the women went out and fled from the tomb. They said nothing to anyone. For they were afraid of...*

[3] This can be the only reason why Jesus commanded them to meet him in Galilee, since he would ascend to heaven from the Mount of Olives. We can read all about this re-launch of the story by the lake in John 21.

[4] See Matthew 28; Luke 24; John 20–21.

With an ending like that, it is easy to see why the early Christians added two alternative endings of their own. What kind of story ends like that? Well – an unfinished story.

Mark deliberately ends his gospel mid-sentence in order to emphasise to his readers that it is now their move.[5] They do not need to know the details about what Peter did next. If he had not stepped back into the story, they would not be reading Mark's gospel at all. What matters now is not Peter's reaction, but their own. It's their move. What will they do? How will they react to the story they have read? Will they step into the unfinished story and start writing more chapters of their own?

Reading is easy. Taking action is hard. That's why Mark tells us frankly that the women were trembling and bewildered, too afraid to speak to anyone. He invites us to follow their example by overcoming our own fears, just as they did. They eventually told Peter and the disciples what they had discovered, becoming part of the 120 believers who started the first church in Jerusalem.[6] They understood that the story of Jesus wasn't over and that they needed to keep on writing it with their lives.

The women overcame their fears and stepped into the unfinished story. Mark's closing question is simple: Will you?

---

[5] Luke employs this same literary device by ending the story of Acts in mid-air in Acts 28:31.

[6] The 120 believers in Jerusalem in Acts 1:14–15 included both men and women.

Write This (16:9–20)

He said to them, "Go into all the world and preach the gospel to all creation. Whoever believes and is baptised will be saved, but whoever does not believe will be condemned."

(Mark 16:15–16)

It doesn't really matter that we know the other two possible endings of Mark's gospel were not really written by him. They have been preserved in many of the Greek manuscripts because God wants to speak to us as much through them as through the words that were actually written by Mark's hand.[1] Having told us clearly through Mark's original ending that it's our move – that it's time for us to continue the unfinished story – God has preserved for us two of the endings that were written by early Christians as examples of what continuing his story ought to mean for us today.

The first of these additional endings is short but sweet. It doesn't have a verse number because it doesn't appear in most modern translations of the Bible. It simply says:

Then they quickly reported all these instructions to those around Peter. After this, Jesus himself also sent out through them from east to west the sacred and imperishable proclamation of eternal salvation. Amen.

---

[1] Mark 16:9–20 does not appear in the *Codex Vaticanus* or the *Codex Sinaiticus*, two of our most reliable Greek manuscripts of the New Testament. However, it does appear in several other manuscripts.

You have read enough of Mark's gospel by now to recognise that this was not written by him. The language is much more formal and churchy in its style. It was so obviously written by somebody who felt that Mark's original ending was not good enough that it is not included in most modern translations of the Bible. But before we dismiss it and move on, let's note that this is a very early example of somebody trying to continue the unfinished story. God allowed it to be preserved for us in order to show us what those closest to Mark believed continuing the story ought to mean. Whatever else you do personally as you finish this book, make sure that you prioritise the same things as this anonymous early Christian. Tell everyone you can that Jesus is alive and that his resurrection means salvation for the world.

The so-called "longer ending of Mark" was not written by him either. Nevertheless, it is such an ancient addition to the text that it appears as 16:9–20 in most modern translations of the Bible. One of the earliest Christian writers appears to quote from it, and it is also quoted by other early Christians such as Ambrose and Augustine.[2] These verses therefore have some serious pedigree as Scripture, even though Mark did not write them. God wants to use them to show us how we ought to carry on the story.

Verse 9 reminds us that we must share the Gospel with everyone. Mary Magdalene was afflicted by seven demons, but she was not beyond the reach of the Gospel. Jesus invited demonised prostitutes and hardened sinners to step into his story.[3] So must we.

Verses 10–14 remind us that we need faith to continue this

---

[2] Many scholars believe that Justin Martyr is quoting from Mark 16:20 in his *First Apology* (chapter 45), written in *c.*150 AD, because his language is very similar.

[3] Luke 8:2 also tells us that Mary Magdalene was afflicted by seven demons. Some people identify her with the woman in Luke 7:37–39 and John 8:1–11, although the Bible never explicitly states this.

story. At first, the disciples refused to believe that Jesus had been raised from the dead.[4] Even when two of their friends returned from the Road to Emmaus and confirmed that they had seen the risen Jesus, they still refused to listen. The writer tells us that *"Jesus appeared to the Eleven as they were eating; he rebuked them for their lack of faith and their stubborn refusal to believe those who had seen him after he had risen."*[5] The writer clearly has the reader in mind. Do we truly believe Mark's gospel? Do we believe that Jesus has risen from the dead? Do we believe that he healed the sick and demonised? Do we believe that he wants to continue this story through us?

Verses 15–16 remind us that the salvation of the world hinges on our belief in God. Peter and his friends must have felt like the synagogue ruler Jairus. Their hopes had died and their world had ended, until suddenly Jesus appeared and changed everything. He told eleven fearful Galileans to go and preach the Gospel to every nation in the world. This was scary enough, but Jesus makes it worse by telling them that anyone who rejects their message will be eternally condemned.[6] Peter and his friends needed to remember the reassuring words Jesus spoke to Jairus in 5:36: *"Don't be afraid; just believe."*[7]

Verses 17–18 remind us that Jesus has given us all the help we need. Don't skim over these verses because they have been misused by snake-handlers and madmen.[8] God wants us to

[4] Greek masculine endings to the words in 16:10–11 tell us that these doubters were not just among Mary's female friends. They were also among the Eleven.

[5] We can read about these two events in Luke 24:13–49 and John 20:19–29. The Greek word used to describe Jesus *rebuking* the Eleven is a strong one. It was used for the robbers rebuking Jesus in 15:32.

[6] Jesus stresses obedient baptism as well as repentance. Saying that we believe in him is not enough. Actions speak louder than words.

[7] Mark contrasts fear and faith throughout his Gospel. We soon discover why when we carry on the story.

[8] Although Paul experienced this literally in Acts 28:3–6, the writer is probably following the lead of the Old Testament prophets by using *snakes* and *poison* as metaphors for demons and their toxic work in the world.

recognise that any second-century Christian understood that reaching nations would require miracles. God wants us to be concerned and challenged if our experience is very different from that of the second-century church in France:

> *Those who are truly His disciples receive grace from Him to perform miracles in His name, so as to promote the welfare of other people according to the gift which each one has received from Him. For without doubt some truly drive out demons, so that those who have thus been cleansed from evil spirits frequently join themselves to the Church. Others foresee things to come: they see visions, and utter prophetic expressions. Still others heal the sick by laying their hands on them, and they are made whole. Yes, moreover, as I have said, the dead have even been raised and have remained among us for many years. What more shall I say? It is not possible to name the number of the gifts which the Church throughout the whole world has received from God in the name of Jesus Christ... For as she has received freely from God, freely also does she minister to others.*[9]

Verses 19–20 remind us that Mark's gospel is a call to action. Its pace, its intensity and its awkward ending are all meant to catapult us into the story. Mark took his words so seriously that he left Peter and went to preach the Gospel to the Egyptians, even though they dragged him through the streets behind a horse until he died. He surrendered his life to continue this story and, as he did so, he won the nation of Egypt to the Lord.[10]

---

[9] Irenaeus of Lyons wrote this in around 180 AD in his *Against Heresies* (2.32.4). Some Christians need to be reminded that the Holy Spirit still acts today. Others need to be reminded that the Holy Spirit's acts should always send us out of our churches and into the world.

[10] Eusebius tells us that Mark went to Alexandria in Egypt and served there until at least 62 AD (*Church History*, 2.16.1–2 and 24:1). Coptic tradition records the details of his martyrdom in the city.

God has given us two of the endings that were written by early Christians in order to challenge us. How will we continue the story that Mark has started? Will we step into the story like Peter and Mark and Irenaeus and the early Christians? What ending of our own will we write to bring Mark's gospel to its ultimate conclusion?

Go Out (16:19–20)

After the Lord Jesus had spoken to them, he was
taken up into heaven and he sat at the right hand of
God. Then the disciples went out.

(Mark 16:19–20)

If the sign of a good book is that it is hard to put down, Mark's gospel is a very good book. We have reached the final two verses of the last of three endings, but most of us would still prefer to continue reading. Reading is easy. Continuing the story is much harder. We can all find excuses to put it off for another time.

Some people end Mark's gospel and start debating. It's easier to discuss the authorship of these final twelve verses than it is to follow their example. It's easier to doubt some of Mark's story than it is to step into it. Perhaps that's why the final two verses of Mark's gospel end with a command for us to go out and obey.

Some people end Mark's gospel and start praying. They even have a verse for it. They argue from 9:29 that nothing can be done without first devoting ourselves to prayer. Of course they are right, but the words of their prayers also show that they are wrong. They sit down and ask God to go out and save the world. These final two verses tell us that their prayers will never be answered unless they first face up to the fear that keeps them inside praying when they should be out proclaiming.[1] The correct response to the finish of Mark's gospel is not to sit

---

[1] This is one of the reasons why Mark gave us the example of Joseph of Arimathea, the secret believer. He told us literally in 15:43 that *"taking courage, he went."* We need to follow his example.

down and pray for Jesus to go out into the world. We are told straightforwardly: *"He sat at the right hand of God. Then the disciples went out."*[2]

The disciples went out convinced that *Jesus has all authority*. Jesus has been raised up to heaven and has sat down on his throne.[3] That's what a king does when he has done all there is to do. Jesus has sat down on his throne and has given us authority to speak commands in his name and to place our hands on people to convey the Holy Spirit's power to meet their need.[4] His command for us to pray and fast in 9:29 was not an end itself. It had these two great things in mind. Jesus told the disciples to fast and pray in order to counter the unbelief which he rebuked in 9:19. Praying to receive what we already have is not faith. It is fear-filled delay.

In 1786, a 25-year-old shoemaker from England named William Carey dared to voice his desire to step into the story of Mark's gospel. He pleaded with his local church leaders to take seriously the fact that three-quarters of the world had not yet heard the good news about Jesus. Merchants and imperialists were leaving English ports every day in search of money and power, but no Christians were leaving English ports in search of souls. One of the church leaders responded angrily: *"Young man, sit down, sit down! You're an enthusiast. When God pleases to convert the heathen, He'll do it without consulting you or me."*[5] But William Carey refused to sit down. Instead he went out. He stirred an army of believers through his example and

---

[2] The Greek particles *men* and *de* emphasise this contrast strongly in the original text. They tell us literally that *on the one hand* Jesus has sat down and that *on the other hand* this means we need to go out.

[3] The New Testament always describes Jesus' ascension using the Greek passive voice. This emphasises that God the Father raised a human being to heaven and can also therefore bring heaven down to human beings.

[4] Issuing commands in Jesus' name (16:17) and laying hands on people to see them healed (16:18) have been big themes throughout Mark's gospel.

[5] The quotations in this chapter come from S. Pearce Carey's book *William Carey* (1923).

is still known today as "the father of modern missions". It's amazing what God does through ordinary people who pluck up the courage to go out and step into Jesus' story.

The disciples went out convinced that *Jesus has given us a message which must be heard*. This is very important, because many of us have been told that we need to earn the right to share the Gospel with anybody. That's not the story Mark has told us, and it certainly isn't the story we read in these two final verses. They tell us that Jesus has spoken and that our right to speak is not given us by the listener, but by the Lord. The Greek text places the emphasis less on our going than it does on our speaking, because our movement matters far less than our message.[6] Too many people make the mistake of thinking that they will share the Gospel *one day* – when they are older or when they go abroad or when they have a bit more time. These verses tell us that we need not wait to go to foreign nations, like William Carey, before we start proclaiming the Gospel to every creature. Each of us can step into the story of Mark's gospel today.

The disciples went out convinced that *Jesus would make them fruitful as they went*. They knew that it would not be easy. Peter and Mark were killed. William Carey spent seven years in India before he saw a single conversion. Nevertheless, they were convinced that God would be with them and that, if they went, he would come too. The final verse of the gospel tells us literally that *"the Lord worked with them and confirmed his word by the signs that followed it."*[7] It tells us that, if we wait, God waits, but if we go, God goes with us. The first move is ours, but the Lord promises that his move will always follow.

---

[6] Mark 16:15 and Matthew 28:19 do exactly the same thing. In Greek the "going" is a participle and the "preaching" is an indicative. Mark 16:20 reads literally, *"Then the disciples, going out, preached everywhere."*

[7] Mark 16:17 also tells us that miracles will *follow* us as we go. Until we go, we will see nothing.

William Carey learned this during his first seven unfruitful years in India. He wrote in his diary that,

> When I left England, my hope of India's conversion was very strong; but amongst so many obstacles, it would die, unless upheld by God. Well, I have God, and His Word is true. Though the superstitions of the heathen were a thousand times stronger than they are, and the example of the Europeans a thousand times worse; though I were deserted by all and persecuted by all, yet my faith, fixed on the sure Word, would rise above all obstructions and overcome every trial. God's cause will triumph.

In the eighth year, William Carey saw his first Indian conversion. Three decades later, there were half a million believers in his part of India.

Mark's gospel therefore ends with a wonderful promise. It tells us that, if we sit down and pray that God will go out, we will never see the story finished but that, if we trust Jesus has sat down on the throne of heaven and has sent us out, we cannot fail. These final two verses assure us that God will work hard alongside us and will confirm our words by empowering us to perform miracles in his name. They assure us that God wants to complete this unfinished story through us. The only question is whether we have the faith and courage to let him do so.

It is time for you to make your choice, just like William Carey. He told a complacent church before he sailed to India, and he still tells us today: *"Expect great things from God. Attempt great things for God."*

Conclusion:
Step into the Story

"Come, follow me," Jesus said, "and I will send you out to fish for people."

(Mark 1:17)

We have come a long way with Jesus since he stood on the shore of Lake Galilee and commanded Peter to follow him. We have walked a long way with Peter as he discovers what it means for us to step into Jesus' story. But how far we have come with Jesus is not what matters most as we finish Mark's gospel. What matters is how far we are willing to go with Jesus from this moment on.

Over twenty years ago, I stumbled into a Christian meeting in Germany. As I listened to the preacher, I realised that I had never truly made a decision to step into Jesus' story. I knew that deciding to follow Jesus would devastate my drinking and my sinful lifestyle and my many friendships that were centred around those things. It would shatter the way in which my life revolved around myself, instead of around Jesus as my Lord.

That evening felt like any other. Decisive moments in our lives tend to feel very normal at the time. Peter's life didn't flash before his eyes when Jesus called him. He probably felt just like you feel now. I had no idea that I was making the most important decision of my life, but before I went to bed that evening I surrendered my life to Jesus and my life fundamentally changed. As we finish Mark's gospel, you are standing at a similar crossroads. Are you willing to step into Jesus' story?

When I returned home from Germany, I discovered that

deciding to follow Jesus isn't the end of the story, but the beginning. A bit like Peter, I messed up frequently. Jesus forgave me. A bit like Peter, I made stupid mistakes. Jesus patiently taught me at every pit stop along the way. I needed to discover that following Jesus is not so much about his helping me in my plans as it is an invitation to play a role in his plans. I began to sense his call to spend long hours with him, reading the Bible and praying and worshipping. I learned the lesson of Mark 3:14–15. Jesus calls those who follow him, first and foremost, to be with him.

You have already begun to do this by reading this commentary on Mark's gospel. Well done. Are you willing to make this your lifestyle, getting to know Jesus better every single day? Peter had just caught his greatest ever catch of fish when Jesus called him to leave everything behind and follow him.[1] It is never easy to step into Jesus' story, but he told Peter: *You have only one life. Spend it well. Don't sell yourself short. Great though these things are, it is time for you to start living for something better than fish.* Whatever it costs you, are you willing to give it up in order to step deeper into Jesus' story?

It wasn't long before I felt the need to share Jesus' story with other people. Like Peter, I started with those around me – my friends and neighbours and work colleagues – but then Jesus opened my eyes to the harvest fields of the world. I spent a year abroad as a missionary and, when I returned, I found a job at a multinational company where I could share the Gospel with work colleagues from Europe, Lebanon, Saudi Arabia and Egypt. A lot of them laughed at me. Some of them were very rude. Many of them called me names behind my back. But it was nothing compared to what befell Peter and his friends. If we are willing to continue Mark's gospel through our own lives, Jesus

---

[1] You can read about this in Luke 5:1–11 and in *Straight to the Heart of Luke*.

promises to be with us as we call other people to step into his story too.

After I left the business world to become a church leader, I was ambushed by a friend from Africa. He pointed out that I was reading Mark's gospel selectively, as a European. I was filtering out all of its references to supernatural healing. He persuaded me to visit a church as a guest speaker and, the night before I preached, he told me that he had billed it as a healing service.

This doesn't make him sound like a very good friend, but I'm deeply grateful. He prepared me by showing me that Luke begins the book of Acts by describing his gospel as an account of *"all that Jesus began to do and teach"* – in other words, Jesus wants to carry on doing and teaching through us. As a result, I preached the following day about the leper in Mark 1:40–45: *"'If you are willing, you can make me clean'... 'I am willing. Be clean!'"* When I offered to pray for anyone who needed similar healing, what happened next surprised me more than anyone.

The first woman to respond had a jabbing pain behind her eye. When I commanded it to go, the pain disappeared. Another woman had been suffering from a terrible sore throat for the previous eight months. She was instantly healed too. A man was unable to bend his knee or walk without pain. When I laid hands on him and commanded the knee to be healed, he started leaping around the room with excitement. A few weeks later, he sent me a message from a walking holiday which he was enjoying with his family, completely pain-free. Did everyone get healed that morning? No. I've only told you about the three that did. But when I called unbelievers to respond to the Gospel at the end of my message, I could not believe my eyes. More people responded to the Gospel that morning than I had seen respond during the entire previous year.

I'm not pretending to be anything. I have so much to learn on this journey that I feel as though I am only just getting started. I am simply trying to help you to believe that God will do amazing things through you if you step deeper into his story. Mark's gospel isn't just a history book. It is also a manual. It is a description of what your life can become.

What is so great about the story of your life as it currently stands? What makes it too precious for you to surrender it into Jesus' nail-pierced hands? What is of such great value that you would rather throw away the life Jesus offers you than do without it? Jesus issues you a warning and a promise as you make your decision at the end of Mark's gospel: *"Whoever wants to be my disciple must deny themselves and take up their cross and follow me. For whoever wants to save their life will lose it, but whoever loses their life for me and for the gospel will save it."*[2]

Come on. Don't turn down the invitation of a lifetime. As you finish Mark's gospel, tell Jesus that you are willing to give up everything to step into his story.

---

[2] Mark 8:34–35.

STRAIGHT TO THE HEART SERIES

TITLES AVAILABLE: OLD TESTAMENT

ISBN 978 0 85721 001 2

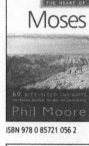

ISBN 978 0 85721 056 2

ISBN 978 0 85721 252 8

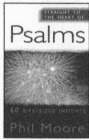

ISBN 978 0 85721 428 7

ISBN 978 0 85721 426 3

STRAIGHT TO THE HEART SERIES

TITLES AVAILABLE: NEW TESTAMENT

ISBN 978 1 85424 988 3

ISBN 978 0 85721 253 5

ISBN 978 0 85721 642 7

ISBN 978 1 85424 989 0

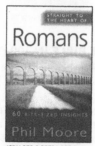

ISBN 978 0 85721 057 9

ISBN 978 0 85721 002 9

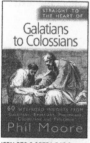

ISBN 978 0 85721 546 8

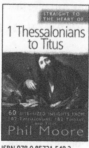

ISBN 978 0 85721 548 2

ISBN 978 0 85721 668 7

ISBN 978 1 85424 990 6

GAGGING JESUS
Things Jesus Said We Wish He Hadn't
Phil Moore

If you ever suspected that Jesus wasn't crucified for acting like a polite vicar in a pair of socks and sandals, then this book is for you. Fasten your seatbelt and get ready to discover the real Jesus in all his outrageous, ungagged glory.

ISBN 978 0 85721 453 9

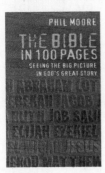

THE BIBLE IN 100 PAGES
Seeing the Big Picture in God's Great Story
Phil Moore

Written in a punchy and engaging style, this crisp, clear summary provides a handy reference tool enabling the reader to see how the Bible fits together. Despite its many authors and vast time frame, there is a core narrative that runs throughout the text.

ISBN 978 0 85721 551 2

JESUS, RIGHT WHERE YOU WANT HIM
Your biggest questions. His honest answers
Phil Moore

Written in a punchy and easy-to-read style, this is a starting point for those who want to address key issues and get answers to the big questions, such as: Hasn't religion been the cause of appalling violence? Aren't Christians a bunch of hycocrites? And isn't the Bible full of myths and contradictions?

ISBN 978 0 85721 677 9